INSIGHT GUIDES

Eating in New York

Restaurants, Bars, Diners, and Cafes

ABOUT THIS BOOK

New York City does not have to work hard to sustain its reputation as a culinary capital. A new wave of successful contemporary restaurants, and a new generation of innovative young chefs, are keeping it firmly on top. Good restaurants are found all over the island, thanks to the gentrification of Manhattan over the past decade. Areas once considered dangerous or run down, like the Lower East Side and the East Village, are undergoing a culinary explosion; even the normally docile Upper West Side is now home to several destination restaurants. Other places worth a subway trip or a cab ride are popping up in Brooklyn and Queens. You only have to look at the concentration of restaurants in each area to realize that eating out in New York remains a fundamental part of daily life.

With such an abundance of eateries, however, the choice can be overwhelming. To help you make an informed decision, we assembled a team of writers with a passion for food and asked them to give us a rundown of recommended restaurants for the neighborhoods they live in, work in, relax in, or love to eat in. We have divided the city into nine districts, with an additional chapter covering the Outer Boroughs. Each chapter begins with an overview of the area and the type of restaurants you might find there, pinpointing any markets, food shops or other gastronomic landmarks worth mentioning. To help narrow down your choice, we also give our top five recommendations for each area.

The Listings

The listings are organized by type of cuisine or establishment. Each restaurant is given a price code *(see panel on opposite page)* for an idea of how much you can expect to spend. The reviews are kept short and to the point; they aim to give an overall impression of the restaurant's food, style and ambiance, and the level of service. On the whole, they are positive recommendations, but any negative aspects, such as slow service or high noise levels, are pointed out. Please bear in mind that, because the information is based on the experience of one person and because both quality and service are bound to be variable in most

restaurants, these reviews should be used only as a guide. They are supplemented by a shortlist of cafes and bars for each area.

The Contributors

The guide was compiled by Insight editor Cathy Muscat, with the help of a variety of expert writers living and working in New York.

Mimi Tompkins, a broadcast and print journalist based in New York who is currently developing a radio program called The Food Experience, wrote the chapters covering Flatiron, Union Square and Gramercy, West Village and NoHo, and Midtown, and the features on Cooking Schools and Brunch. Stephen Brewer (Upper West Side, Chelsea, and the Midtown chapter with Mimi, and the features on Markets, Late-Night Dining and New York Experiences) is a long-time travel journalist who has dined all over the world but continues to think the eating is best in New York.

Bridget Freer is a freelance journalist who has been happily living, working, and eating in New York for the past five years; she wrote the chapters on Tribeca, Downtown, SoHo and Further Afield, covering the Outer Boroughs, and the features on Burgers, Pizza, and Food Carts.

Jill Rabelais (Lower East Side and East Village, Upper East Side) writes reviews for ManhattanI.com, a website for professionals in the restaurant and hotel business. Editorial back-up was given by Siân Lezard and Martha Ellen Zenfell and the book was proofread by Sylvia Suddes.

How to use this guide

Each restaurant review contains the following information:

Address and grid reference: after each address we give a street location and a corresponding grid reference. This refers to the map in the introduction to each area chapter, on which each restaurant is plotted. Subway stations are also marked.

Opening times: B=breakfast, Br=brunch, L=lunch, T=Tea, D=dinner. Specific opening times are not given, except where they are exceptional.

Price codes: $ = under $25, $$ = $25–40, $$$ = $40–60, $$$$ = 60+
These prices are based on the cost of an average 3-course dinner per person including half a bottle of house wine, or the cheapest wine available, and any cover or service charge. Lunch is often cheaper.

Website: where the restaurant has its own website with up-to-date information on menus and prices, this has been given.

Editorial

Series Editor **Cathy Muscat**
Editorial Director **Brian Bell**
Art Director **Klaus Geisler**
Picture Manager **Hilary Genin**
Photography **Britta Jaschinski**
Production **Linton Donaldson, Sylvia George**
Cartography **Zoë Goodwin, Laura Morris**

Distribution

UK & Ireland
GeoCenter International Ltd
The Viables Centre, Harrow Way
Basingstoke, Hants RG22 4BJ
Fax: (44) 1256-817988

United States
Langenscheidt Publishers, Inc.
46–35 54th Road,
Maspeth, NY 11378
Fax: (718) 784-0640

Canada
Thomas Allen & Son Ltd
390 Steelcase Road East
Markham, Ontario L3R 1G2
Fax: (1) 905 475-6747

Worldwide
Apa Publications GmbH & Co. Verlag KG (Singapore branch)
38 Joo Koon Road, Singapore 628990
Tel: (65) 6865-1600.
Fax: (65) 6861-6438

Printing

Insight Print Services (Pte) Ltd
38 Joo Koon Road, Singapore 628990
Tel: (65) 6865-1600.
Fax: (65) 6861-6438

First Edition 2004

CONTACTING THE EDITORS
Although every effort is made to provide accurate information, we live in a fast-changing world and would appreciate it if readers would call our attention to any errors or outdated information that may occur by writing to:

Insight Guides, P.O. Box 7910, London SE1 1WE, England. Fax: (44) 20-7403 0290. insight@apaguide.co.uk

www.insightguides.com

Introduction

Listings

Features

Directory

Maps

For individual zone maps, see area chapters

◁ **Pearl Oyster Bar**

18 Cornelia St, West Village [page 67]

Oysters, clam chowder, bouillabaisse, lobster roll – all deliciously fresh and expertly prepared.

▽ **Spice Market**

*403 W. 13th St, Chelsea [page 50]*Samosas, sushi, and big flavors in a wonderfully exotic setting.

△ **Florent**

69 Gansevoort St, Meatpacking District [page 50]

Offering French flair and a relaxed atmosphere, this popular neighborhood cafe has been serving burgers, salads, and boudins for 20 years.

▽ **Bouley**

120 W. Broadway, Tribeca [page 108]

Inspired cuisine, sumptuous surroundings, and immaculate service make this one of the city's best restaurants.

△ **Katz's Delicatessen**

205 E. Houston St, Lower East Side [page 73]

For delicious deli classics in a dingy but hallowed canteen.

△ **Balthazar**

80 Spring St, SoHo [page 91]

For the best brasserie experience this side of Paris.

△ **Craft**

43 E. 19th St, Gramercy Park [page 32]

Create your own meal by choosing from the freshest of ingredients and stating your preferred method of cooking.

△ **Daniel**

60 E. 65th St, Upper East Side [page 123]

French haute cuisine at its highest in this temple of gastronomy.

▽ **Boathouse**

Central Park [page 120]

For the most Woody Allenesque of New York brunch experiences.

◁ **Peasant**

194 Elizabeth St, Little Italy [page 95]

Chic and rustic Italian food cooked in white-hot, wood-burning ovens.

Bubby's
Restaurant & Bar
OPEN

Eating Out in New York

In the city that never stands still, change is as commonplace as red-checked tablecloths. Eat with attitude

New York is a place where anything can happen. Traffic, noise, innovation and outrageous street life all come together in a frenzied non-stop rhythm. So quick are its inhabitants to embrace change that by the time anyone thinks they understand New York, their understanding is obsolete, for this is a city that never stands still.

New York has always had a reputation as a culinary melting pot. From Jewish delicatessens to Mexican taco joints to the United Nations' Delegates Dining Room, people have enjoyed a staggering range of food at every price range. They can order a 95¢ hot-dog at Gray's Papaya or a $99 hamburger with white truffles at DB Bistro Moderne. Its top-drawer restaurants take pride in serving the best of French cuisine.

But New York is not a city to rest on its laurels. Innovations come fast and, as you would expect, in your face. The first signs of visible food are always the silver carts parked on most street corners. Such a hit were these from the beginning that it could arguably be claimed that New Yorkers invented the concept of chowing down while standing up outside. In previous years, these carts mainly peddled soggy pretzels and overboiled hotdogs. But now you can nibble on an empanada (a South American savory pastry), on chow fun noodles, on wholegrain pancakes and fruit, on chocolate-truffle cookies or a coconut or mango ice. As often as not these will be dispensed by men in crisp white jackets, without a mustard stain in sight.

Opposite: open for business in Tribeca

Sullivan St Bakery's Roman-style pizza has little in common with that archetypal New York street food, the slice – except, of course, that it is sold by the slice. The bakery's Jim Lahey, the city's premier bread-maker, applies the principles he learned in Rome (use only high-grade flour and wild yeast, plus fresh, all-natural ingredients) to his roster of pizzas, which are accessorized only minimally. His most significant slice is the seductively simple pizza pomodoro, reminiscent of ripe fruit and olive oil, with a thin coat of tomato puree. That's it. The flavors mingle nicely at room temperature, making this pizza even better when cold – itself a modern take on a typical way of eating.

The current rising star in fine dining is New American cuisine, fast overtaking French as the city standard. Nostalgics can still savor the quintessential Manhattan experience at places like the Oyster Bar in Grand Central Terminal or the clubby '21' in Midtown. But think the sizzle of *Sex and the City* rather than the crooning of Frank Sinatra and soon you'll find dozens of creative, innovative American restaurants generating excitement these days, including Craft, WD-50 and the Mermaid Inn. All of these feature fresh American ingredients mixed with hip, New York know-how.

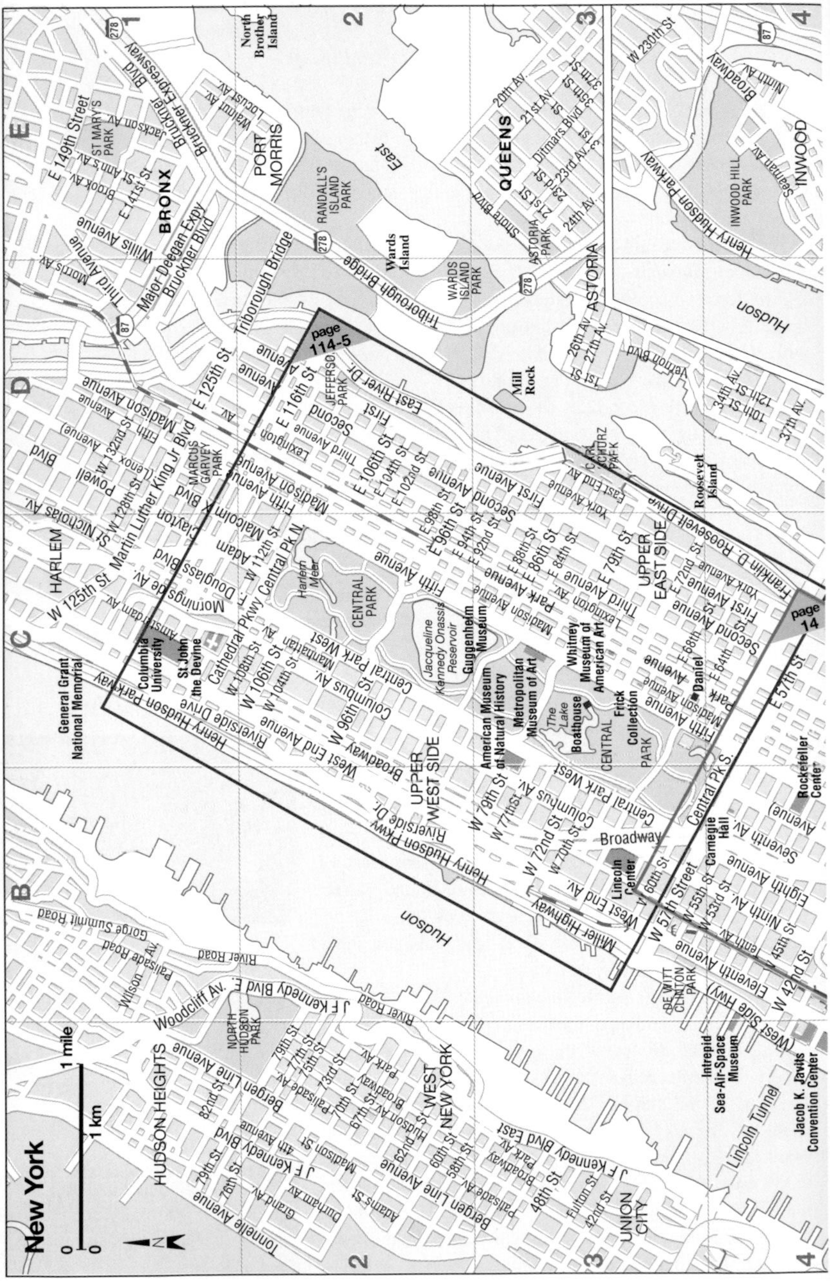
New York
0 1 mile
0 1 km
N
HARLEM
BRONX
PORT MORRIS
QUEENS
ASTORIA
INWOOD
UPPER WEST SIDE
UPPER EAST SIDE
HUDSON HEIGHTS
WEST NEW YORK
UNION CITY
CENTRAL PARK
ST MARY'S PARK
RANDALL'S ISLAND PARK
Wards Island
WARDS ISLAND PARK
ASTORIA PARK
INWOOD HILL PARK
NORTH HUDSON PARK
MARCUS GARVEY PARK
JEFFERSON PARK
CARL SCHURZ PARK
DE WITT CLINTON PARK
North Brother Island
Mill Rock
Roosevelt Island
Hudson
East
page 114-5
page 14
General Grant National Memorial
Columbia University
St John the Devine
Harlem Meer
Jacqueline Kennedy Onassis Reservoir
Guggenheim Museum
American Museum of Natural History
Metropolitan Museum of Art
Whitney Museum of American Art
The Lake
Boathouse
Frick Collection
Daniel
Lincoln Center
Carnegie Hall
Rockefeller Center
Intrepid Sea-Air-Space Museum
Jacob K. Javits Convention Center
Lincoln Tunnel
Triborough Bridge
Major Deegan Expy
Bruckner Expressway
Bruckner Blvd
Henry Hudson Parkway
Franklin D. Roosevelt Drive
East River Dr.
Riverside Drive
Riverside Dr.
Miller Highway
West Side Hwy
W 125th St
E 125th St
E 116th St
E 106th St
E 96th St
E 86th St
E 79th St
E 57th St
W 96th St
W 79th St
W 72nd St
W 57th Street
W 42nd St
E 149th Street
Third Avenue
Willis Avenue
Madison Avenue
Fifth Avenue
Park Avenue
Lexington Av.
Second Avenue
First Avenue
York Avenue
Broadway
West End Avenue
Columbus Av.
Central Park West
Central Pk S.
Amsterdam Av.
Morningside Av.
Cathedral Pkwy Central Pk N.
Malcolm X Blvd
Adam Clayton Powell Blvd
Martin Luther King Jr Blvd
St Nicholas Av.
Frederick Douglass Blvd
Eighth Avenue
Ninth Av.
Tenth Av.
Eleventh Avenue
Seventh Av.
J F Kennedy Blvd
J F Kennedy Blvd East
Bergen Line Avenue
Palisade Av.
Boulevard East
Woodcliff Av.
River Road
Gorge Summit Road
Tonnelle Avenue
Vernon Blvd
Ditmars Blvd
Shore Blvd
Seaman Av.
W 230th St
278
87

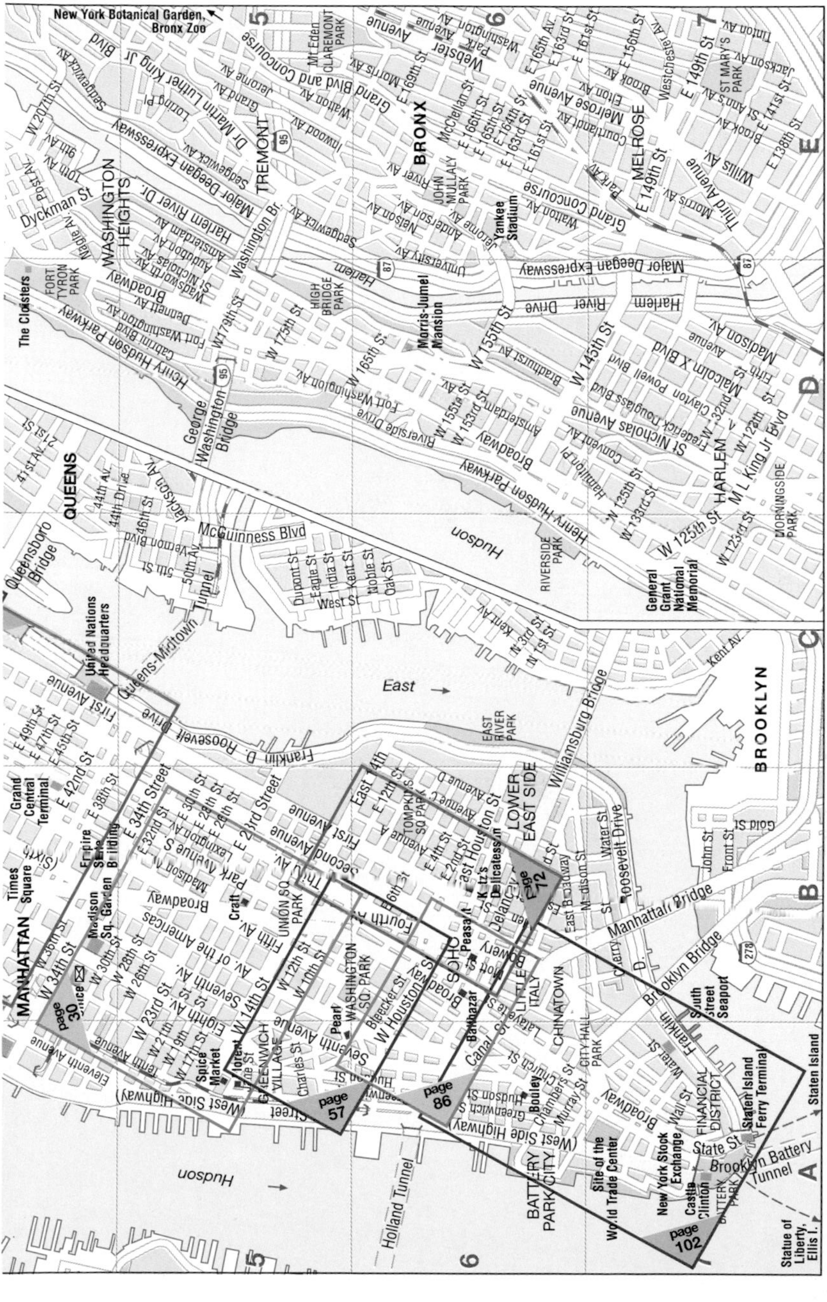
New York Botanical Garden, Bronx Zoo
MANHATTAN
BRONX
QUEENS
BROOKLYN
WASHINGTON HEIGHTS
TREMONT
MELROSE
HARLEM
GREENWICH VILLAGE
SOHO
LITTLE ITALY
CHINATOWN
LOWER EAST SIDE
FINANCIAL DISTRICT
BATTERY PARK CITY
The Cloisters
FORT TYRON PARK
HIGH BRIDGE PARK
JOHN MULLALY PARK
CLAREMONT PARK
ST MARY'S PARK
MORNINGSIDE PARK
RIVERSIDE PARK
EAST RIVER PARK
TOMPKINS SQ PARK
UNION SQ PARK
WASHINGTON SQ PARK
CITY HALL PARK
BATTERY PARK
Yankee Stadium
Morris-Jumel Mansion
General Grant National Memorial
George Washington Bridge
Queensboro Bridge
Williamsburg Bridge
Manhattan Bridge
Brooklyn Bridge
Queens-Midtown Tunnel
Holland Tunnel
Brooklyn Battery Tunnel
United Nations Headquarters
Grand Central Terminal
Times Square
Empire State Building
Madison Sq. Garden
South Street Seaport
Site of the World Trade Center
New York Stock Exchange
Castle Clinton
Staten Island Ferry Terminal
Staten Island
Statue of Liberty, Ellis I.
Spice Market
Craft
Pearl
Balthazar
Peasant
Katz's Delicatessen
Bouley
Hudson
East
page 30
page 57
page 72
page 86
page 102
Henry Hudson Parkway
Harlem River Dr.
Major Deegan Expressway
Grand Concourse
Franklin D. Roosevelt Drive
West Side Highway
McGuinness Blvd
Broadway
W 34th St
E 42nd St
W 125th St
W 145th St
W 155th St
Canal St
W Houston St
East Houston St
A
B
C
D
E
5
6
7

MIDTOWN

Where to find the best of the best – so many of the city's exceptional dining experiences are to be had in this part of town

Midtown, the slice of Manhattan that stretches between the East and Hudson rivers from 34th to 59th streets, is a powerful, hyperactive sky-scraping hub where corporate headquarters, flashy department stores, and big-city hotels sit cheek by jowl. The Empire State Building, Rockefeller Center, and the Chrysler Building are just three of the city's many architectural icons that soar among them. Fifth Avenue cuts the area in half from north to south, with Times Square, the 'Crossroads of the World', and the Theater District on the east side, and Park Avenue and the United Nations to the west. What all this means is that there is plenty to see and do – and of course eat – in Midtown. When it comes to food, what makes Midtown stand out from other Manhattan neighborhoods is that whatever your craving or budget, you'll find something to suit.

Something for everyone

Some of the finest and most expensive restaurants in the world can be found in Midtown; Four Seasons *(see page 17)*, Le Cirque 2000 *(see page 20)*, Alain Ducasse at Essex House *(see page 19)*, and Le Bernardin *(see page 25)*, to name but a few. Many of the mainstays of Manhattan dining are here too, with the 90 year-old Oyster Bar at Grand Central Station *(see pages 25–26)* winning the prize for longevity.

Midtown is also fertile ground for aspiring and established chefs to show off their talents, and the neighborhood is continually brightened by the opening of restaurants as varied as Daniel Boulud's DB Bistro Moderne *(see page 20)* and Raymond Mohan's Caribbean Plantain Cafe *(see page 24)*.

Restaurateurs, cottoning on to the idea that New Yorkers and their visitors enjoy eclectic food, have elevated ethnic food to new heights in Midtown, providing a United Nations' worth of dining experiences, from swish Swedish smörgåsbord fare at Aquavit *(see page 25)* and elegant Indian cuisine at Dawat *(see page 23)*, to upscale Greek at Molyvos *(see page 22)* or Franco-Thai fusion at Vong *(see page 26)*. There's even a hot new culinary neighborhood: Ninth Avenue, long known for its ethnic markets, is these days lined with new restaurants, some of which are well worth the walk that far west.

To the east, Second Avenue is likewise chock-a-block with eateries that service denizens of the surrounding office towers and residential highrises. Over on Columbus Circle, the new Time Warner Center towers high above Central Park and houses a glitzy shopping mall, complete with what has to be the world's most upscale food court. Diners (provided they have reserved well in advance) can choose between such temples of haute-cuisine as Per Se, by Thomas Keller of Napa Valley's French Laundry fame, and V, an haute-cuisine steakhouse by Jean-Georges Vongerichten. If you can't procure a table, settle for a walk through the outlet of Whole Foods in the cellar, said to be Manhattan's largest grocery store and certainly one of its most appealingly stocked.

***Opposite:* Blue Fin at the Times Square Hotel**

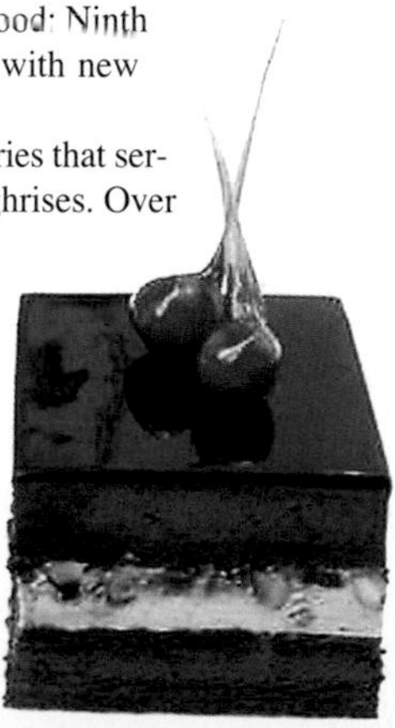

While the Midtown dining scene, like so much else in Manhattan, defies any sort of logical categorization, we can offer a few generalities, but do keep in mind that there are many, many exceptions to these rules. Looking for glitz? Many of the more rarified restaurants are on the east side of Midtown, around Park Avenue. Going to the theater? That's easy. You'll probably want to eat in the Theater District (roughly, the blocks from West 42nd to West 50th Street between Broadway and Ninth Avenue). Want to know some places to avoid? That's easy, too – Times Square, not to be confused with the adjacent Theater District, has almost as many overpriced and bad eateries as it does bright lights.

Midtown restaurants can be mightily expensive, so to save you the embarrassment of lapsing into a choking spasm when the bill arrives remember to check your wallet and credit card limits. Many Midtown restaurants are surprisingly affordable, too; as a rule of thumb, you'll find a larger selection of inexpensive and moderately priced restaurants in Midtown West, especially along Ninth Avenue.

Forward planning

When it comes to dining out in Midtown, it pays to do your homework in advance (that's where this guide comes in handy). While you can risk being spontaneous in the more compact districts farther downtown, in Midtown it's a good idea to secure a reservation, especially if you plan on dining before or

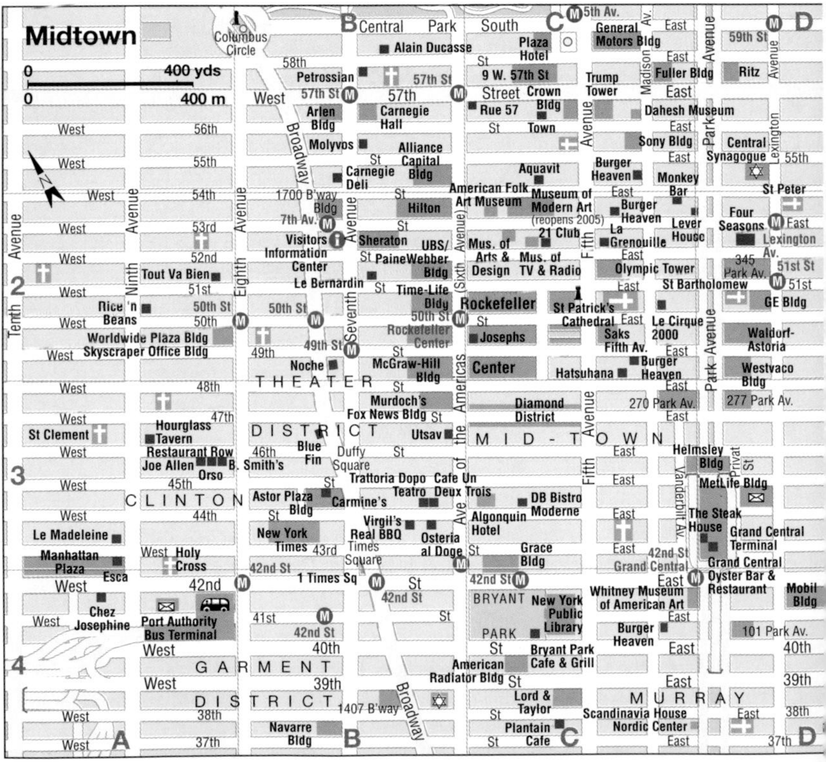

after the theater. Indeed, many of the better restaurants get booked up months in advance, so reserve as far ahead as possible. While you won't necessarily end up having a bad meal if you set out without a place in mind, you may miss out on some truly exceptional dining experiences. Plus, Midtown is big, and the distance between blocks deceptively long. So if you do want to wander round before deciding, it's advisable to at least have an idea of where you're headed to save you the misfortune of wandering hungry and sore-footed through the concrete canyons.

Eating out in Midtown is a good excuse to get dressed up. Restaurants here, especially the more expensive ones, tend to have a more formal dress code than those elsewhere in town. Men are suited (or at least jacketed) and women go glamorous and groomed for a night on the town.

One last tip: avoid Sundays. Many Midtown restaurants close that day, and many – geared to a corporate lunch and dinner crowd – are closed for lunch on Saturday as well. Should you find yourself looking for Sunday dinner, head west – restaurants in this part of Midtown serve theatergoers, and are more likely to be open on Sunday evening. The easiest way to find a meal is simply to head to the block of 46th Street between Eighth and Ninth avenues; here, on so-called Restaurant Row, are more than two dozen restaurants, most of them open seven evenings a week. Another good stretch of spots to choose from is on 2nd Avenue between 50th and 60th Streets.

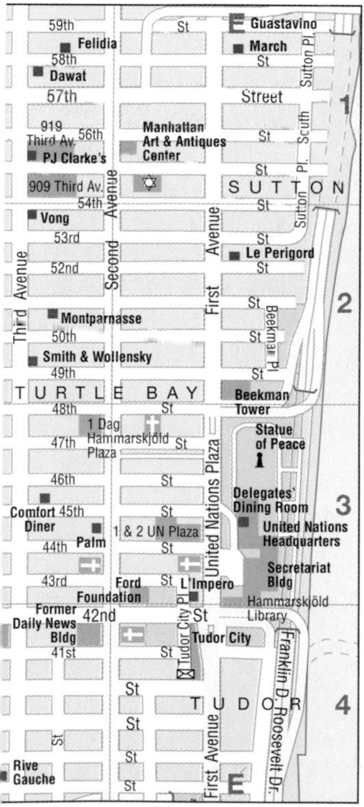

FIVE OF THE BEST

Le Bernardin: for ethereal eating, where the seafood is heaven-sent
Four Seasons: ingenious American cuisine in an iconic Mies van der Rohe setting
L'Impero: an Italian newcomer that's making a splash
Lever House: classic American elegance in a vintage highrise
Palm: one of Midtown's most appealing steakhouses

Carnegie Deli, for an authentic New York experience

American

'21' Club
21 W. 52nd St (bet. Fifth and Sixth aves) [C2]. Tel: 212-582-7200. Open: L and D Mon–Fri, D only Sat. **$$$$** *www.21club.com*
It feels a lot like Sinatra's Manhattan at this clubby New York enclave of the wealthy and powerful, where US royalty has been dining since Prohibition. The classic dishes (steak, oysters, rack of lamb) are superbly executed, and the wine cellars legendary.

Bryant Park Cafe and Grill
25 W. 40th St (bet. Fifth and Sixth aves) [C4]. Tel: 212-840-6500. Open: L Wed, Sat, Sun; D Tues–Sun. **$$–$$$** *www.arkrestaurants.com*
A wall of glass and an enormous terrace make the most of one of New York's most idyllic dining venues, the leafy Bryant Square Park. A menu of expertly grilled and roasted fish and meats shows that food is more than an afterthought in this bucolic setting.

B. Smith's Restaurant Row
320 W. 46th St (bet. Eighth and Ninth aves) [A3]. Tel: 212-315-1100. Open: L and D Tues–Sun, D only Mon. **$$–$$$**
Barbara Smith is a former model and host of a lifestyle TV program. Her busy restaurant near the theaters does southern classics with a twist, such as crunchy curried fried oysters dipped in coconut-wasabi sauce, and sweet-potato pie in a crushed pecan crust.

Burger Heaven
20 E. 49th St (bet. Fifth and Madison aves) [C2] Tel: 212-755-2166. Open: 6am–8.30pm Mon–Fri, 7am–7pm Sat, 9am–5.30pm Sun. **$** *www.burgerheaven.com*
Midtown workers are willing to put up with the hellish noontime crush at these burger joints (this is one of many Midtown branches) which can't be beaten for big juicy burgers at bargain prices. Salads, sandwiches, and soups are at hand for less carnivorous appetites.

Carnegie Deli
854 Seventh Ave (at 54th St) [B1]. Tel: 212-757-2245. Open: 7am–4am daily. **$** *www.carnegiedeli.com*
You won't find a more authentic deli experience, and this New York institution is well aware of its

legendary status – the walls are plastered with photos of celebrity regulars, and the lines are long, but the generously stuffed sandwiches are well worth the effort and price.

Comfort Diner

214 E. 45th St (bet. Third and Second aves) [D3]. Tel: 212-867-4555. Open: B, L, and D, 365 days a year, 7.30am–10pm. **$**

A boisterous upscale diner serves a wide selection of comfort food such as macaroni cheese, chili, burgers, and waffles and ice cream. It's popular with office workers from the area's many skyscrapers, so expect a wait at lunch.

Four Seasons 🍴

99 E. 52nd St (bet Lexington and Park aves) [D2]. Tel: 212-754-9494. Open: L and D Mon–Fri, D only Sat. **$$$$** *www.fourseasonsrestaurant.com*

Since it opened 40 years ago this temple to power and money has had a clientele that rivals any *Who's-Who* listing: JFK celebrated his 45th birthday here; Henry Kissinger still comes for lunch. The stunning Philip Johnson minimalist decor is timeless, and the seasonal classics (Dover sole, crabcakes, breast of pheasant, etc.) served in the elegant pool room or the grill room are impeccable.

Guastavino

409 E. 59th St (bet. First and York aves) [E2]. Tel: 212-980-2455. Open: L and D daily. **$$–$$$** *www.guastavino.com*

Who would have thought that the underpinnings of the 59th Street Bridge could be a posh dining room? Well, British magnate Sir Terence Conran did. He named the place for the father-son team who designed the distinctive tile work in the early 20th century and put chef Daniel Orr in charge of a kitchen that turns out a commendable menu of dishes such as roast salmon, rack of lamb, and a wide selection of oysters.

Hourglass Tavern

373 W. 46th St (bet. Eighth and Ninth aves) [A3]. Tel: 212-265-2060. Open: D daily. **$**

An affordable meal in the Theater District can be as scarce as a ticket to a hit show, but this diminutive room shaped, yes, like an hourglass, serves just that. Plus, a meal here really is a meal, with salad and potatoes accompanying the chops and other basic fare.

Joe Allen

326 W. 46th St (bet. Eighth and Ninth aves) [A3]. Tel: 212 581-6464. Open: L and D daily. **$$–$$$** *www.joeallenrestaurant.com*

The star you just saw on stage might be at the next table at this cozy, decades-old Broadway lair. But regulars come here not to gaze but to graze on unexciting yet reliable staples that include meal-size salads, decent burgers and pastas, and, the most memorable dish in the house, hot fudge pudding cake.

Lever House 🍴

390 Park Ave (at 53rd St) [C2]. Tel: 212-888-2700. Open: L and D Mon–Fri, D Sat–Sun. **$$$** *www.leverhouse.com*

The 21-story office tower set the gold standard for modernist archi-

Picasso at the Four Seasons

tecture when it went up on Park Avenue in 1952. More than half a century later, this elegantly polished, ground-floor dining room is doing the same thing for a new breed of Midtown dining. Serving innovatively prepared lobster, chops, and other American fare in an über-chic interior designed by A-list architects, it provides the perfect setting for a power lunch or an intimate dinner.

Above and below right: Michael Jordan's The Steak House NYC

March

405 E. 58th St (bet. First Ave and Sutton Pl.) [E1]. Tel: 212-754-6272. Open: D daily. ***$$$$*** *www.marchrestaurant.com*

In good weather, you can begin and end a meal here over a drink in the pretty garden, but what happens in between, in an intimate, two-level, antiques-filled dining room, is especially noteworthy. Chef-owner Wayne Nish encourages diners to feast on small plates of what can only be described as 'American fusion,' in which Asian and Latin touches transform simple ingredients into culinary delights.

Michael Jordan's The Steak House NYC

Grand Central Terminal, 23 Vanderbilt Ave (bet. 42nd and 43rd aves) [D3]. Tel: 212-655-2300. Open: L and D daily. ***$$$*** *www.theglaziergroup.com*

The food here is good, but the view, overlooking the central concourse of Grand Central Terminal in all its refurbished glory, is extraordinary. The famous basketball player rarely stops by, but his menu offers delicious dry-aged steaks, as well as Mom's recipe of macaroni and cheese.

TIP

For some star gazing – the celestial kind – head to Grand Central Terminal, where 24-carat gold constellations adorn the ceiling of the grand concourse. The station's lower concourse is also one of the liveliest places to find a quick Midtown meal.

Palm

837 Second Ave (bet. 44th and 45th sts) [D3]. Tel: 212-687-2953. Open L and D Mon–Fri, D only Sat. Palm Too at 840 Second Ave (bet. 44th and 45th sts) [D3]. Tel: 212-697-5198. Also open Sun. ***$$$***

There are several Midtown steakhouses, but the Palm duo take the prize for character and charm. You can't beat the selection of steaks, and the decor of framed movie stills and the sawdust on the floor helps make eating here a quintessentially New York experience.

PJ Clarke's

915 Third Ave (55th St) [D1]. Tel: 212-317-1616. Open: L and D daily. ***$*** *www.pjclarkes.com*

This renovated 1860s pub/bar in a townhouse that's nearly lost in a sea of surrounding skyscrapers has a new upstairs bar that's as charming as the original downstairs. Both are great for a beer or basic pub food such as hamburgers, chicken wings, and salads.

Smith & Wollensky

797 Third Ave (49th St) [D2]. Tel: 212-753-1530. Open: L and D Mon–Fri, D only Sat–Sun. ***$$$*** *www.smithandwollensky.com*

This New York institution is usually packed with a boisterous crowd of well-dressed stockbrokers and

Midtown executives. The steaks are huge, and the extensive wine list features only North American wine. For a less expensive option, try the adjacent Wollensky's Grill.

Steakhouse at Monkey Bar
Hotel Elysée, 60 E. 54th St (bet. Madison and Park aves) [C2]. Tel: 212-838-2600. Open: L and D Mon–Fri, D only Sat. **$$–$$$** *www.theglaziergroup.com*
The ghosts of former habitués Tennessee Williams and Tallulah Bankhead (whose pet allegedly gave this glamorous Art Deco retreat its name) seem to waft past monkey murals amid a refreshing hush. While the menu sticks to the basics of the steak, chop, and lobster variety, all are unfailingly prepared to perfection.

Town
15 W. 56th St (bet. Fifth and Sixth aves) [C1]. Tel: 212-582-4445. Open: B, L and D Mon-Fri, D only Sat, Br only Sun. **$$$**
Grown up and glamorous, this striking yet subdued room in the Chambers Hotel is well suited to the straightforward preparations of chef Geoffrey Zakarian. The freshest fish, juiciest duck, and other ingredients are flavored with a hint of apple and a range of surprising tastes to create dishes that are solid enough to be classics yet exciting enough to be memorable.

Virgil's Real BBQ
152 W. 44th St (bet. Broadway and Sixth Ave) [B3]. Tel: 212-921-9494. Open: L and D daily. **$$** *www.virgilsbbq.com*
Forget the diet at this fun southern restaurant serving delicious piles of ribs, biscuits and gravy, Texas red chili, and some of the best brisket in NYC. The hickory smoke from the grill hanging in the air adds to the barbeque experience.

French

Alain Ducasse at Essex House
155 W. 58th St (bet. Sixth and Seventh aves) [B1]. Tel: 212-265-7300. Open: Mon–Sat D, Thur–Fri L. **$$$$**
www.alain-ducasse.com
How much is a meal worth? The place to research the question is this haughty French gastro-temple, the most expensive restaurant in town, where the namesake chef delivers the heavenly goods – medallions of Maine lobster, roasted rack of milk-fed veal, clear Iranian caviar with cauliflower cream, etc. – on prix-fixe menus that start around $150 and waft to $300. Lunch is a steal at $65.

Cafe Un Deux Trois
123 W. 44th St (bet. Sixth Ave and Broadway) [B3]. Tel: 212-354-4148. Open: L and D daily.
$$–$$$
www.cafeundeuxtrois.biz
Basic French fare is served in this clamorous, high-ceilinged brasserie that caters to a pre- and post-theater crowd. Steak frites, onion soup, and roast chicken are among the classic

Did you know?
There's a street for everything in New York, including one for restaurants – Restaurant Row, as 46th Street between Eighth and Ninth avenues is known, has at least two dozen of them, including several of our choices (Hourglass Tavern, Joe Allen, and Orso.)

French standards on offer. The service can be brusque but will get you to the show on time.

Chez Josephine

414 W. 42nd St (bet. Ninth and 10th aves) [A4]. Tel: 212-594-1925. Open: D only Mon–Sat. ***$$–$$$*** *www.chezjosephine.com*
Josephine Baker dazzled French cabaret patrons in the 1920s and '30s. These days her adopted son Jean-Claude pays homage to her at this entertaining French restaurant of classics (magret de canard, steak frites, etc.) with it's high-camp French bordello decor. It's all in good fun, the warmth here is real, and the food is good.

Le Cirque 2000

NY Palace Hotel, 455 Madison Ave (bet. 50th and 51st sts) [C2]. Tel: 212-303-7788. Open: L and D Mon–Sat, D only Sun. ***$$$$***
A spectacle as much for its opulent, circus-themed decor as the sumptuous versions of classic dishes such as rack of lamb or sauteed veal. Moguls and city bigwigs jostle for the best tables in a social circus that's as ostentatious as it is unforgettable.

DB Bistro Moderne

55 W. 44th St (bet. Fifth and Sixth aves) [C3]. Tel: 212-391-2400. Open: L and D Mon–Sat, D only Sun. ***$$$$*** *www.danielnyc.com*
So *moderne* that the menu is organized by ingredients (check out the arugula section), chef Daniel Boulud's bistro is awash in Art Deco glitz and well-heeled publishing types and trendy tourists. The foie gras and truffle burger is typical of the kitchen's culinary surprises.

La Grenouille

3 E. 52nd St (bet. Fifth and Madison aves) [C2]. Tel: 212-752-1495. Open: L Tues–Fri, D Sat. ***$$$$*** *www.la-grenouille.com*
This 40-year-old classic is still one of New York's most important restaurants, serving impeccably prepared Gallic dishes such as grilled Dover sole, quenelles, and soufflés. The floral displays are stunning, the lighting flattering, and the clientele discerning and high-powered.

La Madeleine

403 W. 43rd St (bet. Ninth and Tenth aves) [A3]. Tel: 212-246-2993. Open: L and D daily. ***$$–$$$*** *www.lamadeleine.com*
The pretty, glass-roofed garden and standard French fare (such as grilled salmon or steak with béarnaise sauce) at reasonable prices are a winning ticket at this pre-theater favorite. Drop in for a bite before a Wednesday matinee and

Daniel Boulud's Bistro Moderne

Le Cirque 2000

you might find yourself humming Stephen Sondheim's tune, 'Here's to the Ladies Who Lunch.'

Montparnasse

230 E. 51st St (bet Third and Second aves) [D2]. Tel: 212-758-6633. Open: L and D daily. **$$–$$$** *www.montparnasse.com*

A somewhat undiscovered gem of a bistro that feels like Paris thanks to the red banquettes, framed Art Deco posters and linen tablecloths. But what's really French is the wide selection of wines available by the glass, the excellent service, and such hearty but refined classic bistro dishes as steak-frites with red wine sauce and braised chicken fricassee.

Le Périgord

405 E. 52nd St (bet. FDR Drive and First Ave) [E2]. Tel: 212-755-6244. Open: L and D Mon–Fri, D only Sat–Sun. **$$$$** *www.leperigord.com*

A long-established bastion of French cuisine where efficient waiters in starched white jackets and table captains in tuxedos serve excellent classics (rack of lamb, sole meunière, etc.) in a hushed, dignified atmosphere. The kitchen has produced some of the city's best chefs.

Petrossian

182 W. 58th St (at Seventh Ave) [B7]. Tel: 212-245-2214. Open: L and D daily. **$$$$** *www.petrossian.com*

You might not get to sip champagne out of a slipper at this sleek Art Deco outpost of the famed Parisian purveyor of caviar, but you can settle for dipping into the Caspian eggs with a gold-plated spoon. Foie gras, smoked sturgeon, and French inspired lamb and fish dishes are also on the menu.

Rive Gauche

560 Third Ave (at 37th St) [D4]. Tel: 212-949-5400. Open: L and D daily, Br Sat–Sun. **$$** *www.rivegauchenyc.com*

An attempt to bring a little bit of Paris to the canyon of Midtown skyscrapers, this late-night bistro serves good classic dishes such steak-frites, escargots, fresh ravioli, and roast chicken. Not a standout, but a comfortable, reasonably priced choice in the area.

Rue 57

60 W. 57th St (at 6th Ave) [C1]. Tel: 212-307-5656. Open: L and D daily. **$$–$$$**

The culinary boundaries of this large, bustling two-story bistro extend far beyond France, with

TIP

Don't get rained out of a picnic in the park – head to the bamboo tree-filled atrium of the IBM building at 57th St and Madison Ave, the perfect spot for an al-fresco snack, whatever the weather.

Dawat, for Indian haute cuisine

dishes on offer ranging from sushi to American classics and Italian pastas. Somehow it works – the food is delicious, and the atmosphere is upbeat, making it a good choice after a show at nearby Carnegie Hall.

Tout Va Bien

311 W. 51st St (bet. Eighth and Ninth aves) [A2]. Tel: 212-582-7200. Open: L and D Mon–Sat, **$–$$**

True to the name, all is indeed well with the world at this trusty oldtime theater district favorite. A good-natured wait staff keeps appreciative regulars satisfied with sweetbreads, liver, kidneys and other French fare that remains refreshingly untouched by nouvelle concepts. The $22 prix-fixe menu is great value.

Global

Delegates' Dining Room

United Nations, 4th Fl., First Ave at 46th St [E3]. Tel: 212-963-7626. Open: L only, Mon–Fri. **$$$**

Enjoy spectacular views of the East River and a taste of UN living in this sparingly decorated dining room. The buffet-style menu changes bi-weekly and features international cuisines, from Swedish to Mongolian. There's a tough security check to get in (bring photo ID), and men must wear jackets.

Greek

Molyvos

871 Seventh Ave (bet. 55th and 56th sts) [B1]. Tel: 212-582-7500. Open: L and D daily. **$$$**

Wooden tables and blue tiles will whisk you to an Aegean island, as will some of the best versions of Greek staples to be found this side of the Atlantic – melt-in-the-mouth dolmades, expertly prepared octopus, wood-grilled lamb chops, and homey moussaka and pastitsio. Only the bill will remind you that you're in New York.

Indian

Dawat

210 E. 58th St (bet. Third and Second aves) [D1]. Tel: 212-355-7555. Open: L and D Mon–Sat; D only Sun. ***$$$***
www.restaurants.com/dawat
The cuisine of the subcontinent goes haute amid elegant surroundings at what is arguably the finest Indian in New York. Curries, tandooris, biryanis, and all the other familiars are elevated to new levels, and even spinach leaves (battered, lightly fried, and emerging from the kitchen as bhaja) are works of art.

Utsav

1185 Ave of the Americas (bet. 46th and 47th sts) [B3]. Tel: 212-575-2525. Open: L and D daily. ***$$***
Midtown towers create the backdrop for a meal in this glass room, where the emphasis is on elaborate fish preparations, seafood curries, and other Indian delights, many of which are rarely encountered on New York Indian menus. Despite the faux Taj Majal setting, the offerings can be enjoyed for a relative song at the lunchtime buffet and prix-fixe dinners.

Italian

Carmine's

200 W. 44th St (bet. Broadway and Eighth Ave) [B3]. Tel: 212-221-3800. Open: L and D daily. ***$–$$*** *www.carminesnyc.com*
Need a place to feed a hungry mob? This cavernous mess hall of a room fits the bill with large tables and family-size portions of southern Italian pastas and parmigianas that are more notable for quantity than quality.

Felidia

243 E. 58th St (bet. Second and Third aves) [D1]. Tel: 212-758-1479. Open: L and D Mon–Fri. D only Sat. ***$$$$***
This is where it all began for star TV chef Lidia Bastianich, but fame, it seems, has neither gone to her head nor affected her cooking. This comfortable outpost in a stylish townhouse is still all about wonderful food. The robust northeastern Italian dishes are polished, inspiring, and served in generous portions; the wine-list is impressive.

L'Impero 🍴

45 Tudor City Pl. (bet. 42nd and 43rd sts) [E3]. Tel: 212-599-5045. Open: L and D Mon–Fri, D only Sat. ***$$$$***
www.limpero.com
This sensational newcomer, set in a quaint square isolated from the din of Midtown, right by the United Nations, is here to stay. The updated Italian fare by Scott Conant is delicious (try the fricassee of seasonal mushrooms or the roasted orata rossa with lobster reduction), and the atmosphere sophisticated and comfortable. A winner.

Orso

322 W. 46th St (bet. Eighth and Ninth aves) [A3]. Tel: 212-489-7212. Open: L and D daily. ***$$***
www.orsorestaurant.com
For many theater regulars, the best part of a performance is a meal at this warm Italian pre- and post-show hangout, where the quality of the pastas, thin-crust pizzas, and

TIP

Need more than just food to keep lunch or dinner exciting? Step right in to one of Midtown's fun themed restaurants. The **Hard Rock Cafe**, now a middle-aged classic, is popular as ever (221 W. 57th St; tel: 212-489-6565); for ghoulish grub, try **Jekyll and Hyde** (1409 Sixth Ave; tel: 212-541-9505); **Mars 2112** offers sci-fi antics (1633 Broadway; tel: 212-582-2112); and **The World**, is a big contender from the weighty World Wrestling Federation (1501 Broadway; tel: 212-398-2563).

robust entrees is as reliable as the chances of seeing a star at the bar.

Osteria al Doge

142 W. 44th St (bet. Sixth Ave and Broadway) [B3] Tel: 212-944-3643. Open: L and D Mon–Sat, D only Sun. **$$–$$$**
www.osteria-doge.com

Dinner at this bustling pre-theater favorite is a show in itself. Take a seat on the second-floor balcony, watch the crowds come and go, and enjoy the antics of overworked waiting staff who fly around the room like actors in a farce. The carpaccios and seafood pastas sometimes miss a cue but more often than not deserve an ovation.

Trattoria Dopo Teatro

125 W. 44th St (bet. Sixth Ave and Broadway) [B3]. Tel: 212-869-2849. Open: L and D Mon–Sat, D only Sun. **$$–$$$**
www.dopoteatro.com

Unlike the 'wolf-it-down' experience of many theater-district chow houses, a meal of Italian basics in this plain, high-windowed dining room or rear garden is always relaxing, and you can rest assured that the staff will have you in your seat when the curtain goes up.

***Below:* potent fruit at Aquavit**

Japanese

Hatsuhana

17 E. 48th St (bet. Fifth and Madison aves) [C2]. Tel: 212-355-3345. Open: L and D Mon–Fri, D only Sat. **$$–$$$**
www.hatsuhana.com

Hot indeed when it came on the scene in the late 1970s, this plain upstairs room introduced many a New Yorker to the delights of raw fish. The sushi and sashimi are still reliably ocean fresh, as the loyal custom of what seems to be most of the Japanese business people in New York will attest.

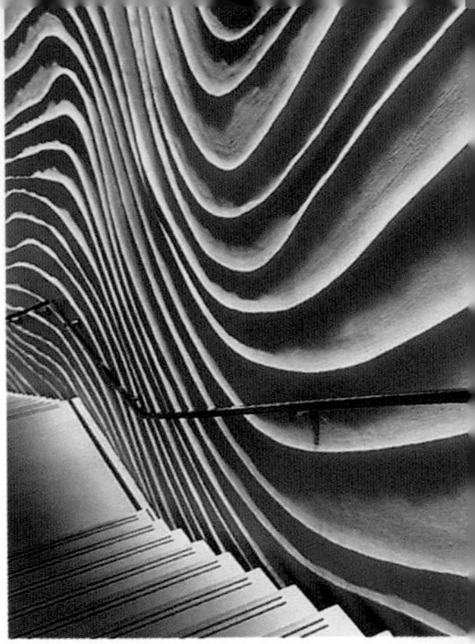

Latin American

Noche

1604 Broadway (bet. 48th and 49th sts) [B2]. Tel: 212-541-7070. Open: L and D Mon–Sat.
$$–$$$

This hopping four-story Latin-inspired hotspot just off Times Square has pulsating music and a stage on the second floor, but the place isn't just a scene; the kitchen also manages to send out delicious upscale versions of classic Latin dishes such as empanadas (flakey pastry filled with beef and onions or spinach and corn), ceviches, tacos, and tamales. On Tuesday and weekend evenings there's live music and late-night dancing.

Plantain Cafe

20 W. 38th St (bet. Fifth and Sixth aves) [C4]. Tel: 212-869-8601. Open: L and D Mon–Sat.
$–$$

A mellow-hued, two-story space at the edge of the Fashion District is doing its part in bringing innovative, affordable Caribbean cuisine into vogue. Plantains are the way to start, served as chips and dipped in salsa, followed by delicious new takes on ceviche, roast pork, curried goat, and other Latin staples.

Left: *Blue Fin seafood restaurant, flashy but fun*

Rice 'n Beans

744 Ninth Ave (bet. 50th and 51st sts) [A2]. Tel: 212-265-4444. Open: L and D daily. **$**
www.riceandbeansrestaurant.com

Small and unadorned, except for a bust of Carmen Miranda, this hole-in-the-wall Brazilian concentrates on hearty basics and a warm atmosphere. Big bowls of caldo verde, a sausage soup, and feijoada, a meat-laden casserole, steam up the windows, while strains of the bossa nova set a steamy mood.

Scandinavian

Aquavit

13 W. 54th St (bet. Fifth and Sixth aves) [C1]. Tel: 212-307-7311. **$$$$** *www.aquavit.org*

The best of Swedish design and cuisine come to the fore in this sparse, multi-level townhouse, ensuring a sophisticated night out and one of Manhattan's most memorable dining experiences. Sweden's beloved herring shows up as a work of art, as do all other manner of fish, venison, and game. Meatballs, smorgasbord plates, and, of course, aquavit, are also on hand, offered on prix-fixe menus. Service is slick. The upstairs AQ cafe is more casual.

Seafood

Le Bernardin

155 W. 51st St (bet. Sixth and Seventh aves) [B2]. Tel: 212-489-1515. Open: L and D Mon–Fri, D only Sat. **$$$$**
www.le-bernardin.com

Trawl no more for the world's best seafood. Here at Le Bernardin, chef Eric Ripert's seafood menu will grab you hook, line, and sinker. His deceptively subtle preparations of anything that swims, from fried calamari to poached salmon to oven-roasted sea bass, are expertly served in simple surroundings. A gastronomic shrine.

Blue Fin

W. Times Square Hotel, 1567 Broadway (bet. 46th and 47th sts) [B3]. Tel: 212-918-1400. Open: B, L, and D daily. **$$$**

It's easy to get swept away by the hype here – in the street-level bar only a glass wall separates you from the hubbub of Times Square, and Austin Powers would feel at home in the 1970s retro, two-floor dining room. The kitchen, though, gets real, sending out salmon, sea bass, tuna, and their scaley kin in deliciously innovative preparations.

Esca

402 W. 43rd St (9th Ave) [A3]. Tel: 212-564-7272. Open: L and D Mon–Sat, D only Sun. **$$$**

The star of this exceptional southern Italian seafood restaurant are the crudo appetizers: starters of raw fresh fish. There are lots of delicious fish dishes to choose from (chef David Pasternack's enticing menu changes daily depending on the day's catch), as well as fresh pasta and gnocchi.

Grand Central Oyster Bar and Restaurant

Grand Central Terminal (at 42nd St and Park Ave) [D3].

Fresh seafood in Times Square

Tel: 212-490-6650. Open: L and D Mon–Sat. ***$$***
Bi-valves rule at this arched-and-tiled 1913 landmark in the bowels of Grand Central Terminal – they show up on the half shell, in several kinds of chowder, in pan roasts, and even in po'boys (a kind of sandwich). A seat at the lunch counter ensures an entertaining bird's-eye view of comings and goings as frantic as those in the main concourse upstairs.

Josephs
1240 Sixth Ave (at 49th St) [C2]. Tel: 212-332-1515. Open: L and D Mon–Fri, D only Sat–Sun. ***$$$–$$$$*** *www.citarella.com*
New Yorkers flock to Citarella markets around the city to procure the freshest seafood, and now the fishmongers have also become restaurateurs. Every fish in the sea seems to feature on the menu, and you can enjoy the day's catch in a breezy, nautical-themed, multi-floored townhouse so close to Radio City you can almost hear the Rockettes tap. You may wish to forego decision-making and try the delectable tasting menu.

Thai

Vong
200 E. 54th St (at Third Ave) [D2]. Tel: 212-486-9592. Open: L and D Mon–Fri, D only Sat/Sun. ***$$$*** *www.jean-georges.com*
In elegant surroundings where ceiling fans whirl above polished teak, über-chef Jean-Georges Vongerichten's marriage of Thai and French flavors results in such outstanding creations as crunchy crab rolls, lobster curries, and a long menu full of other taste sensations. Many places try to imitate the Vong fusion concept, but few can compare to this.

Did you know?
For a few months in 1930, the Chrysler Building, with its radiator-like spires gleaming high above Midtown, was the tallest building in the world. Soon, however, it was eclipsed by the Empire State Building.

Cafes and Bars

For sheer drop-dead glamour, step into **Campbell Apartment** *(tel: 212-953-0409)*, a secret lair in Grand Central Terminal, once the private digs of a magnate. Or, lounge in a leather seat at the **King Cole Bar** *(St. Regis Hotel, 2 E. 55th St, tel: 212-339-6721)*, where the Bloody Mary was invented. Over at the **Algonquin** *(59 W. 44th St, tel: 212-840-6800)* you can still hear Dorothy Parker and other members of the elitist Round Table slurping bourbon and throwing *bons mots* around the paneled room. Their publishing descendants take a tipple down the street, at **Bar 44 at the Royalton** *(Royalton Hotel, 44 W. 44th St, tel: 212-944-8844)*.

For an earthier taste of New York, head over to **Rudy's** *(627 Ninth Ave, tel: 212-974-9169)*, a scruffy neighborhood haunt with bags of atmosphere where drinks are cheap and the hot dogs free.

For a quick, less expensive bite to eat, try **Mangia** *(16 E. 48th St, tel: 212-754-0637, and elsewhere)*, a multi-outlet lunchtime favorite that honors its Italian roots with antipasti, little pizzas, and hot entrees. Alternatively, try **Prêt à Manger** *(1350 Sixth Ave, tel: 212-307-6100, and elsewhere)* which has brought its tasty sandwiches across the Atlantic from London and dispenses them at several Midtown outlets.

A Food Cart Named Desire

If food carts provoke images of chewy hot dogs and overpriced soda, think again. In this city, they are an altogether classier affair

The chances are your first sighting of a cart peddling food will be in Central Park, and the wares on offer will be hot dogs, giant pretzels, a few bags of potato chips, and cans of soda. Such carts should, however, be ignored: the hotdogs will be boiled beyond blandness, the pretzel stale, and the sodas ludicrously expensive. But don't let them put you off. Instead, retrain your eye to spot the licensed vendors with a dazzling variety of foods at bargain prices.

The three 'h's'

The majority of food carts hawk hot dogs, hamburgers, and heros (large, torpedo-shaped sandwiches). If it's got to be a hot dog, make sure it's a good one, such as the impeccable Chicago-style ones (with poppy-seed buns, fried onions, lettuce, cucumber, green relish, mustard, and hot peppers) from the cart run from April to September by the **Eleven Madison Park Restaurant** *(see page 33)* and located on the southwest corner of Madison Square Park. They also sell amazing chocolate-truffle cookies and home-made lemon-verbena squash. Another pedigree dog can be found year-round at **Hallo Berlin** (at Fifth Ave and 54th St). The sausages here include knockwurst, bratwurst, and weisswurst, and are served on a crusty roll with sauerkraut, onions, and the tangy 'house' mustard, which, thankfully, is neither yellow nor from a squeezy bottle.

International options

For the South American take on the Cornish pasty try an empanada from **Ruben's Cart** (at Broadway and 39th St), where there are at least five different varieties daily. Or try the marinaded, skewered, and grilled meats on the west side of Sixth Avenue at 50th Street, at a stall run by Puerto Ricans and popular with Midtown's office workers, who line up to take polystyrene boxes of food home for dinner. Dressed in spotless white clothes, with two assistants at his side, **Antonio Dragonas** (at 62nd St and Madison Ave) serves inexpensive, Greek-style grilled meats to 200 people a day. And for great Middle Eastern-style kebabs – generous slices of meat rolled up in a soft flatbread – try **Rafiqi's Cart** (Madison and 47th sts); everything is kept impeccably clean and fresh.

The lines for the **NY Dosas Cart** at the southern edge of Washington Square Park can go round the square and back again, but patience is a virtue, as delicious, ultra-healthy meals can be had for just $5. Another Indian vegetarian option is **Govinda's** (at Park Ave and 52nd St). For breakfast, there are oatmeal or wholegrain pancakes and fruit, and at lunch, $5 gets you a daily changing medley of sautéed vegetables, brown rice, pasta, or potatoes.

Down in Chinatown, look out for the **Chow Fun Noodle Cart** (at Pike St and East Broadway). They specialize in the long rolled noodles called chow fun that the vendor snips off at your required length before dressing them with three different sauces of your choice and a handful of sesame seeds.

And for the best coffee from a cart – or possibly from anywhere in Manhattan – make for **The Mudtruck** (at Fourth Ave and 8th St) in Astor Place. The mild, but rich, shot of espresso is the perfect wake-up call.

New York dogs cut the mustard

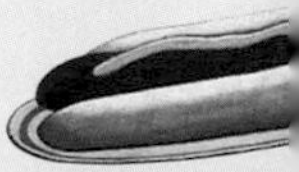

Area 2: Flatiron, Union Square and Gramercy

FLATIRON, UNION SQUARE, AND GRAMERCY

Food fanatics and fashionistas alike flock to this former industrial area, which straddles Midtown and downtown Manhattan

Since the mid-1980s, this part of town has flourished into one of the city's most notable areas for restaurants. This is where you'll find the empires of celebrity chefs including Bobby Flay (Mesa Grill, Bolo); Rocco DiSpirito (Union Pacific, Rocco's), Anthony Bourdain (of Les Halles restaurant and author of *Kitchen Confidential*, an hilarious, revealing account of life as a chef), restaurateur Danny Meyer (Union Square Cafe, Gramercy Tavern, Eleven Madison Park, and Blue Smoke), plus countless other high-quality hotspots. drawing in crowds of food fanatics and fashionistas.

Flatiron and Union Square

The old Flatiron District due north of Union Square is named after the spectacular Flatiron building, erected in 1902 and located at the spot where Fifth Avenue, Broadway, and 23rd Street meet. The surrounding buildings were built in the 19th century for commercial and industrial use. The regeneration of this area owes a lot to these cast-iron buildings whose cavernous interiors, soaring ceilings, vast windows, and original features are an interior designer's dream, particularly for restaurant designers (think large kitchens and dramatic dining rooms). This style of building has attracted other creative professions, from photography studios and advertising agencies to modeling agencies and media production offices, whose employees provide a constant stream of lunch and dinnertime customers.

Another explanation for the proliferation of great restaurants in the area is its proximity to the Farmer's Market on Union Square. The scene of gatherings and speeches by political radicals in the 19th and early 20th centuries (one Marxist bookstore, Revolution Books, remains at 9 W. 19th St), the park has hosted the market four days a week (Monday, Wednesday, Friday, and Saturday) year-round since 1976. This is Manhattan's most important outdoor market, where farmers from upstate New York and neighboring states come to sell seasonal produce, flowers, and baked goods.

Opposite: bar at the vibrant Turkish Kitchen

Park Avenue South

Stretching up from Union Square is Park Avenue South, a bustling artery jammed with restaurants and nightspots on both sides and reaching almost fever pitch on Friday and Saturday nights. Here, you'll find the steakhouse and cigar bar Angelos and Maxie's (No. 233), seafood bar City Crab (No. 235), Brazilian-Japanese hotspot Sushi Samba (No. 245), top Latin-American restaurant Patria *(see page 39)*, all-night bistro L'Express *(see page 35)*, chic Mexican restaurant Dos Caminos *(see page 38)*, and French steakhouse Les Halles *(see page 36)*. Along 19th, 20th, 21st and 22nd streets

East, between Park and Fifth avenues, are some of the city's best restaurants: Bolo *(see page 41)*, Craft *(see page 32)*, Gramercy Tavern *(see page 33)*, Veritas *(see page 35)*, and Fleur de Sel *(see page 36)*.

During the day, the stretch of 5th Avenue between 23rd and 15th streets is ideal for clothes shopping. Here, you'll find chains such as Banana Republic, Victoria's Secret, Kenneth Cole, and Ann Taylor, along with Paul Smith and beauty stores Aveda and The Body Shop. For a quick bite, there are small New York delis and coffee shops, as well as quality sandwich and salad places such as City Bakery at 3 West 18th Street and Mayrose at 920 Broadway.

Gramercy Park

On the east side of Union Square is Gramercy Park. While the Flatiron and Union Square districts are primarily commercial areas, the Gramercy Park area is mostly residential. This well-heeled enclave centers around Gramercy Park, a

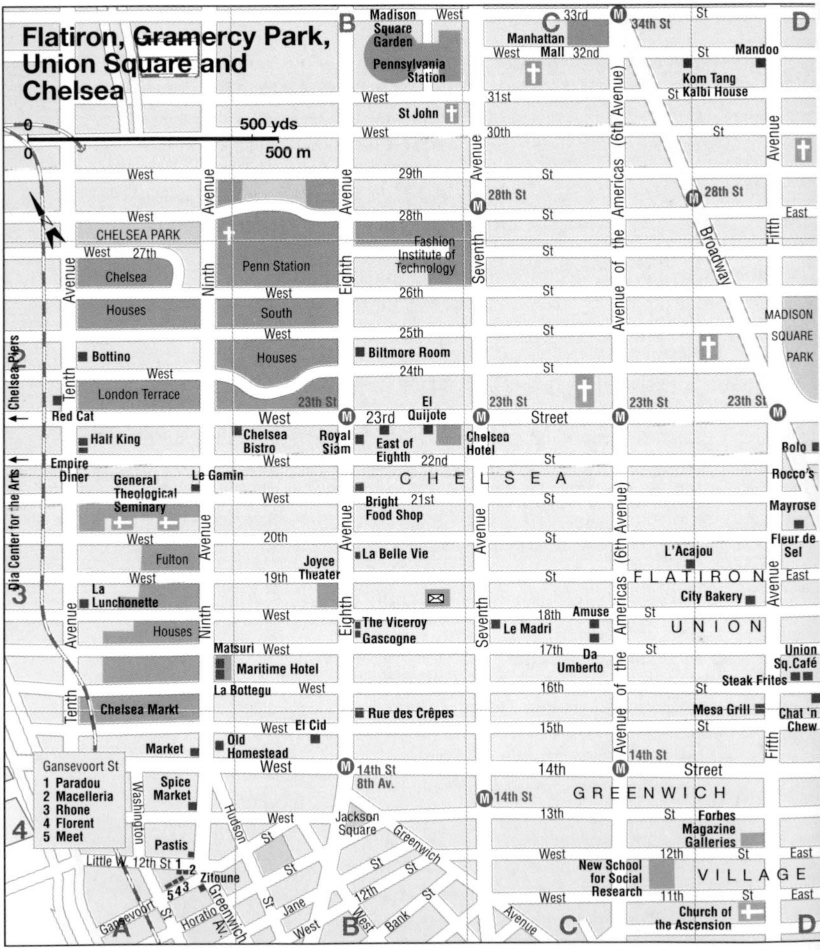

2-acre (.8 sq km) square providing a welcome expanse of leafy greenery. It was built in the mid-1800s and modeled on the genteel residential squares of London. Only residents of the surrounding townhouses have a key to this, Manhattan's only private park, although guests at the Gramercy Park Hotel on the corner of Lexington and 21st are also allowed in.

Running south from Gramercy Park down to 14th Street is the charming Irving Place, named after Washington Irving, author of the *Legend of Sleepy Hollow*. The quiet street is lined with elegant brownstones and punctuated along its length with good restaurants, including the cozy, family-oriented Friend of a Farmer *(see page 33)* at No. 77. Celebrity chef and restaurateur Mario Batali (of Babbo and Lupa fame) has bumped up the glamour quotient of the neighborhood with the opening of his bijou Spanish restaurant Casa Mono *(see page 41)* and the even smaller wine and tapas bar next door, Bar Jamón *(see page 40)*,

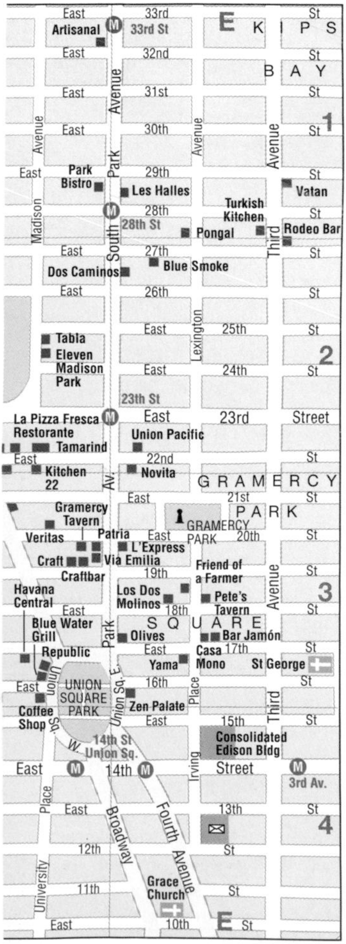

Little India

The mood changes several blocks up at the north end of Gramercy Park on Lexington Avenue, where Manhattan's Little India is found – an area known affectionately as 'Curry Hill.' Here, for several blocks, the avenue and neighboring streets are dotted with Indian and Pakistani restaurants and grocery stores. The most famous food store (est. 1944) is Kalustyan's at 123 Lexington – two floors of Indian and Middle Eastern spices, grains, canned goods and prepared food. A few good choices for eating on this stretch include a restaurant spin-off of the food store Kalustyan's Masala Café at 115 Lexington; the vegetarian Pongal at 110; and Vatan down the block and around the corner on 3rd Avenue at 29th Street *(see page 37)*.

Five of the Best

Blue Water Grill: great seafood, bar and brunches in an elegant setting
Chat 'n' Chew: huge portions of delicious comfort food American-style
Craft: New York hotspot with a do-it-yourself menu.
Mesa Grill: Bobby Flay's southwestern fare is as flamboyant as the chef himself
Novità: quality Italian fare at reasonable prices in a sophisticated atmosphere

Craft, one of the city's biggest success stories

Did you know?

The triangular structure of the Flatiron building became the world's first steel-framed skyscraper when it was erected in 1902, and remains one of New York's most photographed sights.

American

Blue Smoke

116 E. 27th St (bet. Park Ave S. and Lexington) [E2]. Tel: 212-447-7733. Open: L and D daily. ***$$$*** *www.bluesmoke.com*

Restaurateur Danny Meyer does down-home barbeque dog-gone good. His huge portions of ribs and Texas-style beef brisket make this a meat-eaters' paradise. The decor is casual but sophisticated, and the ceiling soaring. Food is also served in the downstairs jazz club.

Chat 'n' Chew

10 E. 16th St (bet. Fifth Ave and Union Sq. W.) [D3]. Tel: 212-243-1616. Open: L and D daily; Br Sat–Sun. ***$$***

A cheap 'n' cheerful restaurant with a rustic feel – perfect for freshly squeezed lemonade and macaroni and cheese. Expect big portions and delicious desserts including homemade apple or blueberry pie. A good place to bring the kids or for a casual date, though the service could be better.

City Bakery

3 W. 18th St (bet. Fifth and Sixth aves) [C3]. Tel: 212-366-1414. Open: L and D daily. ***$***

This is not your average deli: it has soaring ceilings, minimalist modern decor, chic patrons, and the most imaginative gourmet salad bar in the city. You can also order sandwiches, get great desserts, or sip on perhaps the best hot chocolate in Manhattan – they even make their own marshmallows and hold a hot-chocolate festival in February.

Coffee Shop

29 Union Sq. W. (16th St) [D3]. Tel: 212-243-7969. Open: B, L, and D daily, till late. ***$$***

A great place for a casual meal or drink and a spot of people-watching, this glorified diner bustles with a disproportionate number of good-looking people, mostly models and struggling actors. The menu offers a choice of simple pasta dishes and burgers, alongside Brazilian specialties such as shrimp baiano (shrimp sautéed with peppers, garlic, and coconut) or moqueca stew (shrimps, clams, and scallops poached in a caruru sauce).

Craft

43 E. 19th St (bet. Broadway and Park Ave S.) [D3]. Tel: 212-780-0880. Open: L and D Mon–Fri, D only Sat–Sun. ***$$$$***

Chef Tom Colicchio (of Gramercy Tavern fame, *see page 33*) encourages creativity in his customers, who are invited to concoct their own meal. The menu is split into sections (vegetable, sides, meat, and fish) and cooking methods, and you choose the combination (e.g. roasted dourade, potato gratin, sautéed peas, and baby bok choy). The top-quality ingredients are rich in flavor, and the decor is cutting-edge elegant (check out the leather wall). Some call it foodie heaven, but it's a nightmare for the indecisive on a first date. Wildly popular.

Craftbar

47 E. 19th St (bet. Broadway and Park Ave S.) [D3]. Tel: 212-780-0880. Open: L and D daily. **$$$**

Little sister to Craft next door, Craftbar offers a cheaper, less complex way to enjoy the delicious New American creations by Tom Colicchio, such as veal-and-ricotta meatballs, whipped salt cod, or braised rabbit. For an even more casual spin-off try 'Witchcraft' next door, which does sandwiches such as Sicilian tuna with shaved fennel, black olives, and lemon on a baguette, or grilled gruyère with caramelized onions on rye. Craftbar operates a no-reservation policy so expect long lines.

Eleven Madison Park

11 Madison Ave (24th St) [D2]. Tel: 212-889-0905. Open: L and D daily. **$$$$**

Formerly a bank lobby, the majestic dining room here, with soaring marble ceiling, makes a dramatic setting for Danny Meyer's high-class New American dishes. Concoctions such as spice-dusted duck breast with fois gras, Napa cabbage, and Armagnac sauce, or seared Arctic char with black truffle vinaigrette, salsify, and pea shoots are served by chef Kerry Heffernan with aplomb. A treat.

Friend of a Farmer

77 Irving Pl. (bet. 18th and 19th sts) [E3]. Tel: 212-477-2188. Open: B, L, and D Mon–Fri, Br and D Sat–Sun. **$$**

It feels like a Vermont bed and breakfast in this cozy and casual restaurant that serves hearty portions of American fare. Great for family eating and brunches, and for basic dishes such as lasagne, meatloaf, banana bread, and apple pie.

Gramercy Tavern

42 E. 20th St (bet. Broadway and Park Ave S.) [D3]. Tel: 212-477-0777. Open: L and D daily. **$$$$**

Danny Meyer's New American Gramercy Tavern has been a triumph since it opened in the early 1990s. It draws in crowds every day of the week to the large bar area up front, or to the more formal back room. The neo-colonial decor is both comfortable and sophisticated, and the updated classic American cuisine is always top-notch; dishes include braised veal cheeks with gnocchi and morels, seafood stew, and rack of baby lamb. To follow, choose from 85 different types of cheese (one of the best cheese courses in the city.)

Kitchen 22

36 E. 22nd St (bet. Broadway and Park Ave S.) [D2]. Tel: 212-228-4399. Open: D only Mon–Sat. **$$** *www.charliepalmer.com*

This bustling New American restaurant attracts young professionals who come for the moderately priced comfort food, and the wine at $25 or $35 a bottle. The prix-fixe menu ($25) includes dishes such as golden roast chicken, and roast salmon with a fennel crust. Other regulars crowd in at the bar, enjoying the well-priced martinis. No reservations.

Mayrose

920 Broadway (21st St) [D3]. Tel: 212-533-3663. Open: L and D daily; Br Sat–Sun. **$**

This retro-diner's home-baked hot dogs, macaroni and cheese, and meatloaf are good but not thrilling.

***Below:* Eleven Madison Park's dining room, and Gramercy Tavern's kitchen**

Landmark pub, Pete's Tavern

The main attractions here are the soaring ceilings, huge picture windows, and fashionable crowd of models and creative types who work in the area.

Mesa Grill

102 Fifth Ave (bet. 15th and 16th sts) [D 3–4]. Tel: 212-807-7400. Open: L and D daily. ***$$$–$$$$*** *www.mesagrill.com*

Food Network star chef Bobby Flay wows crowds with his delicious, inventive southwestern creations mixing sweet and sour flavors, and smoke and spice, in dishes such as wild-boar satay with a maple glaze, or 16-spice chicken. Everything here, from the eclectic menu to the fabulous lofty ceilings, is as bold and imaginative as the chef himself.

Pete's Tavern

129 E. 18th St (Irving Pl.) [E3]. Tel: 212-473-7676. Open: L and D daily. ***$$*** *www.petestavern.com*

This is one of the city's most historic pubs, and reportedly where O. Henry wrote *Gift of the Magi*. It still draws an illustrious crowd of writers, celebrities, and locals, who come for the history and the comfortable, though somewhat dingy tavern atmosphere, more than for the basic pub fare.

Rodeo Bar

375 Third Ave (27th St) [E1]. Tel: 212-683-6500. Open: L and D daily. ***$*** *www.rodeobar.com*

Great for honky-tonk, fiddlin', or alt-country sounds while munching on southwestern fare of brisket, ribs, cat-fish, or enchiladas. An added pleasure is the Tex-Mex decor – saddles and cow skulls on the walls – and the crunch of peanut shells on the floor.

Union Pacific

111 E. 22nd St (bet. Park Ave S. and Lexington Ave) [E2]. Tel: 212-995-8500. Open: L and D Mon–Sat, D only Sun. ***$$$$*** *www.unionpacificrestaurant.com*

The ascent of TV chef Rocco DiSpirito (of *The Restaurant* fame) began here at his soothing, sophisticated Asian-inspired New American place serving creative fare such as black cod with avocado and pickled mango or tiger-shrimp stuffed rabbit. Some say it's losing its footing at the expense of DiSpirito's TV show filmed at nearby Rocco's 22; others say it's still firmly on track.

Union Square Cafe

21 E. 16th St (bet. Fifth and Union Sq.) [D3] Tel: 212-243-4020. Open: L and D daily. ***$$$$***

After nearly 20 years in business, Danny Meyer's New American restaurant remains a firm city favorite. This is largely down to chef and co-owner Michael Romano's consistently good daily specials, ranging from lobster shepherd's pie and red-wine-braised prime rib of beef, to monkfish, manila clams, and rock shrimp in Catalan garlic, almond, and tomato sauce. The casually elegant surroundings and, above all, the warm, respectful nature of the informed waiting staff keep this restaurant at the top.

Veritas

43 E. 20th (bet. Broadway and Park Ave S.) [D3]. Tel: 212-353-3700. Open: D only daily. **$$$$**
www.veritas-nyc.com

Critics have hailed chef Scott Bryan's spare, but inventive New American cuisine as 'flawless' and 'intelligent' (dishes on a recent menu included juniper-crusted venison with braised red cabbage, and slow-poached Atlantic salmon with braised escarole, zucchini, and saffron). The atmosphere is sophisticated and relaxing, but the undisputed star here is the wine cellar, stocked with a superb selection, including rare French vintages, at reasonable prices.

Asian

Republic

37 Union Sq. W. (bet. 16th and 17th sts) [D3]. Tel: 212-627-7172. Open: L and D daily. **$**
www.thinknoodles.com

Large and noisy but stylish, with communal wood benches, Republic is like a huge gourmet canteen. The portions of noodle dishes are mammoth too. For great value, try the steamy, delicious, affordable 'meals-in-a-bowl.'

French

L'Acajou

53 W. 19th St (bet. Fifth and Sixth aves) [C3]. Tel: 212-645-1706. Open: L and D Mon–Fri, D only Sat. **$$**

When the craving for French brasserie food hits, try this neighborhood institution. It's big on reliably satisfying classics from the Alsace region, such as thick chops, sausage, and herring. The food is accompanied by excellent wines and served in delightful Art Deco surroundings. Long popular with media-industry locals.

Artisanal

2 Park Ave (32nd St) [D1]. Tel: 212-725-8585. Open: L and D daily. **$$$**

A boisterous French brasserie with red banquettes and white tablecloths and an enormous cheese selection. A large part of the menu is devoted to classic bistro cooking such as steak-frites or sole meunière, but most fun is the gooey cheese fondue served with hunks of freshly baked bread.

L'Express

249 Park Ave S. (20th St) [E3]. Tel: 212-254-5858. Open: daily, 24 hrs. **$$**

Artisanal, for traditional French brasserie fare

Late-night revellers flock to this bistro in the small hours to snack on escargots, onion soup, and salade frisée. Thanks to the affordable fare and appealing bistro decor (tin ceiling, fans, and red banquettes) it's a tight squeeze in here pretty much round the clock.

Fleur de Sel

5 E. 20th St (bet. Fifth Ave and Broadway) [D3]. Tel: 212-460-9100. Open: L and D Mon–Sat, D only Sun. ***$$$$***

The talents of Brittany-born chef Cyril Renaud shine at his sophisticated, welcoming French outpost. Vermont goat's cheese and artichoke ravioli with caviar beef in Dijon mustard jus, or Colorado lamb loin with rosemary tomato jus, sweet pepper confit, and a fromage blanc tart are typical of the kind of refined yet flavor-packed dishes this culinary wizard creates. Pricey, but many think it's worth it.

Below and bottom: Tabla, for Indian-inspired American food

Les Halles

411 Park Ave S. (bet. 28th and 29th sts) [D1]. Tel: 212-679-4111. Open: L and D daily. ***$$$*** *www.leshalles.net*

This French steakhouse packs in the crowds, who come to soak up the very French atmosphere and deliberate over the expansive menu of classics such as cassoulet, mussels steamed in white wine, blood sausage with caramelized apples, or duck-leg confit with salade frisée. Best-selling author Anthony Bourdain used to cook here, but you're unlikely to find him in the kitchen unless it's in his capacity as 'consultant'. The butcher's shop next door means you can try and do it yourself at home. There's a second branch near Wall Street.

Park Bistro

414 Park Ave S. (bet. 28th and 29th sts) [D1]. Tel: 212-689-1360. Open: L and D Mon–Fri. ***$$$*** *www.parkbistro.com*

With its creaky wood floors, red banquettes, and limited elbow room, this cozy French restaurant feels like the real thing. The lobster salad with black-truffle vinaigrette, creamy seafood medley in puffed pastry, duck confit in a sauce of port and lingon berries, and other such refined dishes are consistently delicious. A neighborhood favorite.

Steak Frites

9 E. 16th St (bet. Fifth Ave and Union Sq. W.) [D3]. Tel: 212-

463-7101. Open: L and D daily; Br Sat–Sun. **$$** *www.steakfritesnyc.com*
Generous cuts of steak paired with delicate French fries is the specialty of this spacious restaurant with high ceilings, white-linen tablecloths, and comfortable wooden bar. But there's more to the menu than just steak – fish and seafood dishes such as steamed mussels, bouillabaisse, and wild salmon are equally tasty.

Indian

Pongal
110 Lexington Ave (bet. 26th and 27th sts) [E2]. Tel: 212-696-9458. Open: L and D daily. **$$** *www.pongal.org*
This Kosher vegetarian restaurant, specializing in the food of Gujarat, Punjab, and southern India, is a good choice on this block filled with Indian eateries and grocery stores. There's a wide choice of dosai (thin crisp crêpes with fillings of potatoes and onions, cilantro and rice, etc.), and the kala chana (black chickpeas in a creamy tomato and onion sauce) and iddly (steamed lentil and rice cakes) are excellent.

Tabla
11 Madison Ave (25th St) [D2]. Tel: 212-889-0667. Open: L and D Mon–Fri; D only Sat, Sun. **$$$$**
Floyd Cardoz's Indian-inspired New American restaurant is as much loved for its rich decor in shades of jade and coral, as for its original fusion of flavours and ingredients such as Vermont baby lamb with tandoori eggplant, English peas, mint, taro, and green cardamom; or crisped soft-shell crab with chilled mung bean noodles, cucumber, and roasted mango vinaigrette. For a less-expensive option, or to sample hors d'oeuvres, try Bread Bar downstairs.

Tamarind
41–3 E. 22nd St (bet. Broadway and Park Ave S.) [D2]. Tel: 212-674-7400. Open: L and D daily. **$$$** *www.tamarind22.com*
The elegant, modern dining room sets this multi-regional Indian restaurant apart from its competitors, and the menu is interesting too. As well as classics such as saag paneer, there are American-Indian fusion creations such as pan-seared tuna with toasted black sesame seeds and cayenne, or Cornish game hen with tamarind sauce and garlic soup. Some say it's past its prime and a little pricey, but for a taste – along with a cup of tea – try the Tea Room next door.

Vatan
409 Third Ave (29th St) [E1]. Tel: 212-689-5666. Open: D only, Tues–Sun. **$$** *www.vatanny.com*
Vatan is decorated like a northern Indian village, with artificial banyan trees and thatched rooftops over booths. There's no choosing dishes here – for a fixed price, waitresses serve a generous selection of mild, medium, or hot vegetarian dishes from Gandhi's home region of Gujarat. They include chana masala (chickpeas in a cream sauce), saag paneer, and lentil cakes.

Italian

Novità
102 E. 22nd St (bet. Park Ave S. and Lexington) [E2]. Tel: 212-677-2222. Open: L and D daily. **$$$**
This northern Italian restaurant is much appreciated by its regulars, who like the fact that it remains an undiscovered gem. What makes it so successful are the delicious, freshly prepared dishes such as pappardelle with lamb ragu and porcini mushrooms, red snapper in

TIP
If you need a snack and a break from shopping, try **Eisenberg's Sandwich Shop** (174 Fifth Ave between 22nd and 23rd sts.), which serves pastrami sandwiches people travel miles for.

tomato broth, or rack of lamb roasted with mustard and rosemary. Add the sophisticated decor, gracious service, and reasonable prices, and you have a winner.

La Pizza Fresca Ristorante

31 E. 20th St (bet. Broadway and Park Ave S.) [D2]. Tel: 212-598-0141. Open: L and D Mon–Fri, D only Sat–Sun. **$$**

This small, friendly restaurant is famous for its authentic Neapolitan pizzas. They are made with hand-pressed dough topped with a sauce of San Marzano tomatoes and cooked to thin-crust perfection in brick ovens. There are 16 different kinds of pizza on the menu, from basic margarita (tomato sauce, olive oil, and garlic) to cime di rapa (broccoli, sausage, and fresh Italian buffalo mozzarella. They also serve great fresh pasta.

Rocco's

12 E. 22nd St (bet. Broadway and Park Ave S.) [D2]. Tel: 212-353-0510. Open: D daily. **$$$**
www.roccosrestaurant.com

Celebrity chef Rocco DiSpirito's latest creation is a restaurant inspired by his Italian-US upbringing. His mother helps out, and her meatballs are featured on the vast menu which includes pasta, baked lemon shrimp, broiled quail in red-wine sauce, and fried baby artichokes. DiSpirito turned the launch of the restaurant into a reality TV series, and the patrons tend to be curious tourists; the critics have been less enthusiastic, and many say the food has paid the price of TV fame.

Via Emilia

240 Park Ave S. (bet. 19th and 20th sts) [D3]. Tel: 212-505-3072. Open: L and D Mon–Fri, D only Sat. **$**
www.viaemilianyc.com

Don't let the plain, unpretentious decor of brick walls and wood banquettes fool you – this small North Italian neighborhood restaurant serves delicious bolognese dishes such as lasagne and tortellini (of the four fillings, the pumpkin with butter and sage is simple but delectable) at quite reasonable prices. Other recommended dishes include gnoccho fritto (puffy fritters served with cured meats), washed down with a chilled glass of quality lambrusco from an impressive list of Italian wines.

TIP

The nation's largest cooking school, the Institute of Culinary Education, is on 23rd Street, between Sixth and Seventh avenues. It offers several half-day classes every day. Go to (www.ice-culinary.com).

Japanese

Yama

122 E. 17th St (Irving Pl.) [E3]. Tel: 212-475-0969. Open: L and D Mon–Fri, D only Sat. **$**

Some complain that the decor and service are mediocre, but most agree that this is compensated for by the delicious, creative food. There are very generous servings of sushi and tempura, too. Just expect a wait at the door.

Latin American

Dos Caminos

373 Park Ave S. (bet. 26th and 27th sts) [E2]. Tel: 212-294-1000. Open: L and D daily. **$$$**
www.brguestrestaurants.com

This chic Mexican serves imaginative, upscale versions of classic dishes. Try the fresh guacamole, tacos stuffed with tequila-and-lime-marinated shimp and lobster, or the Florida red snapper with coconut rice, lentils, and a passion-fruit sauce. The decor by designers Yabu Pushelberg is hip yet warm. If you want to make a night of it, there are 100 types of tequila to choose from. The second branch, in SoHo (475 W. Broadway at Houston St), is a runaway success.

Charming local Italian, Novità

Havana Central
22 E. 17th St (bet. Broadway and Fifth Ave) [D3]. Tel: 212-414-2298. Open: L and D daily. **$$** *www.havanacentral.com*
With its high ceilings, huge hanging fans, and green-and-terracotta walls, this place has a sleek, casual mood – think Havana in the 1950s. The delicious, varied menu features traditional Cuban dishes including Ropa Vieja (beef, pepper, and onions), or delicious barbequed ribs with mango habanero ginger, which some say are the best in New York.

Los Dos Molinos
119 E. 18th St (bet. Irving Pl. and Park Ave S.) [E3]. Tel: 212-505-1574. Open: L and D Tues–Sat. **$$**
The hip atmosphere here combines with a kitsch western decor (Route 66 signs and voodoo dolls on the walls, and cacti hanging from the ceiling). The firey southwestern food of nachos, burritos, and ribs, and the delicious margaritas, draw in a rumbustious crowd including New Yorkers homesick for Arizona.

Patria
250 Park Ave S. (20th St) [D3]. Tel: 212-777-6211. Open: L and D Mon–Fri, D only Sat–Sun. **$$$** *www.patria-restaurant.com*
Considered one of the city's top Latin American restaurants, the hip, multi-leveled Patria serves inventive Nuevo Latino dishes. These include red snapper with crab-crusted yuca and a guajillo chile lobster broth, and crispy duck's leg over sweet plantains sautéed with a reduction of apple cider and mustard seeds. The decor is suave and festive, and, despite changing chefs a couple of years ago, the restaurant still holds the title of 'Latin star' in the Flatiron district.

***Right:* Outdoor terrace of the vibrant Blue Water Grill. *Below:* subdued lighting at the Turkish Kitchen**

Mediterranean

Olives

W. Union Square Hotel, 201 Park Ave S. (E. 17th St) [E3]. Tel: 212-353-8345. Open: 7am–midnight daily; Br Sat–Sun. **$$$**

The bar area of this Mediterranean restaurant is pretty lively at night, but the sleek, modern dining room remains comfortably sedate. Either area is perfect for digging into Todd English's bold, flavorful cuisine, shown off in dishes such as seared yellow-fin tuna loin with curry polenta, ginger spinach, and blood orange vinaigrette; or crispy Long Island duck breast with chorizo basmati, golden raisin glaze, and eggplant purée.

Middle Eastern

Turkish Kitchen

386 Third Ave (bet. 27th and 28th aves) [E1]. Tel: 212-679-6633. Open: L and D Mon–Fri, D only Sat, Br and D Sun **$$**

The vibrant red walls, multicolored kilims, and Turkish music are part of the intoxicating fun at this large, bustling restaurant that specializes in authentic Istanbul cuisine. The meat-oriented menu features chicken and lamb kebabs with rice, grilled lamb with garlic, yoghurt, and tomato sauce, and steamed beef dumplings.

Seafood

Blue Water Grill

31 Union Sq. W. (16th St) [D3]. Tel: 212-675-9500. Open: L and D Mon–Fri, D only Sat, Br and D Sun. **$$$**
www.brguestrestaurants.com

A vibrant, two-level restaurant in a former bank (est. 1904) with marble floors, high ceilings, and an outdoor terrace. It's one of the city's most popular restaurants due to its sophisticated but easy-going ambiance, and well-priced, varied menu. Dishes include fresh lobster, Maryland crab cakes, and sushi.

Spanish

Bar Jamón

125 E. 17th St (bet. Irving Pl. and Third Ave) [E3]. Tel: 212-253-2773. Open: 2pm–2am daily. **$$**

Star chef and gourmet entrepreneur Mario Batali goes Spanish with two tiny adjacent bar/restaurants near Gramercy Park *(see Casa Mono, below)*. Bar Jamón, the

The popular roof terrace bar of the Gramercy Park Hotel (2 Lexington Ave at 21st St, tel: 212-475-4320) is great for taking in the air on summer nights and the views at any time.

smaller of the two, does excellent Spanish wines and dishes of chorizo and cheese with hunks of fresh bread to patrons sitting at two long communal tables. Crowded, boisterous, open late, and a hit.

Bolo

23 E. 22nd St (bet. Broadway and Park Ave S) [D2]. Tel: 212-228-2200. Open: L and D Mon–Fri, D only Sat–Sun. $$$ www.bolorestaurant.com

The cuisine at Bobby Flay's Spanish restaurant is a more refined version of his playful creations at the Mesa Grill *(see page 34)*, although no less imaginative or satisfying. The menu offers tantalizing dishes like horseradish-and-potato-crusted red snapper with red pepper-and-black olive relish, or pork tenderloin filled with walnut romesco, with a sauce of caramelized dates and shallots. The decor is equally inventive – note the wall collages and tiles.

Casa Mono

52 Irving Pl. (at 17th St) [E3]. Tel: 212-253-2773 Open: L and D daily. $$

Sister to Bar Jamón *(see above)*, Casa Mono is intimate and cozy, with wooden tables and a bar facing an open grill, where the staff whip up small delectable dishes. Off-beat meat products, such as cock's combs with green chilis, or tripe with chickpeas, are the stars here, although for the faint of heart there's a good selection of more traditional tapas from fried anchovies to lamb chops.

Vegetarian

Zen Palate

34 Union Sq. E. (16th St) [E3]. Tel: 212-614-9291. Open: L and D daily. $$ www.zenpalate.com

A multi-leveled yet calm vegetarian restaurant with a vast menu of evocatively named dishes, such as Jewel of Happiness (tempura mushrooms, bean steaks, and bran oats on a bed of mashed squash with sweet peas in a sage aromatic sauce). The food is mostly Asian-influenced, but there are some Mexican and US-style dishes as well. No alcohol.

Cafes and Bars

If you want to draw the evening out, many of the restaurants in the area have atmospheric bar areas, usually front of house, where you can enjoy an aperitif or digestif, or come in for a drink even if you're not eating, such as the four-star **Gramercy Tavern** *(see page 33)* and **The Blue Water Grill** *(see page 40)*. **Lola** *(30 22nd St W., bet. Fifth and Sixth aves, tel: 212-675-6700)* is a great bar/restaurant where you can sip a cocktail while listening to live jazz and R 'n' B. Another choice is **Morrell's Wine Bar and Café** *(900 Broadway, bet. 19th and 20th sts)*, where you can order a glass (or several) from a list of 150 wines. Historic pubs including **Pete's Tavern** *(see page 34)* and **Old Town Bar** *(45 E. 18th St, bet. Broadway and Park Ave S., tel: 212-529-6732)* are great for soaking up the atmosphere of Old New York. **The Coffee Shop** *(29 Union Sq. W. at 16th St, tel: 212-243-7969)* is a good place for a drink or coffee any time of the day. **L'Express** *(249 Park Ave S., at 20th St, tel: 212-254-5858)* is open 24/7 for a drink or a bite to eat. **City Bakery** *(3 W. 18th St, at Fifth Ave, tel: 212-366-1414)* and **Mayrose** *(920 Broadway, at 21st St)* are both good for a coffee, pastry, or snack. **ABC Carpets** *(888 Broadway at 20th St)* has a great cafe in the back on the first floor. **Barnes & Noble**'s *(33 17th St E., bet. Broadway and Park Ave S., tel: 212-253-0810)* in-store cafe is perfect for browsing through a magazine over a cup of coffee.

Indoor and Outdoor Markets

New York's markets offer a dazzling array of high-quality produce and specialty foodstuffs to its discerning customers

The more time you spend in the city's busy, clamorous restaurants, the more you might be led to believe that New Yorkers never eat at home. They certainly eat out more than most people, but when they cook at home, no mere supermarket will suffice. Instead, they seek out the gourmet and specialty markets to purchase their goods. Even if you're not planning to wield a spatula while in New York, you may nonetheless wish to step into some of these food shops to see the goods on display, stock up on ingredients that may not be readily available back home, nibble on cheese or some other delectable snack, or, in some, simply sit down and enjoy a meal.

City markets

A good way to see New Yorkers in their element is to stroll through the **Union Square Greenmarket** *(Broadway at 17th St, tel: 212-477-3220)*. Some 200 purveyors of produce, cheese, and other goods, all of it grown and produced on family farms, converge here every Monday, Wednesday, Friday, and Saturday. The action moves indoors at nearby **Chelsea Market** *(75 Ninth Ave, bet. 15th and 16th sts, tel: 212-727-1111)*, where several dozen bakers, butchers, fishmongers, and other food merchants are gathered together in an aromatic former Nabisco biscuit factory where the Oreo cookie was invented.

All over the city there are markets-cum-grocery stores, lively emporia that compete to outdo each other in the range of exotic gourmet goods on offer. King of these stores is **Zabar's** *(2245 Broadway, at 80th St, tel: 212-787-2000)*, close to three-quarters of a century old but not to be accused of resting on its laurels. The selection of cheeses, coffees, and prepared foods is constantly expanding, the smoked fish counter is a city institution, and the second-floor kitchenware department can't be outdone in terms of selection and price. You can enjoy Zabar's highly touted pastries and bagels, along with sandwiches and soups, at the serve-yourself cafe next door (a great place to sit and view the parade of pedestrians marching up and down Broadway).

A neighbor to Zabar's, **Citarella** *(2135 Broadway, at 75th St, tel: 212-874-0383)*, once just a fish market, is noted for the exotic scaled creatures on sale and for its elaborate watery window displays; the market has now branched out into quality meats, cheeses, and prepared food, and has opened Josephs, one of the finest seafood restaurants in the city *(see page 26)*. Nearby **Fairway** *(2127 Broadway, at 74th St, tel: 212-595-1888)* makes itself known with mountains of fruits and vegetables heaped on to sidewalk displays.

Union Square Greenmarket

Inside, shelves overflow with a vast selection of basic foodstuffs as well as cheeses, olives, baked goods, coffees, and prepared meals; a pleasant cafe upstairs serves sandwiches, salads, and more elaborate fare throughout the day and into the evening.

Chelsea Market

Delis to die for

Across town, a trio of gourmet giants caters to well-to-do Upper East Siders. **Grace's Marketplace** *(1237 Third Ave, at 71st St, tel: 212-737-0600)* takes the prize for the widest selection; **Eli's Vinegar Factory** *(431 E. 91st St, bet. First and York aves, tel: 212-987-0885)*, occupying a former vinegar factory, has a stupendous selection of breads and an atmospheric cafe; and **Agata and Valentina** *(1505 First Ave, at 79th St, tel: 212-452-0690)* elevates the notion of the neighborhood Italian market to new heights.

Downtowners with generous food budgets stock up at **Dean and DeLuca** *(560 Broadway, at Prince St, tel: 212-226-6800)*; the rest of us browse through the aisles laden with exquisite foods and high-line kitchenware and gasp at the prices. If you feel overwhelmed, take refuge in the trendy coffee bar and brace yourself with an espresso. Slightly more pedestrian are the prices at **Jefferson Market** *(450 6th Ave at 11th St, tel: 212-533-3377)*, where the excellent selection ranges from pantry basics to gourmet treats.

At Grand Central Terminal, a cavernous hall in the newly restored landmark houses the food stalls of **Grand Central Market** *(Park Ave at 42nd St, tel: 212-340-2347)*. Vendors here sell everything from pastries and produce to prosciutto and prawns; if you're staying in Midtown, this the place to stock up on hotel-room snacks.

Finally, a quick tour of the city's truly specialized gourmet shops would include: for cheese, olives, and salamis, **Alleva Dairy** *(188 Grand St, at Mulberry St, tel: 212-226-7990)*; for homemade chocolates, **Li-Lac** *(120 Christopher St, at Bleecker St, tel: 212-242-7374)* and **Mondel** *(2913 Broadway, at 114th St, tel: 212-864-2111)*; for one of the largest selections of cheese imaginable, **Murray's** *(257 Bleecker St, at Cornelia St, tel: 212-243-3289)*; for shepherd's pie, tea bags, and all else British, **Myers of Keswick** *(634 Hudson St, between Horatio and Jane sts; 212-691-4194)*; and for caviar, **Petrossian Boutique** *(182 E. 58th St bet. Lexington and Third aves, tel: 212-245-2217)*.

Chelsea and the Meatpacking District

Think Chelsea, think scene. These blocks between Sixth Avenue and the Hudson River buzz with unusually high intensity

Chelsea means different things to different New Yorkers. The neighborhood's main drag, Eighth Avenue, between 14th and 23rd streets, is the epicenter of gay New York, now overshadowing its predecessor, Greenwich Village's Christopher Street, in this respect. The blocks west of Tenth Avenue, roughly between 18th and 22nd streets, are currently home to the city's trendiest art galleries, many of which have moved up here from SoHo. And the little wedge of blocks around the far west end of 14th Street constitutes the ultra-hip Meatpacking District; the area was once (and, in some ways, still is) little more than a messy concentration of industrial buildings focused on the meat trade, but nowadays its restaurants and bars are the 'meet' markets most in evidence. There's also a little pocket of Korean shops and restaurants at the northern edge of the neighborhood, around 32nd Street between Sixth and Eighth avenues. Alluring as these scenes are, Chelsea's hip and eclectic character does not necessarily make the neighborhood a restaurant mecca. Scenes, alas, do not always signal great dining, with buzz all too often considered more important than brilliant cuisine.

The art scene and the Meatpacking District

In the blocks west of Tenth Avenue, former warehouses and taxi garages now house the Chelsea gallery scene. The Dia Center for the Arts, a three-floor showplace for contemporary artists that hosts temporary exhibitions and houses a permanent collection, sets the stage at 548 West 22nd Street, between 10th and 11th avenues. Among its neighbors are Gagosian (at 555 W. and 24th St) and Mary Boone (at 541 W. and 24th St). Thin and sleek as many of the patrons of these galleries are, they are not averse to a good meal – hence the popularity among the art crowd of such fashionable nearby restaurants as Red Cat *(see page 49)*.

***Opposite:** 20-year old Florent bustles from the middle of the day to midnight*

The Meatpacking District comprises the blocks around the far west end of 14th Street. One of the main reasons for venturing this far west is to dine and socialize, even if many of the patrons over here are wafer-thin models who look as if they haven't eaten for days. Take your pick of a whole new battery of eateries and a few old standards, such as the ever popular Florent *(see page 50)*, open day and night. New restaurants, boutiques, and galleries open all the time here, but the neighborhood has charms that extend beyond such outposts of consumerism. Many of the substantial brick buildings date to the 1880s, when these blocks became the location for the Gansevoort Market. The cobblestone streets end at the Hudson River and a new waterside promenade. The Chelsea Market, at Ninth Avenue and 15th Street, just beyond the northern edge of the district, is a dreamland for food fetishists – a dozen or so bakeries, meat markets,

kitchen suppliers, and other shops of a gastronomic bent based in former warehouses. Another recent conversion just up Ninth Avenue is the white-tiled Maritime Hotel, with porthole-shaped windows that belie its original mission as a home for aged sea-men. Nowadays, anyone over 40 is going to feel over the hill in the 1950s-style lobby lounge and two in-house restaurants *(see reviews for Matsuri and La Bottega, pages 52 and 51).*

FIVE OF THE BEST

Florent: popular round-the-clock hangout
Gascogne: Gallic classics served in a delightful summer garden
Paradou: light French fare in a mellow indoor/outdoor setting.
Red Cat: sophisticated US-style cuisine in chic, urbane surroundings
Spice Market: nouvelle Asian cuisine in an exotic setting

Historic Chelsea

Until 15 years ago or so Chelsea was just a rather drab New York neighborhood. At the turn of the 20th century the stretch of Sixth Avenue between 14th and 23rd streets, known as Ladies' Mile, was lined with fashionable department stores; these huge emporia now house 21st-century chainstores. If you head west of Eighth Avenue along 20th or 21st streets, you'll pass through historic Chelsea, a pleasant enclave of row houses that surround the leafy precincts of the 19th-century General Theological Seminary. The Chelsea Hotel, on 23rd Street between Seventh and Eighth avenues, has been home to notable bohemians for a century.

Some of the neighborhood's best restaurants are older, more established places (such as Le Madri, *see page 52*, Gascogne, *page 50*, and Da Umberto, *page 52*) that dispense excellent meals regardless of the social whirl that's spinning around them. In fact, many very good Chelsea restaurants, El Cid *(see page 53)* among them – are physically removed from the action, too, tucked away on rather drab side streets. (So, when looking for a serious dining experience in Chelsea, do your research ahead of time and get an idea of where you're heading before you set out.)

It's also a good idea to reserve a table in Chelsea, especially on weekends. On the other hand, if you come here on a summer weekend, you might wonder what all the hype is about. That's when many of the locals and restaurant regulars head out to Fire Island, the Hamptons, and other retreats, rendering the neighborhood a virtual wasteland. Rather surprisingly, at any time of year Chelsea is a good place to head if you're dining alone – many restaurants, such as Chelsea Bistro and Le Madri, will serve you a meal at the bar, where you might feel more comfortable dining solo than you would at a table.

Late-Night Dining

Countless restaurants from classy gourmet spots to Hopperesque coffee counters stay open around the clock to feed the city that never sleeps

Where you choose to enjoy a late-night bite is likely to depend more on the part of town you happen to be in when hunger strikes than the quality and type of cuisine you demand or the ambiance in which you want to enjoy it. Even so, any number of *boites de nuits* around town provide food and experiences that make it well worth your while to seek them out.

Leading the pack for gourmet fare is **Balthazar** *(open Mon–Thur until 1.30am, Fri until 2.30am, Sat until 3.30am, and Sun until 12.30am, see page 91)*, the SoHo bistro that will transport you across the Atlantic any time of day but exudes an especially romantic 'Paris by Night' feeling once the clock strikes twelve. **Le Zinc** *(open Sun–Thur until 2am, Fri and Sat until 3am, see page 108)* is unfailingly chic at any hour, and the kitchen does not let down its guard as the night wears on. French fare is also served in sophisticated and chic surroundings at the **Brasserie** *(100 East 53rd St, tel: 212-751-4840, open Mon–Sat until 1am)* located at the foot of the Seagram Building, a classic skyscraper by Mies van der Rohe.

Also French, but much more casual and buoyant at any hour, is **Florent** *(open Mon until 5am, Thurs–Sun, 24 hours; see page 50)* a favorite with downtown clubgoers. SoHo's raucous **Blue Ribbon** *(open daily until 4am, see page 88)* gets crowded but the food is imaginative and the oyster bar worth the wait. The sister venue in Brooklyn *(see page 143)* is also a roost for night owls.

Other Downtown night stops that are as much of a scene as the clubs' patrons are coming from, are the **Empire Diner** *(open 24 hours, see page 48)* a flashy expanse of chrome that serves anything from pancakes to pasta; and the **Coffee Shop** *(open Sun, Mon until 2am, Tues–Sat until 5am; see page 32)* where Brazilian food and drink is served by a wait staff blessed with model-perfect looks.

Another sort of comfort food is on offer at **Kiev** *(117 Second Ave at Seventh St, tel: 212-420-9600, open 24 hours)* where the harsh lighting keeps weary patrons awake to enjoy borscht, potato pancakes, kasha, and other eastern European classics. **Sarge's** *(548 Third Ave, bet. 36th and 37th sts, tel: 212-679-0442, open 24 hours)* likewise obliges with matzo-ball soup and mountainous deli sandwiches. If you happen to be wandering on Upper Broadway and get the feeling that brightly lit **Tom's** *(2880 Broadway, at 112th St; tel: 212-864-6137; open 24 hours)* looks uncannily familiar, you're not dreaming: it's where Jerry Seinfeld and his pals hung out – and remember, they didn't come here for the food.

Empire Diner, open 24/7.

Empire Diner, an American classic

TIP

Pack a picnic at Chelsea Market, 75 Ninth Avenue, where you can buy everything from a pickle to a pie. For a delicious fresh loaf, try Amy's Bread. Then, head down to the promenade along the Hudson River to eat. The piers have been restored and are a great place to relax and watch the sunset or the activity along the water.

American

Amuse

108 W. 18th St (bet. Sixth and Seventh aves) [C3]. Tel. 212-929-9755. Open: L and D daily. **$$**

Formerly Harvey's Chelsea, where New Yorkers drank seriously for decades, this place has undergone several transformations, emerging most recently as a low-lit, fashionably modern suite of rooms where only the well-worn tile floor and grand old bar remain. The menu is meant for sampling and sharing, and dishes such as the Gruyère and smoked ham gougères, cod and potato cakes, and grilled chorizo are so satisfying that you may be tempted to try everything.

East of Eighth

254 W. 23rd St (bet. Seventh and Eighth aves) [B2]. Tel: 212-352-0075. Open: L and D daily. **$–$$**

There's something for everyone in this two-floor bar/bistro, both on the menu (from burgers to chicken breast) and among the mixed clientele of straights and gays. The scene is relatively subdued, though – in fact, the upstairs dining room and garden are among the neighborhood's nicest retreats.

Empire Diner

210 Tenth Ave (at 22nd St) [A2]. Tel: 212-243-2736. Open: daily, 24 hours. **$–$$**

A slick, stainless-steel version of the roadside eateries that once lined US byways, this diner is open around the clock to feed clubbers with eggs, burgers, and other lunch-counter standards. Before the night crew arrives, a dinner crowd can enjoy pasta and fare that's a tad more elaborate.

Half King

505 W. 23rd St (at 10th Ave) [A2]. Tel: 212-462-4300. Open: B, L, and D Mon–Fri, Br and D Sat–Sun. www.halfking.com

Just the sort of easygoing place that Chelsea could use more of – the bar room and lounge-like dining room serve as a gallery for artists and photojournalists, and the garden is a snug retreat; the crowd is local and friendly; and the fish and chips, shepherd's pie, burgers, and other pub fare is good and fairly priced. A sense of community prevails on Monday evenings, when authors and journalists take the floor for readings.

Old Homestead

56 Ninth Ave (bet. 14th and 15th sts) [A4]. Tel: 212-242-9040. Open: L and D daily. **$$$** *www.oldhomestead.com*

An old-fashioned steakhouse is now a little out of place in trendy Chelsea. But this 135-year-old institution was here first, and its veteran staff still keeps legions of carnivores happy.

Red Cat 🍴

227 Tenth Ave (bet. 23rd and 24th sts) [A2]. Tel: 212-242-1122. Open: D daily. ***$$–$$$***
www.theredcat.com
One of Chelsea's more grown-up eateries is as much a work of art as the pieces hanging in the galleries surrounding it. In a warm, wood-paneled room, chef Jimmy Bradley transforms classic American fish and meat dishes into delicious, elegantly flavored, elaborate creations.

The Viceroy

160 Eighth Ave (at 18th St) [B3]. Tel: 212-633-8484. Open: L and D Mon–Fri; B, L, and D Sat–Sun. ***$–$$***
Though the buffed patrons seem more interested in looking at the passers-by than what's on their plates, the bistro food here is worthy of attention. The crisp fries, served the Belgian way in a paper cone, are a good accompaniment to most of the dishes on offer, even at the ever-popular brunch.

Asian

Biltmore Room

290 Eighth Ave (bet. 24th and 25th sts) [B2]. Tel: 212-807-0111. Open: D daily. ***$$$***
Acres of marble, a padded phone booth (now intended for cellphone users), and other eclectic decorative flourishes in this club-like space come from the old Biltmore Hotel, although, unfortunately, that establishment's famous clock is not here. The menu, meanwhile, is Asian/Continental, with mint, mango, lime, and cayenne infusing everything from shrimp to crab cakes.

Kom Tang Kalbi House

32 W. 32nd St (bet. Fifth Ave and Broadway) [C1]. Tel: 212-947-8482. Open: 24 hrs daily. ***$***
When in K-town, as West 32nd Street is known, do as a Korean does: take a seat at one of the brazier-equipped tables and grill up a plate of kalbi – delicious, deboned short ribs.

Mandoo

2 W. 32nd St (bet. Fifth Ave and Broadway) [D1]. Tel: 212-279-3075. Open: L and D daily. ***$***
The name means 'dumpling' in Korean, and that's the stock in trade in this plain but busy room – in fact, the specialty of the house is made right in the window. Mandoo are filled with many different kinds of meat and vegetables, and while you can make a meal of them, soup, noodles, and other dishes are also available.

Rhône

63 Gansevoort St (bet. Greenwich and Washington sts) [A4]. Tel: 212-367-8440. Open: D daily. ***$$***
As you might guess from the name of this minimalist restaurant, wines of the Rhône region take center stage here. But the inventive Franco-Asian cuisine is equally satisfying.

Red Cat, sophisticated and urbane

TIP

Looking for an urban escape? Step into the tree-shaded campus of the General Theological Seminary, the entrance of which is at 175 Ninth Avenue.

Royal Siam

240 Eighth Ave (bet. 22nd and 23rd sts) [B2]. Tel: 212-741-1732. Open: L and D daily. **$**

Unlike its glossier neighbors, this brightly lit, no-frills local favorite doesn't offer much in the way of ambiance. Little matter: the satays, noodles, and spicy seafood dishes are tasty; service is friendly; and the prices are low—a relatively rare, winning combination.

Spice Market

403 W. 13th St (at Ninth Ave) [A4]. Tel: 212-675-2322. Open: Br, L, and D daily. **$$**
www.jean-georges.com

Step into this vast, two-floor warehouse space and you'll be transported into another world that is exotic and fun. Chef Jean-Georges Vongerichten oversees a spicy menu inspired by Asian street fare that includes samosas, sushi, and fish and meat dishes that are as exciting as the surroundings.

Belgian

Markt

401 W. 14th St (at Ninth Ave) [A4]. Tel: 212-727-3314. Open: L and D daily. **$$**

Much of the thrill of being in this cavernous restaurant, with tables that spill on to the sidewalk, is being part of a beautiful crowd. Taking second place is the Belgian food, from mussels to waterzooi, which eventually makes it to the table, despite the uneven service.

French

Chelsea Bistro

358 W. 23rd St (bet. Eighth and Ninth aves) [B2]. Tel: 212-727-2026. Open: D daily. **$$–$$$**

Appearances go a long way when it comes to romance, and the Chelsea Bistro's cozy bar and hearth provide intimate environs for wining and dining a loved one. Just as important, the kitchen sends out excellent versions of standard Gallic fare, including generous portions of steamed mussels and a memorable tarte tatin.

Florent

69 Gansevoort St (bet. Greenwich and Washington sts) [A4]. Tel: 212-989-5779. Open: 24 hours daily. **$–$$**
www.restaurantflorent.com

An old timer that hold its own amid a neighborhood of upstarts, this 20-year-old cafe plastered with maps keeps a loyal gang of regulars happy with burgers, salads, boudins (sausage), and other vaguely French fare.

Le Gamin Cafe

183 Ninth Ave (at 21st St) [A3]. Tel: 212-243-8864. Open: B, L, and D daily. **$**

If you need a break from the surrounding art galleries, try this corner oasis, which looks just as appealing as the Parisian cafes it's meant to imitate. The casual ambiance matches the appealing menu of croque monsieurs, crêpes, salads...

Gascogne

158 Eighth Ave (bet. 17th and 18th sts) [B3]. Tel: 212-675-6564. Open: D only Mon, L and D Tues–Sat, Br and D Sun. **$$**
www.gascogneny.com

Even without the romantic dining rooms and pretty garden, this outpost of the south of France would warm the heart with its unabashedly unslimming classics. Foie gras and duck show up in several tempting variations, and the cassoulet is among the best in town.

La Lunchonette

130 Tenth Ave (at 18th St) [A3]. Tel: 212-675-0342. Open: L and D daily. **$$**

A lot of New Yorkers consider this dark, unadorned bistro to be their secret hideaway, and that's much of the charm. At times the service is slightly below par, but the chef never fails to take the job seriously.

Paradou

8 Little West 12th St (bet. Ninth Ave and Washington sts) [A4]. Tel: 212-463-8345. Open: D only Mon–Fri; L and D Sat–Sun. **$–$$**
www.paradounyc.com

What might seem like just another Meatpacking District bistro is a real gem – too bad the small, bright room and lovely garden are no secret. Even so, it's worth trying to squeeze in to enjoy one of the city's best selections of wines by the glass, served alongside toasted sandwiches, Provençal tarts, and other delicious tidbits.

Pastis

9 Ninth Ave (at Little West 12th St) [A4]. Tel: 212-929-4844. Open: B, L, and D daily. **$$**
www.pastisny.com

It seems like French bistro fare is available on almost every corner in Manhattan, so cuisine alone can't explain the unflagging appeal of this Meatpacking District cousin to Keith McNally's Balthazar *(see page 91)*. The steak frites and other standards are excellent, as is the breakfast fare, but the real draw is the young, beautiful clientele.

Rue des Crêpes

104 Eighth Ave (bet. 15th and 16th sts) [B4]. Tel: 212-242-9900. Open: L and D Mon–Fri, Br and D Sat–Sun. **$**

The eponymous offerings at this simply decorated spot are so authentic you could be in Paris. Order a savory crêpe filled with ham or cheese, then follow it with a sweet concoction, for one of the cheapest meals around.

Italian

La Bottega

88 Ninth Ave (at 16th St) [A3]. Tel: 212-243-8400. Open: D daily. **$$**

Hordes of diners flock to this casual restaurant in the Maritime Hotel, especially in warm weather when tables spill on to a terrace. The fact that the hearty pasta, fish, and chicken dishes, and pizzas (served in an adjacent pizzeria) are not just an afterthought is a nice surprise.

Preparing for lunch at Paradou

Meet in the Meatpacking District

Da Umberto

107 W. 17th St (bet. Sixth and Seventh aves) [C3]. Tel: 212-989-0303. Open: L and D Mon–Fri; D only Sat. **$$**

The dining spotlight never seems to shine on this small, plainly decorated, side-street trattoria, but the loyal clientele of neighborhood hipsters and old crones doesn't seem to worry – they prefer not to share one of the city's best Italians.

Bottino

246 Tenth Ave (bet. 24th and 25th sts) [A2]. Tel: 212-206-6766. Open: L and D Tues–Sat, D only Sun–Mon. **$$**
www.bottinonyc.com

A favorite with the Chelsea gallery gang, Bottino is decorated in the soothing minimalist style and set around a lovely interior garden; wherever you sit, noise levels remain low enough to permit easy conversation. Well matched to these grown-up surroundings is a basic, satisfying menu of deftly prepared pasta, meat, and fish.

Macelleria

48 Gansevoort St (at Ninth Ave) [A4]. Tel: 212-741-2555. Open: L and D Mon–Fri, Br and D Sat–Sun. **$$$**
www.macelleriarestaurant.com

The name is Italian for 'butcher shop,' as befits this simple but chic dining room in a former meat warehouse. Salads, pasta, antipasti, and wines are decidedly Italian, while steaks and chops are prime American cuts. Reservations are essential at the weekend.

Le Madri

168 W. 18th St (at Seventh Ave) [C3]. Tel: 212-727-8022. Open: L and D Sun– Fri; D Sat. **$$–$$$**
www.lemadri.citysearch.com

In a handsome, wood-floored room, diners feast on a bounty of homey Tuscan country classics such as pasta with rabbit sauce and roast chicken stuffed with wild herbs. The same fare can also be enjoyed at the small, friendly bar.

Japanese

Matsuri

88 Ninth Ave (at 16th St) [A3]. Tel: 212-243-6400. Open: D daily. **$$**

You would expect a restaurant that takes its name from a summer festival to be, well, festive, and this cavernous space in the bowels of the Maritime Hotel certainly is that. Paper lanterns and a dramatic, wooden ceiling set the mood, but it soon becomes clear that serving only the freshest sushi and sashimi is serious business here.

Latin American

Bright Food Shop

216 Eighth Ave (at 21st St) [B3]. Tel: 212-243-4433. Open: Br and D daily. **$$**

A former divey lunch counter, this place now serves upscale fare that combines southwestern/Mexican and Asian flavors in unusual creations such as spicy hand rolls and herb-encrusted fish fillets. Gourmet grocery items are on sale next door.

Did you know?

The red brick and wrought-iron pile at 222 West 23rd Street is the notorious Chelsea Hotel, one-time home to writers Thomas Wolfe, Dylan Thomas, Vladimir Nabokov, and punk musician Sid Vicious.

Rocking Horse Cafe
182 Eighth Ave (bet. 19th and 20th sts) [B3]. Tel: 212-463-9511. Open: daily, L and D. ***$–$$***
While the menu in this pleasant cafe, with large windows open to the street, ventures into ambitious dishes such as chops and elaborate stews, it's best to stick to the simpler empanadas and enchiladas. Fabulous margaritas, too.

Mediterranean

Meet
71–3 Gansevoort St (bet. Greenwich and Washington sts) [A4]. Tel: 212-242-0990. Open: D only Mon–Fri, Br and D Sat–Sun. ***$–$$$*** *www.the-meet.com*
The playfulness of this meeting place in the Meatpacking District extends from the name to a water trough in which you can wash prior to dining. There's a more serious mood in the kitchen, where creative fish, meat, and pasta dishes are prepared; sandwiches and salads are served in the hip cafe next door.

Zitoune
46 Gansevoort St (at Greenwich St) [A4]. Tel: 212-675-5224. Open: D only Mon–Fri, Br and D Sat–Sun. ***$$***
Morocco comes to the Meatpacking District thanks to this chic, ambiant haven with its soft lighting and exotic decor. Couscous, tagines, and other North African basics are flavorful and beautifully presented.

Spanish

El Cid
322 W. 15th St (bet. Eighth and Ninth aves) [B4]. Tel: 212-929-9332. Open: D daily. ***$$***
Paella, claimed by aficionados to be the city's best Spanish, is the dish of choice in this small, cheerful, and crowded room. Great tapas, too.

El Quijote
226 W. 23rd St (bet. Seventh and Eighth aves) [B2]. Tel: 212-929-1855. Open: L and D daily. ***$–$$***
This worn but cheerful bastion of bohemia beneath the Chelsea Hotel has introduced generations of New Yorkers to the pleasures of Spanish cuisine – and continues to do so. The crowd is mostly young, but the meat and seafood dishes are strictly old world, and, invariably, delicious.

Cafes and Bars

If you drink, you're in the right place, because Chelsea is full of bars. If you're gay, you're especially lucky, because many of these watering holes cater mainly to men. None of these *boites* is slicker than **G** *(225 W. 19th St, tel: 212-929-1085)* and **xlChelsea** *(357 W. 16th St, tel: 212-995-1400).* At the other end of the spectrum are comfortable, old-fashioned places, such as **Chelsea Commons** *(242 Tenth Ave, tel: 212-929-9424)* and **Flannery's** *(205 W. 14th St, tel: 212-929-9589)* – proof that such bars do still exist in painfully hip Chelsea.

Even little corner cafes here often give off the neighborhood's chic vibe. Take the **Big Cup** *(228 Eighth Ave, tel: 212-206-0059)* – it's really a gay bar in which alcoholic drinks have been replaced with coffee and pastries. **F&B** *(209 W. 23rd St, tel: 646-486-4441)* adds hot dogs and bratwurst to its namesake frites and beignets, served up in Euro-chic surroundings.

Chelsea is home to a number of places for those with a sweet tooth. Head over to **Eleni's Cookies** *(tel: 212-255-7990)* and the **Fat Witch** *(tel: 212-807-1335)*, both in Chelsea Market *(75 Ninth Ave)*, or go for broke at **Krispy Kreme** *(265 W. 23rd St, tel: 212-620-0111)*, where the famous donuts provide a quick sugar fix.

Area 4: West Village and Noho

West Village and NoHo

Take refuge from the frenetic city in the leafy streets of this historic neighborhood. Bask in the calm of its cute cafes and bijou restaurants

The structure of this charming neighborhood, made up of a maze of narrow streets, is at odds with the grid formation and unrelenting urbanism of the rest of the city. This is one of the few places in New York you need a map to find your way around. The leafy streets and elegant townhouses, the plethora of bijou restaurants, cafes, and boutiques, the slow and gentle pace of life, lend the area a character that's more European than American.

From hippy to hip

Greenwich Village, or the West Village as its known to New Yorkers, has always set itself apart from the rest of Manhattan. It has a long history of being at the edge. The townhouses were built here in the mid-1800s by wealthy families fleeing contagious diseases downtown (Bank Street got its name when banks from Wall Street set up temporary home here during a plague). When industry on the waterfront developed, those families moved uptown. Their grand houses were gutted and converted into small apartments, and waves of immigrants from Ireland, Italy, and China took over.

The area's reputation as a center of free-thinking and alternative lifestyles built up over the decades as artists and intellectuals, bohemians, and beatniks, civil rights' and gay rights' activists made it their home. These days parts of the Village are still on the cutting edge – of fashion that is. The outer reaches of the West Village, dubbed the Far West, are attracting media attention for their proximity to the hot Meatpacking District *(see page 45)*, as well as for the new boutiques and restaurants nestled in the quiet streets, the beautifully refurbished piers along the Hudson River, and the equally stunning modern apartment buildings overlooking the piers by architect Richard Meier with dwellings owned by celebrities such as Nicole Kidman and hotel impresario Ian Schrager.

Throughout Greenwich Village in fact, the Greek Revival and Federal townhouses on the interior streets, the former scruffy domains of impecunious bohemians, are being snapped up for millions of dollars by the royalty of film and fashion. With pedigree actors like Gwyneth Paltrow, Sarah Jessica Parker, and Julianne Moore, and glossy magazine editors such as Graydon Carter of *Vanity Fair* and Anna Wintour of *Vogue*, taking up residence, Greenwich Village has returned to its original incarnation as an exclusive, fashionable, and very expensive enclave.

Opposite: Downtown's distinctive architecture

A literary landmark

The artistic and intellectual history of the area is weighty: this is where some of the greatest artistic works of the modern era were created. Such illustrious inhabitants as e e cummings, Dylan Thomas, Edgar Allan Poe, Eugene O'Neill, Edith Wharton, Jackson Pollock, Anaïs Nin,

Woody Allen, Jimi Hendrix, and Bob Dylan drank and fought in the bars here, wrote and painted in the apartments. The political radical Thomas Paine, whose writings helped ignite the American Revolution, was a regular at many of the area's sing-along bars. In the 1960s the iconic left-wing newspaper *The Village Voice* was launched on Greenwich Avenue and 10th Street.

Little remains of the area's artistic and bohemian past, which is an increasingly distant memory. Chumley's *(see page 58)*, a haunt of the literary crowd of the 1940s and 1950s, is virtually untouched. Another survivor is the White Horse Tavern *(see page 67)*, where, in 1953 Dylan Thomas had one too many before he died at nearby St Vincent's Hospital. Apart from a few other tangible remains, Manhattan's hippy Bohemia only lives on in song and legend.

Shopping and Eating

High rents may have closed down most of the old cafes and bookstores, but the area retains its charm, thanks to the architecture, the trees, and the erratic streetplan, not to mention the hundreds of characterful restaurants that line the streets, many of extremely high quality.

Hudson Street between Christopher and Bank streets, and Greenwich Avenue between Sixth Avenue and Hudson, are flanked with good casual choices. Bleecker Street, which cuts through the heart of the West Village, changes character quite radically from one end to the other. Close to Hudson Street it is quiet and elegant, lined with chic boutiques such as Marc Jacobs, Cynthia Rowley, and Lulu Guinness, along with antique shops and several good restaurants like Paris Commune *(see page 63)* and The Miracle Grill, that serve down-to-earth southwestern fare, at No. 415. Right in the middle of this stretch of streets is a new Manhattan star: Magnolia Bakery at the corner of 11th Street. The sugar-starved and the nostalgic line up out the door and up the block at nights and on weekends, anxious to sink their teeth into the bakery's old-fashioned iced cupcakes (it leapt to fame thanks to a cameo appearance on the television show *Sex and the City*).

Bleecker Street then crosses Christopher Street, a major artery of gay life in the city, and heads across Seventh Avenue to what's left of the Village's Italian immigrant community. Here you'll find a smattering of Italian specialty shops, including one of the city's best butchers, Ottomanelli's at No. 281.

Five of the Best

AOC: good, simple French food, evoking Paris without pretense
Babbo: Mario Batali's adventurous Italian is hailed as one of Manhattan's best
Gotham Bar & Grill: an elegant New York gourmet classic with a good bar
Jefferson: imaginative Asian cuisine in a sparsely elegant setting
Pearl Oyster Bar: fabulously fresh seafood carefully prepared at reasonable prices

Manhattan's most famous cheese shop, Murray's, is at the corner of Cornelia Street selling literally hundreds of types of cheeses, and supplying these to many of the city's top restaurants. Fun Cornelia Street itself has four or five very good restaurants, all worth trying, including Pô *(see page 65)* where celebrity chef Mario Batali got his start (he has since left); and Pearl Oyster Bar *(see page 67)*, one of Manhattan's best seafood restaurants.

Past Sixth Avenue, heading up to New York University and Washington Square Park, the atmosphere on Bleecker and its satellite streets hots up. On weekends and in the evenings the area teems with students and tourists who pile into the bars and restaurants, or stand out on the streets with a drink and a cigarette (thanks to the city's strict no-smoking laws). This was hippy heaven in the 1960s, where musicians such as Bob Dylan, the Mamas and the Papas, and Jimi Hendrix played the clubs and lived in tiny walk-up apartments. For a taste of that time, visit Matt Umanov's guitar shop, or have a coffee at Caffe Reggio on MacDougal Street. The buzz that's missing in the quieter parts of the West Village can certainly be found in this stretch of Bleecker Street.

NoHo

Greenwich Village ends at Broadway, where it becomes – somewhat unofficially – NoHo, which stands for North of Houston Street. Twenty years ago this part of town was rundown, dangerous, and deserted at night, but has evolved into a safe and chic area of lofts and boutiques, with a few fashionable restaurants, including Bond Street *(see page 66)* and Il Buco *(see page 64)*.

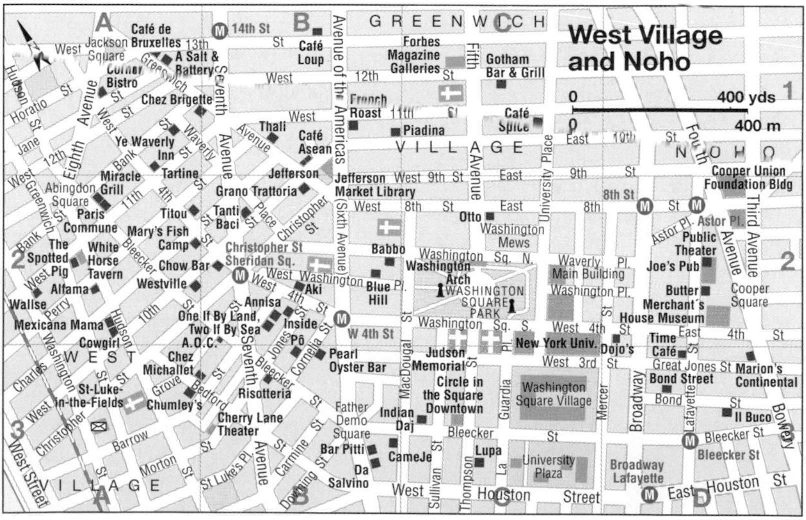

Chumley's, a time capsule of the Village's literary heyday

American

Annisa

13 Barrow St (bet. Seventh Ave and W. 4th St) [B2]. Tel: 212-741-6699. Open: L and D daily. **$$$$** *www.annisarestaurant.com*

Anita Lo is being hailed as one of the nation's great new chefs thanks to her inspirational New American cooking. She draws from a wide range of influences in such adventurous dishes as miso-marinated sable fish with crispy silken tofu, or boneless spare ribs stuffed with shrimp and with a shrimp roe sauce. The serene minimalist space (cream walls and red chairs) is as refreshing as the cuisine.

Blue Hill

75 Washington Pl. (bet. Sixth Ave and Washington Sq. W.) [B2]. Tel: 212-539-1776. Open: daily, D only. **$$$$** *www.bluehillnyc.com*

A mellow, sophisticated spot in a Village brownstone that gets rave reviews for its pretty main room (and small garden out back) and superb, beautifully conceived American dishes the chef creates from fresh food from his family's farm, such as poached duck with a stew of organic carrots and toasted spices, crabmeat lasagne, or grass-fed lamb loin. A find that many say is underrated.

Butter

415 Lafayette St (bet. Astor Pl. and E. 4th St) [D2]. Tel: 212-253-2828. Open: Mon–Sat, D only. **$$$$** *www.butterrestaurant.com*

A current hot-spot, where the fun is in the scene and the DJ, not the food. Celebrity names and wannabes can be spotted in the upstairs dining room with its vaulted ceiling and dim lighting, or in the more intimate lounge downstairs.

Chumley's

89 Bedford St (bet. Barrow and Grove sts) [A3]. Tel: 212-675-4449. Open: daily, D only. Br Sat/Sun. **$**

A bar serving pub grub that's a time trap for those nostalgic for the Village's intellectual heyday. There's no sign outside. Just open the door and step into the past. The apparently unchanged interior is dark, cramped, and lined with books by and photos of illustrious former regulars such as e.e. cummings, Eugene O'Neill, and F. Scott Fitzgerald.

Corner Bistro

331 W. 4th St (at Jane St) [A1]. Tel: 212-242-9502. Open: L and D daily, closes 3.30am. **$**

Hamburger purists call this long-time Village favorite a prime spot for a beer and a 'burg. It's dark and dingy, and the food is served on paper plates, but that doesn't seem to bother the people who crowd in here all week long.

Cowgirl

519 Hudson St (at W. 10th St) [A2]. Tel: 212-633-1133. Open: L and D daily. **$$**

Annie Oakley would feel right at home at this rumbustious

Did you know?

Greenwich Village is sometimes called the West Village by locals, and the East Village is a separate neighborhood; it is not part of Greenwich Village.

southwestern restaurant that serves heaps of hearty Texas specialties such as fajitas, guacamole, burgers, cornbread and chili. The tongue-in-cheek 1950s ranch decor adds to the fun.

Gotham Bar & Grill

12 E. 12th St (bet. Fifth Ave and University Pl.) [C1]. Tel: 212-620-4020. Open: L and D daily. **$$$$**

Still pulling them in after 20 years, chef Alfred Portale is considered the pioneer of vertical cuisine. His sculptural, architectural dishes such as Chinese-spiced duck breast with seared foie gras and caramelized mango, or wild striped bass with green lentils and red wine sauce are a delicate balance of form and flavors. The atmosphere is elegant and inviting thanks to high ceilings and a lively bar area up front.

Inside

9 Jones St (bet. Bleecker and W. 4th sts) [B2]. Tel: 212-229-9999. Open: daily, D only, Br Sun. **$$$**

Sleek and upscale in design but intimate in feel, this relatively undiscovered neighborhood gem serves imaginative high-quality New American cuisine (quail with rhubarb marmalade, grouper with leek brandade) at very fair prices. The service is excellent too.

Marion's Continental

354 Bowery (bet. E. 4th and Great Jones sts) [D3]. Tel: 212-475-7621. Open: daily, D only, last seating 11:30pm. **$$**
www.marionsnyc.com

Fifties kitsch decor of plastic palm trees, patio lights, and framed movie-star photos are part of the fun at this quirky retro joint. So are the potent cocktails served to the casually trendy at the comfortable bar up front. The fare (steak, chicken dishes) is surprisingly good too.

One If By Land, Two If By Sea

17 Barrow St (near Seventh Ave South) [B2]. Tel: 212-228-0822. Open: daily, D only. **$$$$**
www.oneifbyland.com

Located in an historic Village townhouse, this elegant restaurant is considered one of the city's most romantic (and the mayor's favorite). The house specialties of beef wellington and rack of lamb are impeccable; so is the service and the selection of wines, but such charm doesn't come cheap.

The Spotted Pig

314 W. 11th St (at Greenwich St) [A2]. Tel: 212-620-0393. Call for hours. **$$**

The latest addition to Mario Batali's ever-expanding Manhattan empire, this tiny, casual restaurant

celebrates the pig and the pub with concoctions by chef April Bloomfield (from the River Café in London.) A hit even before it opened its doors, Batali does here for pub food what he did for the pizza at Otto, elevating it to gourmet status but keeping the prices down. Sit on plump cushions at small tables or perch on a stool and dig into chicken-liver parfait, squid and mussel salad, pork sausage with lentils, or slow-braised beef shin with risotto. Wash it all down with a beer or a glass of wine from the substantial wine list and congratulate yourself for being fashionable.

Time Café

380 Lafayette St (at Great Jones St) [D3]. Tel: 212-533-7000. Open: L and D daily. **$$** *www.timecafenyc.com*

A huge open restaurant with lovely high ceilings that feels like an upscale coffee shop. Good for basic American food such as grilled chicken, steak, tuna, and many sandwiches, but more fun is people watching on the outdoor terrace, or having a drink and a snack in Fez, the moody Moroccan-inspired bar and jazz club in the back.

Westville

210 W 10th St (bet. Bleecker and W. 4th sts) [A2]. Tel: 212-741-7971 Open: L and D daily. **$** *www.westville-nyc.com*

Delicious hot dogs, burgers, sandwiches, and salads all made with top-quality ingredients. It's a tiny spot with only a smattering of tables so it can get crowded and there have been complaints about slow service, but this is a nice addition to the neighborhood and a great place to stop for a light lunch or dinner. Good for take-out and delivery too.

***Below:* tall food in the big city. *Bottom:* charming and historic Ye Waverly Inn**

Ye Waverly Inn

16 Bank St (at Waverly Pl.) [A1]. Tel: 212-929-4377. Open: D only Tues–Sat, Br and D Sun. **$$$** *www.yewaverlyinn.com*

Located in a pre-Revolution carriage house complete with working fireplaces, low ceilings, and crooked floor, this intimate restaurant is a little bit worn around the edges, but is without a doubt one of the most romantic in the city. It's the charm that stars here, though – the classic American and French dishes veer towards the mediocre.

Asian

Café Asean

117 W. 10th St (bet. Greenwich and Sixth aves) [B1]. Tel: 212-633-0348. Open: L and D daily. **$$**

This inviting, rustic restaurant with a small garden serves an eclectic choice of Southeast Asian dishes (Vietnamese, Thai, and Malaysian), at very fair prices. Chive and shrimp dumplings, Malaysian coconut curry chicken, and sirloin steak and green onions marinated in a soy-based sauce are among the many delicious offerings.

Chow Bar

230 W. 4th St (at W. 10th St) [B2]. Tel: 212-633-2212. Open: daily, D only. **$$**

An upscale but casual Pan-Asian restaurant that draws in a crowd of young professionals who enjoy the clubby atmosphere, potent cocktails, and the varied menu including sake-steamed fish, sesame-seared tuna, or noodles and stir fry.

Jefferson 🍴

121 West 10th St (at Greenwich Ave) [B1]. Tel: 212-255-3333. Open: daily, D only. **$$$**

This high-quality Asian-fusion newcomer is a winner with its

Wallsé, showcase for fine Viennese cuisine

striking minimalist interior and view of the leafy gardens across the street – a beautiful setting for its creative dishes such as snapper with caramelized mango, baby leeks, and coconut candlenut foam; or roasted quail stuffed with figs in a plum-wine sauce. An upscale offshoot of Simpson Wong's Café Asean two doors away.

Austrian

Wallsé

344 W. 11th St (Washington St). Tel: 212-352-2300. Open: daily, D only. ***$$$–$$$$***
www.wallserestaurant.com
Tucked away on a bucolic corner of the West Village, this New Austrian bistro showcases contemporary versions of classic Viennese cuisine (schnitzel, smoked trout) in a sleek, elegant decor with Art Nouveau flourishes. Smokers are offered chic designer capes in winter to puff in style outside. Some say it's charm at a high price, others say it's worth it.

French & Belgian

AOC

314 Bleecker St (at Grove St) [B2]. Tel: 212-675-9463. Open: L and D daily. ***$$***
The waiters are French, conversations around you are in French, and most of all, the duck confit, lamb chops, endive salad, and lamb shank are served as simply and perfectly as in a French bistro. Unlike other hurried New York spots, here *le savoir vivre* reigns, and you can linger and chat as long as you like if no one needs your table. The pretty garden out back is an added bonus. This AOC (which stands for *l'aile ou la cuisse* – wing or thigh) is not to be confused with the more upscale A.O.C restaurant several blocks away.

Café de Bruxelles

118 Greenwich Ave (at W. 13th St) [A1]. Tel: 212-206-1830. Open: L and D daily. ***$$–$$$***
This Belgian brasserie, complete with white lace curtains and a copper-zinc counter, is famous for

TIP
Life in the Village gets off to a slow start in the mornings, and many boutiques and restaurants don't open until noon.

Bleecker Street, quiet and elegant at one end, bright and buzzing at the other

its moules-frites – in fact its French fries recently made the cover of gourmet magazine, *Saveur*. Other mussel-based dishes and hearty stews are on the menu, and there's a wide selection of Belgian beers.

Café Loup

105 W. 13th St (bet. Sixth and Seventh aves) [B1]. Tel: 212-255-4746. Open: L and D Sun–Fri, D only Sat. **$$–$$$**

A well-loved institution in the Village since 1977, mostly for its low-key atmosphere and its above-average bistro fare such as fillet of yellowfish tuna, rack of lamb, or pan-roasted chicken breast. The casual bar at the front is a magnet for local writers and journalists.

CamaJe

85 MacDougal St (bet. Bleecker and Houston sts) [B3]. Tel: 212-673-8184. Open: L and D daily. **$–$$** *www.camaje.com*

The atmosphere may be casual, but this small restaurant is anything but casual about its food. Chef Abigail Hitchcock prepares top-notch French bistro dishes with imagination and heart (rabbit braised with saffron; coriander-crusted tuna; or scallops cooked with Thai green curry). The reasonable prices make this a real find for foodies.

Chez Brigette

77 Greenwich Ave (bet. Bank St and Seventh Ave S.) [A1]. Tel: 212-929-6736. Open: L and D daily. **$**

Brigette has passed away but her minuscule restaurant lives on as a neighborhood institution, serving her basic but hearty French dishes such as roast leg of lamb or veal stew. There are only about eight bar stools at the two counter tops so it can be a tight squeeze but at just $5.95 for lunch or dinner, who's complaining.

Chez Michallet

90 Bedford St (bet. Grove St and Barrow sts) [A3]. Tel: 212-242-8309. Open: daily, D only. **$$$**

So French it's almost a cliché, this romantic restaurant with linen tablecloths and hushed tones is located on one of the more charming street corners of the West Village. The menu of sophisticated classics (magret de canard; rack of lamb with red wine and rosemary sauce) and the good wine list don't disappoint. The prix-fixe menu is good value. Be sure to reserve a table in advance.

Did you know

Washington Square forms the heart of the Village and was once a dueling ground and site of public hangings. Today it's the unofficial campus of New York University, and a playground for numerous performing artists, skateboarders, and chess players.

French Roast

78 W. 11th St (at Sixth Ave) [B1]. Tel: 212-533-2233. Open: daily, 24 hours. **$$**

Popular around the clock for its delicious cafe and bistro fare (fresh ravioli; steak frites; endive salad with goat's cheese) at reasonable prices and its comfortable flea-market-chic atmosphere. The service can be frustrating, but it's a perfect choice for coffee, any meal, or a late-night drink or snack.

Paris Commune

411 Bleecker St (bet. Bank and W. 11th sts) [A2]. Tel: 212-929-0509. Open: daily, D only. Br Sat/Sun. **$$**

The tin ceiling, the fireplace, and the roaming cat define the character of this warm and charming spot. At weekends generous portions of French toast, waffles, and eggs benedict are served to the hungry hordes who flock here for brunch. The evening menu of classic French and American fare is equally delicious and hearty.

Tartine

253 W. 11th St (at W. 4th St) [A1]. Tel: 212-229-2611. Open: L and D Tues–Sun, Br Sun. **$$**

As with all charming Village venues, you're likely to have to wait in line for one of the dozen tables at this quaint BYOB on a picturesque street corner, but the deliciously simple appetizers (escargots, endive salad) and entrées (sauteed chicken in lemon and sage; grilled salmon) and home-made bread and croissants are worth the wait.

Indian

Café Spice

72 University Pl. (bet. E. 10th and E. 11th sts) [C1]. Tel: 212-253-6999. Open: L and D daily. **$$.** *www.cafespice.com*

The decor and the music may be modern, but the well-prepared dishes are traditional. The tandooris, tikkas, and biryanis are all excellent, if not always as hot and spicy as they might be. There's a take-out branch in Grand Central Terminal.

Indian Daj

181 Bleecker St (bet. MacDougal and Sullivan sts). Tel: 212-982-0810. Open: L and D Mon–Fri; 2–10pm Sat; 1–10.30pm Sun. **$–$$**

Formerly called A Taste of India, this restaurant has been receiving rave reviews which are posted in the front windows for you to read. Far better though to go in and taste the real thing: classic Indian dishes, done simply and at reasonable prices for the area. There's another branch on Staten Island *(287 New Dorp Lane between Clawson and Edison streets).*

Thali

28 Greenwich Ave (bet. W. 10th St and Charles) [B1]. Tel: 212-367-7411. Open: L and D daily. **$**

The special here is the day's 'thali' – a round tray with several small bowls filled with daal, rice, vegetable curries, chutney, and curd, accompanied by rotis, and a dessert. It's nothing fancy, but it's hard to beat the fixed-menu price of ten dollars. Cash only.

Italian

Babbo

110 Waverly Pl. (bet. Sixth Ave and Washington Sq. W.) [B2]. Tel: 212-777-0303. Open: L and D daily. **$$$$** *www.babbonyc.com*

The star of Mario Batali's mini-empire where the master chef pushes the culinary envelope with adventurous concoctions such as ravioli with beef cheeks, or pasta with calf's brain. If you're too

TIP

For those who like to cook at home, Greenwich Village has several top-notch grocery stores selling hard-to-find ingredients. All are in a 10-block radius: **Jefferson Market** *(450 Sixth Ave)* has one of the city's best butchers, a great cheese selection, and a bakery; **Citarella** *(424 Sixth Ave)* is the place to go for fresh fish; and **Gourmet Garage** *(117 Seventh Ave)* has a terrific, high-quality deli.

squeamish to be tempted by such unorthodox ingredients, there are more mainstream, but equally inspired, dishes like duck with chanterelle mushrooms and chicory, or goat-cheese tortellini with dried orange and wild fennel pollen. Sensational wines too.

Bar Pitti

268 Sixth Ave (bet. Bleecker and Houston sts) [B3]. Tel: 212-982-3300. Open: L and D daily. ***$$***

The outdoor terrace of this Village hotspot shares the same fashionable people-watching vantage point as Da Silvano next door *(see below)*, but the attitude and prices are more relaxed. The menu is more rustic than refined but the fresh pasta dishes and hearty mains are delicious. Cash only.

TIP

Every evening, laid-back club **Joe's Pub** *(425 Lafayette St, bet. Astor Place and 4th St; tel: 212-539 8770;* ***$$*** *)* stages quality music acts from American folk, soul, and rock, to Latin jazz and African pop. You can graze on simple appetizers, bowls of fresh pasta, and desserts while watching the performance.

Il Buco

47 Bond St (bet. Bowery and Lafayette St) [D3]. Tel: 212-533-1932. Open: L and D Tues–Sat, Br only Sun. ***$$$*** *www.ilbuco.com*

This charming hideaway, with its large communal wooden tables, fresh pastas, and homey desserts, is a NoHo favorite. Creative mains like wild fennel roasted suckling pig with polenta, or Alaskan king salmon poached in cider with serrano ham, are sophisticated but satisfying. Its critics say it's overpriced; its fans say it's transporting and cheaper than a flight to Italy.

Da Silvano

260 Sixth Ave (bet. Bleecker and Houston sts) [B3]. Tel: 212-982-2343. Open: L and D daily. ***$$$*** *www.dasilvano.com*

The outdoor patio guarantees great people-watching, with frequent celebrity sightings both inside and out. Braised veal shank with saffron risotto, fresh spinach and ricotta-filled ravioli, and other authentic Tuscan-inspired dishes rarely disappoint. But dinner at this New York institution doesn't come cheap. Owner Silvano Marchetto's cafe-restaurant next door is a less expensive, more informal option.

Grano Trattoria

21 Greenwich Ave (at W. 10th St) [B2]. Tel: 212-645-2121. Open: L and D daily. ***$$$***

Don't be deceived by the unassuming air of this relatively undiscovered restaurant. It's a romantic spot, with an atmosphere of easy warmth. The daily specials (eg braised lamb shank with parmesan risotto, horseradish- and apple-crusted fillet of flounder) delivered by personable chef Maurizio Crescenzo are generous and bursting with flavour. A real find.

Lupa

170 Thompson St (bet. Bleecker and Houston sts) [C3]. Tel: 212-982-5089. Open: L and D daily. ***$$–$$$*** *www.luparestaurant.com*

The success of this busy Italian trattoria in the Mario Batali stable is largely down to its simple but authentic dishes, warm atmosphere, great staff, and reasonable prices. Be prepared for a wait.

Otto

1 Fifth Ave (at 8th St) [C2]. Tel: 212-995-9559. Open: daily, 9am–11:30pm. ***$$*** *www.ottopizzeria.com*

Opposite and below: Otto, modern pizza for fashionable foodies

Mario Batali has taken the humble pizza and turned it into an upscale crowd-pleaser. Late-night crowds, fashionistas, and foodies come to enjoy an extensive wine list, great appetizers and thin-crust pizzas with tasty toppings like clam and chili, or fresh tomato and raw fennel. The no-reservations policy means you're likely to have to wait in line.

Piadina

57 W. 10th St (bet. Fifth and Sixth aves) [B1]. Tel: 212 460-8017. Open: daily, D only. **$$**

Located on the ground floor of a townhouse, Piadina is dimly lit, but cozy, serving up rustic and affordable homemade pastas and the house specialty after which the restaurant is named. Originally the staple food of farmers from Romagna in northeastern Italy, piadina is a thin round of stone-griddled bread, filled with prosciutto, sautéed spinach, and cheese. It goes well with a salad. A neighborhood favorite.

Pô

31 Cornelia St (bet. Bleecker and W. 4th sts) [B3]. Tel: 212-645-2189. Open: L and D Wed–Sun, D only Mon/Tues. **$$$**

The quality of food remains high at this small and sophisticated Italian restaurant, former domain of celebrity chef Mario Batali. Porcini-crusted cod and rigatoni with gorgonzola, spicy almonds, and cream are the kind of thoughtfully turned out dishes to expect. The six-course $40 tasting menu is one of the city's best deals. Reserve well in advance.

Risotteria

270 Bleecker St (at Morton St) [B3]. Tel: 212-924-6664. Open: L and D daily. **$**
www.risotteria.com

Nestled in the Italian heart of Bleecker Street, this casual restaurant knows its arborio from its canaroli; this is the place to come for expertly prepared risotto. Asparagus and saffron; gruyère and green onions; or lamb, spinach, and gorgonzola, are just three of the 35 tempting combinations on offer. Lucky patrons wangle a seat at one of the few tables; others perch on stools by the window. Pizzas and sandwiches also available.

Tanti Baci

163 W. 10th St (bet. Seventh Ave S. and Waverly Pl.) [B2]. Tel: 212-647-9651. Open: daily, D only, weekends open late. **$$**

More of a café than a restaurant, but regulars like its coziness and simple but reliable Italian pastas – you choose your own sauce – and salads. The front patio opens up in good weather.

Did you know?

The James Beard House at 167 W. 12th St (at Seventh Ave) is now a club for food enthusiasts who enjoy meals cooked by established and emerging chefs from around the world. Beard, considered the father of American gastronomy, died in 1985.

Mexicana Mama

Japanese

Aki
181 West 4th St (bet. Barrow and Jones sts) [B2]. Tel: 212-989-5440. Open: D Tues–Sun only. $$
Chef 'Siggy' Nakanishi once worked for Japan's ambassador to the West Indies in Jamaica, which explains why jerk chicken is on the menu, along with other imaginative twists to a traditional Japanese sushi- and sashimi-based menu. Delicious and imaginative.

Bond Street
6 Bond St (bet. Broadway and Lafayette St) [B3]. Tel: 212-777-2500. Open: L and D daily. $$$
Five years on, this hip, top-quality restaurant is still crowded with models and fashionistas drawn by the atmosphere, great cocktails, and exquisite sushi and sashimi. Bring a flashlight and an attitude deflector.

Latin American

Mexicana Mama
525 Hudson St (bet. Charles and W. 10th) [A2]. Tel: 212-924-4119. Open: L and D Tues–Sun. $$
This tiny, colorful, Mexican gourmet gem is worth the wait to get in. The menu has a limited selection, but the boldly flavored and beautifully presented dishes are a far cry from your average Tex-Mex fare. A taco here is a culinary masterpiece. Cash only.

Portuguese

Alfama
551 Hudson St (at Perry St) [A2]. Tel: 212-645-2500. Open: L and D Wed–Sat, Br and D Sun, D only Mon/Tues. $$$ www.alfamarestaurant.com
This charming and sophisticated restaurant serves hearty but refined dishes (grilled octopus, sausage, or sardines; fresh clams in white wine sauce). The chef once worked for the Portuguese Consul General in New York and the Portuguese wine list is the most extensive in the city. Live *fado* (Portuguese blues) is performed here on Wednesdays.

Seafood

A Salt and Battery
112 Greenwich Ave (bet. 12th and 13th sts) [A1]. Tel: 212-691-2713. Open: daily 11am–10pm. $ www.asaltandbattery.com

TIP
To calculate the right amount to tip, double the tax charge on the check.

Anglophiles and homesick British expats come here for the ultra-fresh authentic fish 'n' chips. It's primarily a take-out spot, but there are a few stools at the counter. If you fancy a cup of tea and a scone, or bangers and mash, try Tea and Sympathy two doors down.

Mary's Fish Camp

64 Charles St (at W. 4th St) [A2]. Tel: 646-486-2185. Open: L and D daily. ***$$$***
www.marysfishcamp.com

New Yorkers in the know line up for a seat at this temple to East Coast fish specialties, run by a former owner of nearby Pearl Oyster Bar *(see below)*. As in so many of the best neighborhood restaurants, space is limited and it can be crowded, but the freshness of dishes such as lobster rolls, fish chowder, fried oysters, and blueberry pie make any discomfort worth it.

Pearl Oyster Bar

18 Cornelia St (bet. Bleecker and W. 4th sts) [B3]. Tel: 212-691-8211. Open: L and D Mon–Fri, D only Sat. ***$$$***
www.pearloysterbar.com

The old adage 'the best things come in small packages' certainly applies to this little gem, considered by many to be the best seafood restaurant in town. Despite recently expanding its premises, lines of hopeful diners still wait patiently outside. Its popularity is entirely justified. The Maine specialties of lobster rolls, bouillabaise, and oysters are fresh, delicious, and of exceptional quality for such fair prices.

Vegetarian

Dojo's

14 W. 4th St (at Mercer St) [D2]. Tel: 212-505-8934. Open: B, L, and D Mon–Fri, L and D Sat/Sun. ***$***

A favorite with students and modern-day Village bohemians (aka broke artists and freelancers), this basic restaurant serves cheap, filling food in a no-frills environment. Best as a quick stop before the evening's activities. There's a sister branch in East Village *(24–26 St Mark's Place)*.

CAFES AND BARS

Greenwich Village has no shortage of watering holes, including a number of historic landmarks. **The Cedar Tavern** *(82 University Place, at 11th St)* is an old literary haunt that oozes charm and history; **The White Horse Tavern** *(587 Hudson Street at 11th St)*, a pub that opened in 1880, is where Dylan Thomas drank the night he died in 1953. More history can be soaked up over a cup of coffee at **Caffe Reggio** *(119 MacDougal St, bet. Bleecker and W. 3rd sts)*, a tiny cafe that's been open since 1927, or the still-bohemian **Cornelia St Café** *(29 Cornelia St, bet. Bleecker and W. 4th sts)* which holds regular poetry readings and music performances downstairs. For a drink in a more contemporary, upscale environment, try the **Temple Bar** *(332 Lafayette St, bet. Bleecker and Houston sts)*, a darkly lit NoHo bar/club perfect for a late-night drink, or nearby **Fez** *(380 Lafayette St at Great Jones St)*, part of **Time Cafe**, a sultry lounge with a Moroccan theme and an adjacent jazz and cabaret room. The bustling restaurant **Bar Six** *(502 Sixth Avenue)*, with a French feel, has a few tables up front for enjoying a drink. **The Cubby Hole** *(281 W. 12th St, at 4th St)* is a charming laid-back late-night bar run by lesbians and catering to all locals. Finally, **Otto**, Mario Batali's gourmet pizza restaurant *(see page 64)*, has a great bar up front with a wide selection of wines and starters to nibble on.

Brunch in Manhattan

Life in the hyperactive city slows down to a more leisurely pace at weekends when New Yorkers love to wind down with a long and lazy brunch

Although undoubtedly fast, the pace of life in New York is not unequivocally so. On Saturday and Sunday mornings, the city is almost quiet, and restaurants are filled with New Yorkers enjoying a slow start to the day eating brunch in the company of a friend or two, with a lover or spouse, or alone with the newspaper or a book. Saturday and Sunday are days when New Yorkers stroll rather than race. Sunday brunch in particular is a New York tradition.

Most restaurants offer a brunch menu, but there are some stand-out choices. The most picturesque are in Central Park or along the East River: **The River Café** offers stunning views of Manhattan from the Brooklyn side of the East River, as well as an extravagant $35 prix-fixe brunch of crab-meat griddle cakes, oysters or caviar, suckling pig or wild salmon. The sprawling **Tavern on the Green** in lower Central Park with its garden strung with lanterns may by touristy, even tacky, but it's still a pretty place for a lingering meal and is great for families. But in the heart of the park on the edge of a pond dotted with wooden rowboats, the **Boathouse** wins the prize for charm. The menu is good too, with smoked salmon frittata, French toast, or steak and eggs.

Aside from the river and park, one of the prettiest and most relaxed areas of the city to enjoy a leisurely brunch is in the heart of Greenwich Village. The tree-lined streets and beautiful townhouses make this the perfect location for a morning stroll and a long brunch at an intimate restaurant. One of the city's favorites is tiny **Tartine** where a wait is guaranteed, mostly for the restaurant's idyllic location as well as its delicious brunches featuring fresh croissants, baked goods, and omelets. Another good West Village choice is **Paris Commune** around the block from Tartine, where the atmosphere is cozy and sophisticated, and the servings of waffles, pancakes, eggs benedict, and orange juice are fresh and copious. **French Roast** on busy Sixth Avenue (there's another located on the Upper West Side) serves an extensive brunch menu until mid-afternoon. Its comfortable French-bistro feel makes it a neighborhood favorite, although the service can be frustratingly slow.

Sunday brunch is a New York tradition

For an uptown brunch that's hard to beat, head for **Sarabeth's**, which has a branch on the Upper West and East sides. Martha Stewart would feel at

home in this local breakfast favorite where the muffins, waffles, French toast, and other home classics are heartily good. **Barney Greengrass** is another Upper West Side institution, where lines form early on weekends for the great Jewish brunch.

Those looking for a more upbeat scene – and fans of seafood – will enjoy **Blue Water Grill** off Union Square *(see page 40)* and **Aquagrill** in SoHo. Set in a 1925 bank building complete with high ceilings and marble floors and walls, Blue Water Grill also has patio seating and offers a great seafood-oriented brunch menu of seafood platters, oysters, and lobster. Aquagrill, on the edge of SoHo, is a traditional seafood restaurant with a fabulous oyster selection and is in the heart of one of the city's best shopping districts.

But brunching isn't confined to weekends – there are a surprising number of restaurants specializing in brunch all week long. One outstanding choice, in SoHo, is the hip and sophisticated diner **Jerry's**; celebrated Downtown residents such as Susan Sarandon and Nicole Kidman have been known to pop in for eggs benedict and a coffee. Also in SoHo, **The Cupping Room Café** has great breakfast and brunch fare and is perfect for a lazy morning. **EJ's Luncheonette** on the Upper West and East sides and in the Village is an upscale retro diner offering the classic choices of bacon, eggs, waffles, pancakes, and omelets until late in the afternoon.

Arguably the best brunch to be had in the city is at **Balthazar** *(see page 91)*. The extremely popular French restaurant, part of the Keith McNally empire, is normally crowded in the evenings, with reservations hard to secure. On weekday mornings until about noon, however, those in the know (including magazine editors and television producers) come here for meetings, or quiet, leisurely, simple breakfasts of soft-boiled eggs and toast, hot cereal, or omelets.

ADDRESSES

Aquagrill 210 Spring St (at Sixth Ave), tel: 212-274-0505
Balthazar 80 Spring St (bet. Broadway and Crosby St), tel: 212-965-1414
Barney Greengrass 541 Amsterdam Ave (bet. 86th and 87th sts), tel: 212-724-4707
Blue Water Grill 31 Union Sq. W. (at 16th St), tel: 212-675-9500
The Boathouse Central Park W. (enter at 72nd St at Central Park N. Dr.), tel: 212-517-2233
The Cupping Room Café 359 West Broadway (bet. Broome and Grand sts), tel: 212-925-2898
EJ's Luncheonette 432 Sixth Ave (bet. 9th and 10th sts), tel: 212-473-5555; 1271 Third Ave (at 73rd St), tel: 212- 472-0600; 447 Amsterdam (bet. 81st & 82nd sts) 212-873-3444
French Roast 78 W. 11th St (at Sixth Ave) 212-533-2233; 2340 Broadway (at 85th St), tel: 212-799-1533
Jerry's 101 Prince St (bet. Greene and Mercer sts), tel: 212-966-9464
Paris Commune 411 Bleeker St (bet. Bank and W. 11th sts), tel: 212-929-0509
Sarabeth's 423 Amsterdam Ave (bet. 80th and 81st sts), tel: 212-496-6280 and 1295 Madison Ave (bet. 92nd and 93rd sts), tel: 212-410-7335
The River Café 1 Water St (bet. Furman and Old Fulton sts), tel: 718-522-5200
Tartine 253 W. 11th St (at W. 4th St), tel: 212-2292611, *see page 63*
Tavern on the Green Central Park West (bet. 66 and 67 sts), tel: 212-873-3200

Area 5: East Village and Lower East Side

East Village and the Lower East Side

The once-mean streets are now the avant-garde domain of young hipsters who crowd into its sidewalk cafes and cheerfully cheap restaurants

Take a rough neighborhood, the drearier the street the better, find a run-down tenement or industrial space, open a restaurant or club – and hey presto, you have a surefire hit. These days, this is a formula that never seems to miss on the Lower East Side and in the East Village. These two neighborhoods cover a generous swathe of the east side of Lower Manhattan between Broadway and the East River. The Lower East Side runs north from Grand Street to Houston Street and the East Village from Houston Street north to 14th Street; the one thing both neighborhoods have in common is a long history of poverty.

The Lower East Side is synonymous with immigration, and its crowded tenements and teeming streets were home to thousands of Europeans who sailed across the Atlantic in the late 19th and early 20th centuries. Tough as it was to make a go of it here, life was rich and colorful enough to inspire one immigrant, the composer Irving Berlin, to observe, 'Everyone ought to have a Lower East Side in their life.' Asian and Hispanic immigrants followed, arriving later in the 20th century.

The definitive melting pot

You can get a sense of what the neighborhood was once like at the Lower East Side Tenement Museum (97 Orchard Street) where authentically furnished rooms re-create the immigrant experience. You can also get a taste of the old world at a handful of culinary institutions that remain with one foot firmly in the past. Among these is Katz's Delicatessen *(see page 73)*, where signs still urge World War II diners to 'Send a salami to your boy in the army,' and Kossar's Bialystoker Kuchen Bakery on Grand Street, where generations of bakers have been turning out the best bialys, bagels, and pretzels in New York. Sammy's Steak House, on Chrystie Street, is so unselfconsciously locked into an era when no one worried about cholesterol that big vats of schmaltz (chicken fat) appear on the tables.

***Opposite:* Chez es Saada for exotic Franco-Moroccan food.**

***Below:* Flor's Kitchen, a cheerful Venezuelan joint**

The East Village, meanwhile, has less of a pedigree. But what this neighborhood of tenements, housing projects, and a few nice blocks here and there lacks in culture, it makes up for with counterculture. The East Village – which in architecture and history is miles removed from its neighbor the West (Greenwich) Village – has seen the passage of beatniks, hippies, and punks, and entering the mix have been homeless squatters, drop-outs, poets and musicians, and drug addicts. If a bohemia still exists in affluent and homogenized Manhattan – and the matter is up for debate – St. Mark's Place, which cuts through the heart of the East Village, is its main drag.

The neighborhood is not without its landmarks, too. St. Mark's Church in the Bowery, on Second Avenue and

Tenth Street, dates to 1799; the Tenth Street Turkish Baths have soothed work-weary residents for a century; and La MaMa Experimental Theatre on East Fourth Street has been staging avant-garde drama for decades. Some of the area's most noted sights are culinary. A string of brightly lit and fantastically inexpensive Indian restaurants along Sixth Street between Second and First avenues are known collectively as Curry Row; and the Kiev, on Second Avenue, is a remnant of the eateries that once served Eastern European immigrants.

FIVE OF THE BEST

'inoteca: raises Italian sandwiches to an art form with a wine list to match
Jewel Bako: for fabulous market-fresh fish
Katz's Delicatessen: peerless pastrami, wonderful wieners, and other deli classics
Prune: unpretentious and pleasant American-Mediterranean dishes
WD-50: adventurous dining and dishes in a cool location

Alphabet City

While the Lower East Side and the East Village once dozed on the sidelines of the Manhattan fast track, these days they have a new lease of life. They are, in a word, hip. To the amazement and amusement of long-time residents, former tenements once inhabited by immigrants who worked like dogs to move on to better environs now rent for small fortunes. Streets so menacing that only the foolhardy risked them at night are now packed with young graduates starting out on new careers. While once there was never much reason to venture into these neighborhoods, and certainly not at night, they now come alive when the sun goes down. In fact, for many New Yorkers, the only two reasons to visit the Lower East Side and East Village are to drink and to dine.

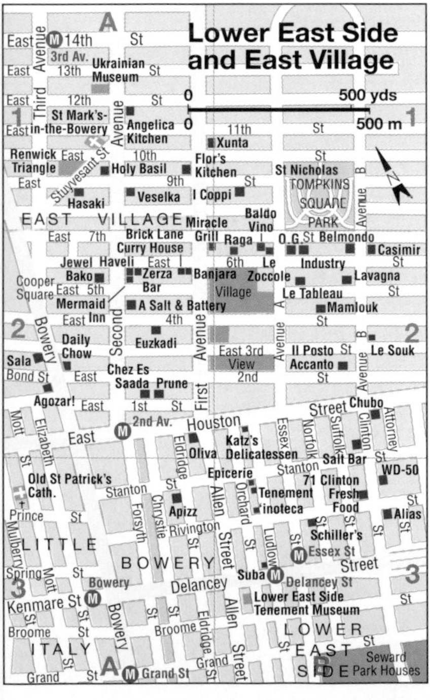

Il Posto Accanto *(see page 78)*, a romantic wine bar at the eastern edge of the East Village known as Alphabet City (so called because the streets are lettered, not named) proves just how cosmopolitan this former no-man's land is becoming. A sense of price consciousness pervades both neighborhoods, as evidenced by bars, coffee shops, and restaurants where a meal won't cost the earth – even at places as trendy and popular as Schiller's Liquor Bar on Rivington Street the tab can remain within the stratosphere.

To witness the Lower East Side renaissance, take a walk down Ludlow and Clinton streets. For a look at the East Village Scene, check out avenues A and B. In both neighborhoods, you'll feel old if you're over 40, unfashionable if you're wearing a color other than black, and out of sync if you show up before 10 o'clock.

American

71 Clinton Fresh Food

*71 Clinton St (bet. Stanton and Rivington sts) [B3]. Tel: 212-614-6960. Open: daily, D only. **$$$$**. www.clintonfreshfood.com*

Chef Wylie Dufresne has moved on, but his legacy continues in this permanently crowded eatery that helped put the Lower East Side on the culinary map. The minimal decor is the perfect backdrop for the contemporary, elegantly prepared dishes such as black bass in a honey wine sauce and venison with sour-cherry compote. A casual atmosphere, but serious food. Reservations necessary.

Alias

*76 Clinton St (at Rivington St) [B3]. Tel: 212-505-5011. Open: daily, D only. **$$$** www.aliasrestaurant.com*

From the outside it looks like a grungy bodega, but inside it's a warm bistro with sleek, modern decor. The tiny space is often filled to capacity thanks to the reasonably priced innovative dishes by chef Anthony Rose such as sauerkraut with braised pork cheek or the oyster and sweet dumpling squash stew (from one of the 'full moon menus' held monthly). Interesting wines offered by the glass.

Industry (Food)

*509 E. 6th St (bet. aves A and B) [B2]. Tel: 212-777-5920. Open: D only Mon–Sat, until 3am Thur–Sat **$$$$** www.industryfood.com*

The velvet rope that goes up to control the crowds late at night is a good indication that this two-story restaurant is more a hip scene than anything else. The decor is Alpine ski-lodge gone wild, there's a garden out back, and a lounge with sultry lighting downstairs. The small menu features homey dishes such as lobster and pancetta bruschetta and skate wing with sweetbreads. Great for people-watching.

Katz's Delicatessen 🍴

*205 E. Houston St (at Ludlow St) [B2]. Tel: 212-254-2246. Open: B, L, and D daily. **$$** www.katzdeli.com*

Founded in 1888, this old-style Jewish deli is a New York institution. The huge space is often filled to capacity, especially on Sunday mornings when a line forms out the

Above and below: Katz's Delicatessen, for a quintessential New York experience

Wylie Dufresne's creative cuisine at WD-50 is winning rave reviews

door and around the block of people hungry for the deli's pastrami on rye or warm beef brisket. The portions are huge, and the service is friendly though brusque. A must for any first-time visitor to the city.

Miracle Grill

112 First Ave (bet. 6th and 7th sts) [A2]. Tel: 212- 254-2353. Open: D only Mon–Fri, Br and D Sat, Sun. ***$$***
www.miracleny.com

With its sunny back garden, festive atmosphere, and the southwestern and Mexican flavors on the menu, this is the place to be on a breezy summer day – if you can get a table (no reservations allowed). The potent margaritas may try to steal the show, but the food is delicious: copious portions of casual, often spicy fare such as cornmeal-crusted catfish in soft tacos, citrus-and-garlic marinated chicken, and the brunch-time huevos rancheros. Flamboyant chef Bobby Flay is long-gone, but his spirit lives on.

Prune

54 E. 1st St (bet. First and Second aves) [A2]. Tel: 212-677-6221. Open: D daily. ***$$$***

Prune is the nickname of chef-owner Gabrielle Hamilton, who has turned this small restaurant into a destination for foodies looking for a fix of excellent and unusual meat dishes. Salivate over the roasted marrow bones and parsley salad, rabbit legs with vinegar sauce, fried dark-meat chicken with cold buttermilk dressing, stewed chestnuts with fresh ricotta, or lentils with fried chicken livers, and Dutch chocolate cocoa cake for dessert.

Salt Bar

29A Clinton St (bet. E. Houston and Stanton sts) [B2]. Tel: 212-979-8471. Open: D daily. ***$$$***

Chef Melissa O'Donnell's seductive spot is one of the new breed of restaurants popping up in New York serving creative but simple dishes featuring seasonal produce (try the wholewheat pasta with mushrooms and pancetta). The vibe is fun and low-key and the staff refreshingly free of pretension. Some seating is communal.

Tenement

157 Ludlow St (bet. Rivington and Stanton sts) [B3]. Tel: 212-

Did you know?

The residents of the East Village and the Lower East Side have long been fans of alternative music, and these areas are full of small clubs where up-and-coming bands strut their stuff. There is a high concentration of record stores, most of which sell vinyl LPs, new and used. DJs form the main clientele.

766-1270. Open: D only Tues–Sun. ***$$$*** *www.tenementlounge.com*
This three-floor space was a tenement building in the early 1900s, its tiny apartments once crammed with immigrants. Today, it gets crowded with night owls digging into large portions of eclectic comfort food from a menu that pays respect to the history of this immigrant quarter: potato and cheese pirogues or pork chops stuffed with dried fruit. There's also a sky-lit cocktail lounge and a DJ most nights.

WD-50 🍴

50 Clinton St (bet. Rivington and Stanton sts) [B3]. Tel: 212-477-2900. Open: D daily. ***$$$$*** *www.wd-50.com*
Risk-taking wonder-chef Wylie Dufresne has left behind the low-key intimacy of 71 Clinton Fresh Food nearby *(see page 73)* and joined forces with Jean-George Vongerichten in this cavernous den of high-art cuisine. Oysters flattened into squares perched on granny smith apple slices with a dab of pistachio puree, or skate curled next to a pile of lemon-flavored gnocchi garnished with hazelnut shavings are examples of his more mannered creations. Some miss the simplicity of his earlier cuisine, but many of his dishes are winning rave reviews.

Asian

Daily Chow

2 E. Second St (at Bowery) [A2]. Tel: 212-254-7887. Open: D daily. ***$$*** *www.dailychow.com*
Locals love this vast, two-floor spot with its chic, industrial feel, sexy lighting, and moderate prices. The wonderful pan-Asian cuisine includes a Mongolian barbeque where diners can create their own dish by choosing their own meats, vegetables, and sauces. The upstairs dining room affords good views.

O.G.

507 E. 6th St (bet. aves A and B) [B2]. Tel: 212-477-4649. Open: D daily. ***$$***
The initials should stand for 'oh-so good' since the exotic fare here is worth shouting about. The simply decorated, candle-lit room is home of some of the best pan-Asian fare in the city with dishes like cracking calamari salad and shrimp dumplings with red-pepper miso. The staff are friendly, prices are low, and the food is outrageously good. Great for groups.

Eastern European

Veselka

144 Second Ave (at 9th St) [A1]. Tel: 212-228-9682. Open: 24 hours. ***$$*** *www.veselka.com*
Hearty Ukrainian specialties are what you'll find at this brightly lit 24-hour diner. The restaurant stays crowded regardless of the time of day, attesting to the quality of the

Ukrainian diner, Veselka

TIP

Along avenues A and B, drug dealers and graffiti-covered walls have been usurped by bars and restaurants with a predominantly young, hip clientele. **Odessa** *(119 Ave A at 7th St)* is a surviving reflection of the neighborhood's Eastern European heritage, where specialties include home-cooked pirogi, blintzes, and borscht.

Brick Lane, one of the better restaurants in Little India, aka Curry Row

comfort fare served. Must-try dishes include the borscht and the cheese- and raspberry-filled blintzes.

French

Casimir
103 Ave B (bet. 6th and 7th sts) [B2]. Tel: 212-358-9683. Open: D daily, Br Sat, Sun. **$$**
This Francophile's heaven offers straightforward, hearty bistro classics (sautéed chicken livers with shallots, grilled boudin, etc.). Prices are gentle, the wine list simple, and the ambiance unpretentious.

Chubo
6 Clinton St (at E. Houston St) [B2]. Tel: 212-674-6300. Open: D only Tues–Sat, Br and D Sun. **$$**
The combination of French, Japanese, and Latin cuisines make this cramped but cozy eatery a good choice for foodies on a budget. The simple two- or three-course menu ($25, $29) offers dishes such as warm frisée salad, miso-glazed monkfish, or Latin-spiced roasted pork medallion. The wine list is small and straightforward, with a few sakes thrown in.

Epicerie
168–70 Orchard St (at Stanton St) [B3]. Tel: 212-420-7520. Open: Daily L and D. **$$**
From the outside this bohemian bistro looks like a corner grocers. Inside, there are two rooms: a sunny dining room and a dark, casual bar. The menu is rustic and reasonably priced, and the crispy chicken is particularly good.

Schiller's Liquor Bar
131 Rivington St (at Norfolk St) [B3]. Tel: 212-260-4555. Open: L and D daily. Until 2am Fri and 3am Sat. www.schillersny.com
Keith McNally (of Balthazar and Pastis fame) spreads his empire of hip bistros eastward, and the crowds have followed. Waits can be long for the basic fare that pays homage to this once working-class immigrant area, with homey dishes such as pork chops with onions, or roast chicken and potatoes available. The wine is in three categories: cheap, decent, and good.

Le Tableau
511 E. 5th St (bet. aves A and B) [B2]. Tel: 212-260-1333. Open: D daily, closed Mon in winter **$$** *www.letableaunyc.com*
A rustic bistro offering well-executed bistro dishes such as artichoke-fennel-potato salad and peppered duck. The reasonable prices draw artists and young people who pump up the energy level, especially on weekends. Reserve.

Indian

Banjara
97 First Ave (at 6th St) [A2]. Tel: 212-477-5956. Open: D only Mon–Fri, Br and D Sat, Sun. **$$**

TIP
If cheap and exotic is your preference, head for 'Little India' on 6th Street, between First and Second avenues. Most restaurants here are inexpensive, stay open late, and some feature live Indian music on weekend evenings.

Chef Tuhin Dutta's subtle cuisine with a French twist makes this restaurant shine out among the stack of Indian restaurants in the area. His menu is a blend of experimental and traditional, the atmosphere calm, and the service polite and professional.

Brick Lane Curry House

306–308 E. 6th St (at First Ave) [A2]. Tel: 212-979-2900. Open: D daily, Br Sat, Sun. **$$**
www.bricklanecurryhouse.com

This above-average Curry Row restaurant challenges its patrons to see how spicy they can go. If you can stand the heat, try the lamb jalfrezi with ginger and chilis.

Haveli

100 Second Ave (bet. 5th and 6th sts) [A2]. Tel: 212-982 0533. Open: L and D daily. **$$**

This simple spot stands apart from the gaudy, brightly lit restaurants of nearby Sixth Street in more ways than one. The decor is understated, service is helpful, and the kitchen executes stellar versions of the classics, beginning with the mixed appetizers. Prices here are a tad higher than at the Curry Row competition, but it's money well spent.

Raga

433 E. 6th St (bet. First Ave and Ave A) [B2]. Tel: 212 388-0957 Open: D only Tue–Sun **$$**

This innovative bistro serves American food with an Indian twist. The bold combination of ingredients and flavors rarely fails. Try the seared scallops with tomatoes and black cardamom.

Italian

Apizz

217 Eldridge St (bet. Rivington and Stanton sts) [A3]. Tel: 212-253-9199. Open: D daily. **$$$**
www.apizz.com

Run by the owners of the excellent Peasant in NoLita *(see page 95)*, the kitchen of this small, inviting, minimalist space turns out hearty dishes cooked in the wood-burning oven. Pizza is a mainstay (Apizz, pronounced Ah-beets, is Italian slang for pizza), but there are other treats such as wild boar lasagne and meatballs with ricotta in tomato gravy. Worth going out of your way for.

Baldo Vino

126 E. 7th St (bet. First Ave and Ave A) [B2]. Tel: 212-979-0319. Open: D daily. **$$**

All the elements of a Tuscan country trattoria are here: the large chalkboard over the bar listing the daily wine selection, the wooden tables and chairs, the painted pottery, and the bowls of deliciously fresh pasta specials such as wild mushroom papardelle, brought to your table by friendly wait staff.

I Coppi

432 E. 9th St (bet. First Ave and Ave A) [B1]. Tel: 212-254-2263. Open: D only Mon–Fri, Br and D Sat, Sun. **$$$**

Transport yourself to Tuscany at I Coppi

Flor's Kitchen, a sunny Venezuelan cafe

This rustic yet sophisticated Tuscan restaurant oozes authenticity thanks to its brick walls, terracotta floors, wood-burning oven, and pretty back garden. The dishes are rustic yet sophisticated (salad of pears with gorgonzola and stracchino cheese, pan-seared duck with Italian bacon and onions roasted in balsamic vinegar). Pricey for the neighborhood, but very romantic.

'inoteca

98 Rivington St (at Ludlow St) [B3]. Tel: 212-614-0473. Open: Daily L and D. ***$$***

A larger, more upscale version of the tiny 'ino in Greenwich Village, this enoteca has the same warmth and casual menu. Here, Italian sandwiches are raised to an art form: hot pressed panini, tramezzini (crustless, cut into triangles). The wine list has over 200 choices from the cheap and cheerful to the divine.

Lavagna

545 E. 5th St (bet. aves A and B) [B2]. Tel: 212-979-1005. Open: D daily. ***$$***
www.lavagnanyc.com

The eclectic choice of well-executed dishes on offer at this trattoria, with its fashionably understated brick wall and wooden tables, could best be described as Northern Italian with an exotic twist. The pork chop with chestnut puree and the spicy roasted fish are stand-outs.

Il Posto Accanto

190 E. Second St (bet. aves A and B) [B2]. Tel: 212-228-3562. Open: Tues–Sun D. ***$$***

This casual but elegant wine bar with a European feel and long communal table is a good place to linger with friends over a bottle of wine and a platter of antipasti. The hot crocks with vegetables and bubbling cheese are delicious.

Le Zoccole

95 Ave A (at 6th St) [B2]. Tel: 212-260-6660. Open: L and D daily. ***$$***

This two-story osteria specializes in the coastal cuisine of Italy's northeast region. In addition to the regular menu, the bar offers a wide selection of tasty bites such as grilled octopus and whitebait ceviche at moderate prices, as well as a good selection of wines by the glass. Decor is minimal, sidewalk seating is available, and the black-clad staff friendly.

Japanese

Hasaki

210 E. 9th St (bet. Second and Third aves) [A1]. Tel: 212-473-3327. Open: L and D Wed– Sun, D only Mon, Tues. ***$$$***
www.hasakinyc.com

Don't be daunted by the line of customers spilling out the door here at peak hours. This tiny restaurant operates a no-reservation

TIP

St. Mark's Place is one of the city's liveliest thoroughfares. Busy sidewalk cafes and restaurants and street vendors selling T-shirts, jewelry and bootleg CDs give it a bazaar-like atmosphere. Stop in at **Dojo** *(Nos 24–26)* for a quick and nutritious vegetarian snack, or take a detour to **McSorley's Old Ale House** *(15 E. 7th St, bet. Second and Third aves)* a true drinking-man's pub that's been in business since the 1850s.

policy. Its popularity is down to the fresh top-grade sushi, sashimi, and tempura. Well worth the wait.

Jewel Bako

239 E. 5th St (bet. Second and Third aves) [A2]. Tel: 212-979-1012. Open: D Mon–Sat. **$$$$**

Husband-and-wife team, Jack and Grace Lamb, have a well-deserved reputation for their uncommon but first-rate sushi choices, and imported rarities such as Japanese spotted sardines and needlefish. Charming, knowledgeable service. Very popular, so reserve well in advance.

Latin American

Flor's Kitchen

149 First Ave (bet. 9th and 10th sts) [A1]. Tel: 212-387-8949. Open: L and D daily. **$** *www.florskitchen.com*

This tiny, blink-and-you'll-miss-it Venezuelan joint has quite a following for its full-flavored simple, homey fare. Prices are very low and service is sweet and earnest. Try the cachapa, fresh corn cakes served with slices of salty farmer's cheese. Long wait at weekends.

Suba

109 Ludlow St (at Delancey St) [B3]. Tel: 212-982-5714. Open: D daily. **$$$** *www.subanyc.com*

Situated in a 1909 tenement building, this sleek Spanish-American has a dining room surrounded by an illuminated shallow moat. Next door, DJs spin world and Latin tracks, and upstairs there's a tapas bar. All rooms are connected by industrial steel staircases and walkways. The inspired dishes (salmon marinated in lemon juice and coconut milk, with green apple and cucumber; grilled sardines with chipotle sauce, red-bean salad, and crunchy guacamole) are whipped up by Portuguese chef Chris Santos.

Middle Eastern

Mamlouk

211 E. 4th St (bet. aves A and B) [B2]. Tel: 212-529-3477. Open: Tues–Sun D, closed Mon. **$$$**

This exotic restaurant with copper-topped Egyptian tables and velvet cushions is held by many to be the best Middle Eastern in the city. It serves a lavish six-course menu that changes daily for just $35. So put yourself in the chef's hands and enjoy a feast including a platter of appetizers, soup, salad, main dishes such as chicken stewed in yoghurt, garlic, and nutmeg, or vegetarian moussaka, and delicious desserts. Two seatings: at 7pm and 9pm.

North African

Chez Es Saada

42 E. First St (bet. First and Second aves) [A2]. Tel: 212-777-5617. Open: D daily. **$$$**

Enter the labyrinth of dark, sexy rooms with low tables and plump cushions, and strewn with rose petals. This ode to colonial North Africa (one of the mosaic tables came from Matisse's favorite hotel in Tangiers) serves a simple menu of French and Moroccan dishes

Enter the exotic world of Chez Es Saada

such as steak frites, couscous, oven-roasted chicken with olives and currants, and crème caramel for dessert. Come for cocktails, or for the weekend bellydancing.

Le Souk

47 Ave B (bet. Third and Fourth sts) [B2]. Tel: 212-777-5454. Open: D daily. **$$**

The tagines at this moderately priced Moroccan restaurant are delicious, but the real draw is the sultry, exotic atmosphere. Stringent anti-smoking laws mean that the hookah pipes are now only decorative, but in summer months you can grab a table outside on the terrace and enjoy a digestive puff.

Zerza Bar

304 E. Sixth St (bet. First and Second aves) [A2]. Tel: 212 529-8250. Open: L and D daily. **$$** *www.zerzabar.com*

A two-story Moroccan-Mediterranean restaurant that pays homage to Casablanca. There's a wide range of scrumptious tagines and couscous dishes served in the elegant dining room upstairs. Start or finish with the signature cocktail, the Shehrazad (vanilla vodka, apple liquor, rose petal water) in the bar/lounge downstairs.

Seafood

A Salt & Battery

80 Second Ave (bet. Fourth and Fifth sts) [A2]. Tel: 212-254-6610. Open: L and D daily. **$** *www.asaltandbattery.com*

Great fish and chips come nostalgically wrapped in newspaper as they once were in Britain. Along with ultra-fresh batter-fried cod and haddock, you'll find deep-fried scallops or chicken chunks, chicken pot pie, and side dishes of baked beans and deep fried beets. (*See page 66 for the West Village branch.*)

Mermaid Inn

96 Second Ave (bet 5th and 6th sts) [A2]. Tel: 212-674-5870. Open: D daily. **$$$** *www.themermaidnyc.com*

This place is reminiscent of a New England seafood shack, its walls decorated with maritime paraphernalia. The food is a refined take on seaside classics such as fish chowder, fried oysters, shrimp cocktail, and seafood au gratin. No reservations, so be prepared to queue.

Spanish

Euzkadi

108 E. Fourth St (bet. First and Second aves) [A2]. Tel: 212-982-9788. Open: D daily. **$$**

The Basque experience kicks off with a welcoming dish of tapenade and thick slices of fresh bread. The food is simple but full-flavored with dishes such as fried bacalao cake served with stuffed peppers, and rabbit braised in a wine and prune sauce. The pretty room is decked in bohemian wall prints and antique mirrors.

Oliva

161 E. Houston St (at Allen St) [A2]. Tel: 212-228-4143. Open: D daily. **$$**

This funky restaurant with just a few tables is a good choice for great tapas such as stuffed Dungeness crab. The staff and bartenders are friendly, and it's a popular spot for sharing a pitcher of margaritas. All this explains explains why the noise level can be high.

Sala

344 Bowery (at Great Jones St) [A2]. Tel: 212-979-6606. Open: D daily. **$$** *www.salanyc.com*

Sala looks so much like a street in Barcelona, you'll feel as though you're sitting in an outdoor restaurant there. The tapas menu offers a choice of dishes in various sizes of both classic and modern Spanish fare, such as bite-sized portions of chorizo and bowls of marinated mushrooms. There's a good selection of Spanish wines, and a downstairs lounge.

Xunta
174 First Ave (bet. 10th and 11th aves) [A1]. Tel: 212-614-0620. Open: D daily, L Sat, Sun. $
Crowded, dark, and grungy it may be, but this spot serves some of the best tapas and sangria in the city. The affordable food and friendly atmosphere draw a young, bohemian clientele, and the noise levels can be high. The cod fishcakes and shrimp grilled with garlic are highly recommended.

Thai

Holy Basil
149 Second Ave (bet. 9th and 10th sts) [A1]. Tel: 212-460-5557. Open: D daily. $$
This candle-lit Thai bistro located on the second floor of a brownstone attracts a hip crowd despite its simple, unpretentious feel. The food is worth crossing town for, especially the shrimp in garlic and black pepper, the sliced crispy duck with basil, onion, and black pepper, or the green papaya salad. Has been named best Thai restaurant by New York journalists.

Vegetarian

Angelica Kitchen
300 E. 12th St (at Second Ave) [A1]. Tel: 212-228-2909. Open: L and D daily. $
This large, bright, warm space with oak picnic-style tables is thought to be the best vegetarian restaurant in the city. Although the vibe is distinctly earthy and bohemian, it attracts young professionals as well as those with nose-rings and tattoos. The pull – inventive cuisine such as marinated tofu and tempeh reuben sandwiches, southern-style cornbread, and the fiery three-bean chili with tofu sour cream.

CAFES AND BARS

The boho-chic neighborhoods of the East Village and the Lower East Side, two areas on the eastern side of the city located just north and just south of Houston Street respectively, are dotted with numerous casual cafes, bars, and alternative music venues.

Unlike the Upper East Side, Irish pubs are few and far between, while French bistros and Italian trattorias are extremely commonplace. The British pub, the **Telephone Bar & Grill** *(149 Second Ave, tel: 212-529-5000)* is located next to the Irish pub **Ryans** *(151 Second Ave, tel: 212-979-9511)*, and hopping from one to the other, and back, is a sport of sorts. The French cafes, whether they stand alone or are attached to an actual restaurant, tend to be charming: **Belmondo** *(98 Ave B, tel: 212-358-1166)*, a lounge and café; **Jules** *(65 St Mark's Pl., tel: 212-477-5560)*, where live jazz can be heard at Sunday brunches, and **Lucien** *(14 First Ave, tel: 212-260-6481)*, a slice of cafe society Parisian-style.

The Italian caffes, like the French, serve wines as well as coffees and most are rustic in feel: **'inoteca** *(see page 78)* and **Le Zoccole** *(see page 78)*. Some even hang chalkboards with daily wine specials: **Il Posto Accanto** *(see page 78)* and **Baldo Vino** *(see page 77)*. Just a couple of elegant bars are found in this area: **Suba** *(109 Ludlow St, tel: 212-982-5714)* with its subterranean bar located two levels down, and the trendy, bi-level **Industry (Food)** *(see page 73)*, another subterranean lounge.

The Best Burgers in New York

When chef Daniel Boulud launched his pricey gourmet burger, the city's bargain staple became a designer commodity

The year 2002 was the year of the burger wars in New York. It all kicked off when celebrity chef, Daniel Boulud, launched the DB burger on an unsuspecting world. This creation, which Boulud reserves for his customers at **DB Bistro Moderne** *(see page 20),* comprises braised short ribs, foie gras, and black truffles wrapped in raw sirloin and oven-roasted until it is medium-rare. The DB weighs in at 9oz and is served in traditional style, inside a bun (albeit one flavored with parmesan); the most shocking thing about the DB, however, is the price – at $59 (or $99 for the double truffle version) it's officially the most expensive commercially available burger in the world.

In a town where the burger is the egalitarian choice of the masses, eaten enthusiastically and two-fistedly, all day, every day, by everybody from the mayor to rooky New York Police Department recruits, this was seen as an over-hyped travesty. However, it happened at a time when business in New York's restaurants was as soggy as yesterday's freedom fries. So instead of showing outrage, scorn, or indifference, the competition decided to treat it as a marketing challenge and wade on in.

Old Homestead *(see page 48)*, an old-fashioned Chelsea steakhouse with a life-sized plastic cow on its roof, was the first place to try to outdo DB, grabbing some of the headlines by announcing their 20oz, $41 burger made with aged Kobe beef. Apparently, they sold 180 the very next day, and the poshest of posh beef patties are still selling well. Not to be outdone, Boulud answered with the 'burger royal,' a $50 foie gras burger topped with shaved white truffles (available only in spring). From then on, all hell was let loose, as every New York restaurant with a grill claimed that its burger might not be the most expensive, or include any gourmet twists, but it was the best. And every food critic who'd ever passed through the Big Apple weighed in with their summary of who packed the best buns in town (as it were).

Pick of the Bunch

If size matters, the whopping Luger burger weighs in at 10oz and is a lunch-only special at **Peter Luger's** *(see page 145)* in Williamsburg. It's made with fresh ground chuck mixed with trimmings from dry-aged porterhouse, and comes on a sesame bun with a slice of raw onion and a crock of fiery mustard. Formerly the most expensive of its kind (until Boulud's 'DB' came along), the $26 burger at **"21" Club** *(see page 16)* attracted tourists, who could then brag to their friends back home about how much they'd spent on a burger in 'Noo Yawk.' The "21" burger is lean ground sirloin with rendered duck fat, cumin, and fresh herbs mixed in. It comes on a silver platter, on to which a tuxedoed waiter will gently spoon ketchup.

For more varieties than Heinz, try **Island Burgers and Shakes** *(766 Ninth Ave, bet. 51st and 52nd sts, tel: 212-307-7934)* offers 63 different burgers including the 'Basic' (no trimmings), the 'Julius' (with Caesar salad in pita bread), the 'Hippo' (curried sour cream, bacon, cheddar and onion on sourdough bread), and the 'Frog' (Boursin, bacon, and onions). These burgers are perfect and never overwhelmed by the accompaniments.

Best-loved by locals are the burgers at the **Corner Bistro** *(see page 58)*, a dark and dingy bar in the West Village. Here, burgers are the only thing on the menu, and they are served on paper plates. Plain as they are, they're juicy, flavorful, and nicely charred. Year after year the lines continue to form. For burgers LA-style there's **Blue 9 Burger** *(92 Third Ave, bet. 12th and 13th sts, tel: 212-979-0053)* in the East Village. This place serves its burgers the way the West Coast like them –- a slender patty of meat on a toasted bun with lettuce, tomato, and Thousand Island dressing.

If you like your burgers served in an unlikely setting, head for a corner of the very grand lobby of the Parker Meridien Hotel. Here, the plainly named **Burger Joint** *(119 W. 56th St, bet. Sixth and Seventh aves, tel: 212-245-5000)* dispenses a blue-collar-style, 4oz burger on a paper plate – in contrast to the distinctly designer surroundings. Spicy, Moroccan-inspired lamb burgers are on offer at **La Sandwicherie** (842 Greenwich St, near Gansevoort St, tel: 212-675-3281), while just across the street from St. Patrick's Cathedral, with the slogan 'The Gates of Heaven – Never Closed,' you can eat the heavenly **Prime Burger** *(5 E. 51st St, at Fifth Ave, tel: 212-759-4729)*; this restaurant was formerly known as Hamburg Heaven and patronized by the likes of Rita Hayworth and Henry Fonda. The name's changed, but the burgers are made to the same recipe.

For the greatest choice of toppings and trimmings, there's the **Rare Bar & Grill** *(303 Lexington Ave, at 37th St, tel: 212-481-1999)*, inside the Shelburne Murray Hill. This place has bunned burgers into which you can sneak foie gras, a fried egg, portobello mushrooms, and five dipping sauces, while unbunned ones come with a wide range of salads. They also have three choices of fries: shoestring, sweet potato, and cottage.

Daniel Boulud's 'DB' burger

Best pedigree has to go to **Westville** *(see page 60)*, where all the food is certified organic and comes from top-notch farmers and suppliers. You can read all about the distinguished herd that your burger derives from as you chow down.

Then there are burgers like a luxury car. Nat King Cole famously called PJ Clarke's bacon cheeseburger, the 'Cadillac of Burgers.' And while the crowd may not be as rakish as it was back then, the newly refurbished **PJ Clarkes** *(see page 18)* still does a mighty fine burger.

Finally, for small but perfectly formed burgers, there's **Pop Burger** *(58–60 Ninth Ave, bet. 14th and 15th sts, tel: 212-337-0555)*, where the mini sirloin burgers weigh in at around six to the pound or 2¾oz each. They come in a toasted brioche bun, and are $5 for two.

CALDO VERDE
*RICES
BROWN STICKY
BASMATI JAPANESE
THAI BLACK RICE
SMALL/LARGE
*BAKED BLACK BEANS
*VEGETARIAN MEATBALLS
*RATATOUILLE
*JERK CHICKEN WINGS
*WARM VIETNAMESE GRILLED LEMONGRASS CHICKEN SALAD
*CHICKEN, TOFU OR SHRIMP SATAY
*THAI BEEF SALAD
*THAI CHICKEN, VEG, TOFU, OR SHRIMP COCONUT CURRY
*WARM LENTIL STEW
*INDIAN CHICKEN CURRY
*RICE BALLS
CARROT OR SPINACH
THAI SHRIMP
*SIDES
*SAUCES
MANGO CHUTNEY
THAI SWEET CHILI
ALEPPO YOGURT
THAI CHILI & GARLIC
SALSA FRESCA
AVACADO SALSA
MANGO SALSA
(SEASONAL)
*SALAD
DRESSINGS
ASIAN CARROT GINGER
CHIPOTLE
GARLIC WOW!
BALSAMIC
AVACADO Y POBLANO
*ASIAN SLAW
*MAKI
GRILLED EGGPLANT SUSHI
*VEG DIM SUM
*SHRIMP DUMPLINGS
*SPECIALS
*TEA SMOKED SALMON SALAD
*TOFU STEAK
*CHICKEN KEBAB
*PAD THAI W/CHICKEN SHRIMP OR TOFU
FRESH
PLEASE ASK
FLAVORS WE
AVAILABLE
WARM PEAR
*THAI BANANA
*INDIAN RICE
*RICE

SoHo and Little Italy

SoHo's rise from 'Hell's hundred acres' to a consumer heaven of chic boutiques and fabulous restaurants has been meteoric

The area now known as SoHo (SOuth of HOuston) has had more dramatic ups and downs than a trapeze artist. It has been in turn: hills roamed by Native Americans, an intimate Dutch village, a poisonous swamp, an upmarket residential community, an industrial wasteland, a bohemian artists' haven, and a chic shopper's paradise.

Historic SoHo

The area's hills were razed in the 1650s to fill in the stream that ran the course of Canal Street because it was thought to be fetid and cause disease. But apart from the missing contours, you can still wander about SoHo today and be aware of its historic zigzags. You can stand at a street corner and see buildings that are named after Native American tribes and once housed theaters patronized by 18th-century toffs. And look across to a beautiful cast-iron industrial building that accommodates one of the few brave gallery owners hanging on despite soaring rents and a designer store where T-shirts start at $150. It's also possible to eat your way through the historical layers of SoHo, as there are restaurants, bars, and cafes reflecting every trace of its past. For example, Spring Street Natural (62 Spring St, at Lafayette) promises that all its organic produce comes from New York farms. And Balthazar *(see page 91)*, the glittering brasserie that makes you feel as if you could look up from your pain-au-chocolat and see the Eiffel Tower reflected in the window, was in fact a shoe warehouse until 1997. It is hard to look round today's SoHo, which has a restaurant on every corner, and imagine it as a food and drink wilderness. But in the 1960s, it was a former industrial area so utterly desolate it was dubbed 'Hell's hundred acres' in the local press. Only a few pugilistic stalwarts such as Fanelli Café *(see page 89)* kept their doors open through the bad old days.

By 1969, the area south of Houston (pronounced HOW-ston, not HEW-ston, and named after William Houston, a lawyer and congressman from Georgia, whose father-in-law first cut this street through his own estate) was ripe for revival, and it was New York's artists who grasped this before the real estate agents or anyone else had a chance to. Painters and sculptors started taking over spacious, but filthy, vermin-infested lofts and converting them into studios, in which they also began to camp out. Andy Warhol, Chuck Close, Frank Stella, Richard Serra, Cindy Sherman, et al, made SoHo their bohemian HQ. So many artists moved in that buildings started carrying the stone label AIR – Artist In Residence – so the fire department would know that the buildings, zoned for industrial use only, were occupied.

***Opposite:* Rice, in Mott Street**

In 1971, SoHo was officially re-zoned as a residential neighborhood, and two years after that the Friends of Cast Iron Architecture managed to get a 26-

block area designated as an historic district, assuring the preservation of the largest concentration of cast-iron buildings in the world. Greene Street has the highest concentration of cast-iron facades in the world – there are 50 in just five blocks – while the stretch between Canal and Grand streets has the longest continuous row of cast-iron facade buildings left standing anywhere.

Once SoHo gained legal recognition as an artistic center, people began streaming in in search of 'the scene,' and early entrepreneurs started catering to their needs. One such was Jerry Joseph, who started in business as an art dealer, but changed career to open Jerry's *(see page 89),* which became the art world's feeding trough. Dean and Deluca is another example of how two worlds collided and created something utterly new in SoHo. In 1972, Giorgio DeLuca opened a little cheese shop on Prince Street in what was still his native Little Italy. Five years later, Joel Dean, a publishing executive with Simon & Schuster, persuaded him to expand it into a lunch counter for SoHo's new community, most of whom did not have kitchens or were passing through. And from that, Dean and Delucca, grew into the huge gourmet, taste-making emporium it now is.

Little Italy

When the term SoHo was first coined in the early 1970s, it referred to the square mile from Houston to Canal Street, between West Broadway and Broadway. The north-south borders haven't changed, but SoHo is now generally accepted to be everything west of the Hudson River to the eastern border of Lafayette Street. The area beyond, from Lafayette to The Bowery, is what's left of Little Italy, although some have re-christened the northern part of that NoLita (for North Of Little Italy), where chic little boutiques and cafes that can't quite afford the SoHo rent lie in waiting. The southern boundaries of Little Italy are being blurred and shunted constantly by incursions from the still-expanding Chinatown. So Little Italy, which once extended across the Village, SoHo, and parts of Tribeca, now lives up to the former part of its name much more than it does the latter.

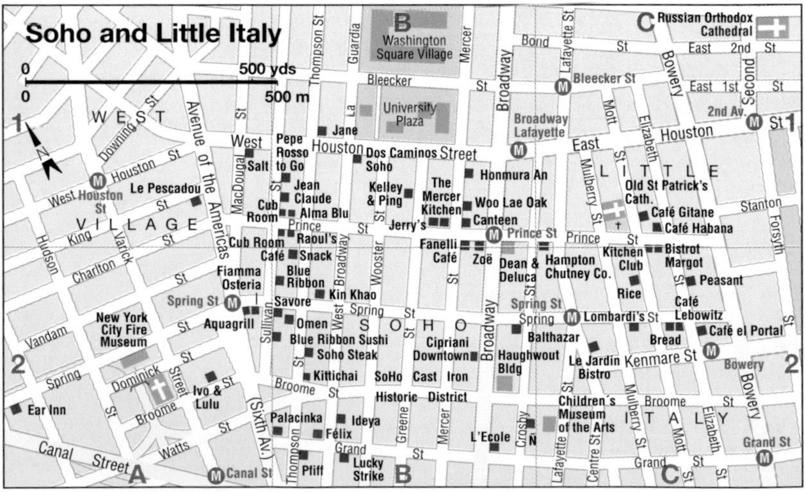

However, there are still fine coffee bars, markets, and restaurants scattered across the area to remind you of how it once was. Two of the best grocery stores for a vestige of the old Italian way of life – good places to buy food for a picnic – are Dom's on Lafayette Street, which specializes in hams and cooked meats, and DiPalo's cheese shop on Grand Street (between Mott and Elizabeth). For a coffee a godfather might relish, try Ferarra Pasticceria, also on Grand (between Mott and Mulberry). And for a slice of Italian-America, try Grotta Azzurra on Mulberry (corner of Broome); it first opened in 1903 but had its heyday in the 1950s when it was a home from home to Frankie and his Rat Pack.

Like all places that have gone through rapid and monumental change, SoHo, NoLita, and Little Italy have their nostalgia-merchants and naysayers. As early as 1974, the New York Times was publishing articles saying SoHo was a victim of its own success. And it's true that throughout the 1970s and 1980s, rents became so high that all the artists fled to cheaper Chelsea and Williamsburg, across the river. With them, the area lost its bohemian edginess, and the only people moving in were luxury-goods stores such as Prada, Burberry, and Versace. By the 1990s, SoHo had been dubbed 'one big shopping mall' by its detractors.

Eating options

Needless to say, the bar, cafe, and restaurant tariffs in SoHo do mostly reflect the area's new 'chichiness'. But, wherever you are in SoHo and surrounds, there's no need to go hungry or thirsty, or to pay through the nose. There are plenty of great places such as Ceci-Cela on Spring Street, Once Upon A Tart on Sullivan, and Le Pain Quotidien on Grand Street where you can grab a coffee and a pastry or soda and a sandwich for a few dollars. Also on Sullivan – a gourmet's paradise – is The Yoghurt Place, a tiny Greek take-out that does delicious filo-pastry pies, gorgeous nutty, honey-flavoured sweets, and, of course, creamy delicious yoghurt, accompanied by fig jam and seasonally changing preserves.

You'll have to pace yourself: take your time, look around, and decide when's the right time to splurge and when to walk on by to the cute little cheap place round the corner. Because while you can pay $30+ for a steak at Balthazar, you can also get it for under $20 at SoHo Steak *(see page 93)*. And while you could pay $20 or more for a plate of pasta at Barolo, you can get one for under $10 at Pepe Rosso to Go *(see page 95)*. As with everywhere: you pays your money and you takes your choice.

Five of the Best

Balthazar: fabulous French brasserie
Blue Ribbon: after-hours haunt of NYC's top chefs
Hampton Chutney Co.: healthy Indian vegetarian – perfect for light meals
Lombardi's: lovely old-style Little Italy pizzeria
Peasant: typical of the New York scene, with very Italian food

Gourmet emporium, Dean & Deluca

Blue Ribbon feeds hungry nocturnals until 4am

American

Blue Ribbon

97 Sullivan St (bet. Prince and Spring sts) [B2]. Tel: 212-274-0404. Open: D daily to 4am. **$$$**

The strict no-reservations policy can mean an infuriatingly long wait, and some complain that the crowd gets a little raucous, but the imaginative food and great oyster bar knocks all other considerations into touch. It's so eclectic as to defy categorisation, but they're obviously doing something right because kitchen gods, including Mario Batalí and Anthony Bourdain, descend here after hours.

Canteen

142 Mercer St (at Prince St) [B1]. Tel: 212-431-7676. Open: L and D daily. **$$$**
www.canteennyc.com

This canteen is every bit as hip as you'd expect, considering that it's located beneath Prada's flagship store. There's something workaday about the whitewashed room, but it's more reminiscent of *2001 Space Odyssey* than anything more mundane. The menu features basics such as pot pies, macaroni cheese, and pizzas, although they are elevated to haute-cuisine status by artful cooking and quality ingredients.

Cub Room

131 Sullivan St (at Prince St) [B1]. Tel: 212-677-4100. Open: L and D Mon–Fri, Br and D Sat–Sun. **$$$**
www.cubroom.com

The bar at the front is often packed with braying bankers, but step around them and you'll be rewarded with a quiet and comfortable brick-walled dining room from which you can watch the SoHo life swoosh by. The staff are attentive without being off-putting, and the food is good – the chocolate soufflé is a marvel. Those on a budget might prefer to go next door to the **Cub Room Café** *(183 Prince St, tel: 212-777-0030, open daily, $)*, which specializes in salads, sandwiches, and American diner favourites such as mac 'n' cheese, burgers and meat loaf.

The Ear Inn

326 Spring St (bet. Greenwich and Washington sts) [A2]. Tel: 212-226-9060. Open: L and D daily. **$**

Established in 1812, the Ear Inn is a contender for oldest bar in Manhattan. The decor is dark, but the atmosphere is welcoming and incredibly relaxed. The clientele, an unholy mix of dockers and artists, has changed little over the

TIP

If you don't want to separate dinner and a movie, go to the **Angelika Film Center** *(18 W. Houston)*, an art-house cinema, known to locals as a great cafe with a picture-house attached. The wraps and sandwiches are good, and the carrot cake and chocolate brownies are delicious.

years. Food is simple and hearty – think massive burgers and surprisingly good seafood. Kids are made welcome; crayons are supplied, for use on the paper tablecloths.

Fanelli Café

94 Prince St (at Mercer St) [B1]. Tel: 212-226-9412. Open: L and D daily. **$**

Want to know what SoHo was like before it was SoHo? Come to Fanelli. The service can be crotchety, but that adds to the sense of character in this handsome pub, which has been serving food continuously since 1874 (it was a speakeasy during prohibition), and the kitchen knocks out a great burger, reasonable pasta, and good sandwiches. Photographs on the walls bear testimony to the Fanelli family's obsession with boxing.

Jane

100 West Houston St (at Thompson St) [B1]. Tel: 212-254-7000. Open: L and D daily, until 1am at weekends. **$$–$$$** *www.janerestaurant.com*

There's nothing plain about this Jane, where huge blow-up photographs of cornfields in the American west perfectly complement the creative dishes crafted from hearty American ingredients. Appetizers and puddings are reliably good, and the complimentary cumin-flavored flatbread is strangely addictive. Main courses can be unpredictable, except for a few standouts such as the steak and the honey-braised pork.

Jerry's

101 Prince St (bet. Greene and Mercer sts) [B1]. Tel: 212-966-9464. Open: B, L, and D daily. **$$** *www.jerrysnyc.com*

Once *the* place for artists, dealers, and collectors to grab a bite and chat about the latest openings. Nowadays, you're more likely to see footsore shoppers in the roomy booths chomping on the fantastic shoestring fries that accompany steaks, burgers, seared tuna, and crab cakes.

The Mercer Kitchen

The Mercer Hotel, 99 Prince St (at Mercer St) [B1]. Tel: 212-966-5454. Open: B, L, and D daily. **$$$$**

If you want a celebrity sighting during your stay in NYC, invest in a meal at the Mercer – it's a magnet to models, movie stars, and musicians. However, the real star is the food. This is where celebrity chef Jean-Georges Vongerichten produces his 'everyday food.' Few eat black truffles, Maine lobster, and warm almond cake on a daily basis, but they probably would if they could afford it.

Pfiff

35 Grand St (at Thompson St) [B2]. Tel: 212-334-6841. Open: L and D daily, Sat–Sun until 1am. **$$**

Don't be put off by the silly name (German slang for highly attractive), this popular bistro is very slick, with incredibly friendly staff. The welcome is boosted by the generous happy 'hour' from 3pm till 7pm. The food is eclectic, inventive, and very good. The single best item is the $4 basket of fries: a golden pile flecked with parsley and served with its own little crock of ketchup.

Salt

58 Macdougal St at W. Houston St [A1]. Tel: 212-674-4968. Open: D daily. **$$$**

As pure and white as, well, a box of salt, this lovely restaurant has a seasonal menu from which you can design your own dinner. Pick your protein from a short but satisfying list that always includes a

Below: *SoHo institution Fanelli's*
Bottom: *Jerry's*

whole fish and a steak, and add two sides. Each night the chef presents several entrées with preselected accompaniments, but the DIY approach is more fun. When listed, the sweet-pea risotto accompaniment is a must-have.

Zoë

90 Prince St (at Broadway) [B2]. Tel: 212-966-6722. Open: L and D Tues–Sun. ***$$$***
www.zoerestaurant.com

You might not think it to look at it, but this elegant SoHo bistro is especially good if you have kids. There's a counter next to the exposed kitchen where children are encouraged to sit to be given little tastes or demonstrations by the chef. Grown-ups, meanwhile, can get stuck in to some seriously smart variations on familiar American classics.

Did you know?

Mare Chiaro *(176½ Mulberry Street between Broome and Grand sts)* is a Mob star in its own right. This *molto Italiano* bar has given background to scenes in the *Godfather* trilogy, Donnie Brasco, and TV's *The Sopranos.*

Asian

Kelley & Ping

127 Greene St (bet. W. Houston and Prince sts) [B1]. Tel: 212-228-1212. Open: L and D daily. ***$$***

Kelley and Ping's cavernous room provides a very stylish backdrop to this cool Pan-Asian noodle shop that's been feeding the starving SoHo hordes since the early 1990s. A good choice for vegetarians.

Kin Khao

171 Spring St (bet. Thompson St and W. Broadway) [B2]. Tel: 212-966 3939. Open: D daily. ***$$***

At first sight Kin Khao can appear to be just another hopping SoHo bar, but beyond the chic types nursing their Cosmopolitan cocktails is a fairly serious dining room. The northern Thai specialties include a deeply spicy but mellow yellow curry in addition to the more familiar red and green

ones, and the green-tea ice creams are the perfect dessert if you want to keep cool.

Kittichai

60 Thompson Hotel, 60 Thompson St (at Broome St) [B2]. Tel: 212-219-2000. Open: daily. ***$$$$***

It's hard to work out who's more gorgeous at Kittichai: the model clientele or the model staff. Either way, this restaurant's modern decor and contemporary take on Thai food are every bit as lovely as those serving and eating it. The people-watching is especially good here in the warmer months, when outdoor tables allow you to view celebrities exit their limos and sashay into the hotel.

Woo Lae Oak

148 Mercer St (bet. Houston and Prince sts) [B1]. Tel: 212-925-8200. Open: L and D daily. ***$$$***
www.woolaeoaksoho.com

Authentically Korean food served in a sleek granite-and-steel setting and presented with more flair than is typical of traditional Korean restaurants. Woo Lae Oak is also free of the linguistic and cultural divide you might feel in the Little Korea dining scene in Midtown.

Eastern European

Café Lebowitz

14 Spring St (at Elizabeth St) [C2]. Tel: 212-219-2399. Open: L and D Mon–Fri, Br and D Sat–Sun. **$**

This take on a Viennese cafe is named after the famed New York humorist, Fran Lebowitz. The wait staff deserve the odd heckle for their slowness and muddle-headedness, but Café Lebowitz is otherwise deadly serious about its satisfying little roster of goulash, schnitzel, burgers, and steak-frites, not to mention the spectacular graham-cracker-crusted Lebowitz cheesecake.

Palacinka

28 Grand St (bet. Thompson St and Sixth Ave) [B2]. Tel: 212-625-0362. Open: L and D daily. **$**

Palacinka – Czech for crepe – offers the rare opportunity to savour the fast-dwindling boho side of SoHo. Savory pancakes come with salad on the side – a fact that should make you feel easier about ordering the dessert crepe with lemon juice, sweet chestnut, or – heaven forbid – the wickedly calorific Nutella and banana.

French

Balthazar (🍴)

80 Spring St (bet. Lafayette St and Broadway) [B2]. Tel: 212-965-1785. Open: B, L, and D daily **$$$–$$$$**

Dinner reservations can be tricky to secure at this gorgeous, glittering Parisian bistro, so at least plump for breakfast, lunch, or a drink at the bar. Delicious daily specials – such as Friday's bouillabaisse and Saturday's braised short ribs – are added to the list of bistro standards, and there's a fabulous three-tiered seafood platter for high days and holidays. One of Manhattan's best restaurants.

Bistrot Margot

26 Prince St (at Mott St) [C2]. Tel: 212-274-1027. Open: L and D Mon–Fri, Br and D Sat–Sun. **$$**

A cute bistro with surprisingly good food at prices that would be remarkable a few blocks to the west. By day, Margot has a laid-back vibe, and you can sit for hours nursing a café au lait – in the garden, if you're lucky. At night, a small selection of hearty French fare such as a memorable carrot soup, boudin blanc, pan-roasted duck, daube, chocolate mousse, and tarte tatin is available.

Café Gitane

242 Mott St (bet. Houston and Prince sts) [C1]. Tel: 212-334-9552. Open: B, L, and D daily. **$**

The onset of Mayor Bloomberg's cigarette-free world was a blow to Le Gitane (named after a French cigarette brand), which somehow looked better shrouded in smoke. However, the young, hip crowd still pile in for delicious light meals and fresh salads. They just take their Gitanes and Silk Cuts outside, in the shadow of St. Patrick's Old Cathedral, between courses.

***Above:* The Mercer Kitchen** **(see page 89)**
***Below:* Cafe Lebowitz**

Bread (see page 94)

TIP
Sullivan Street Bakery *(73 Sullivan St; tel: 212-334 9435)* not only supplies its fantastic crusty breads to the vast majority of New York's restaurants, it also has delicious slices of pizza and gorgeous olive rolls. They make the basis of an excellent picnic or street snack.

L'Ecole

French Culinary Institute, 462 Broadway (at Grand St) [B2]. Tel: 212-219 3300. Open: L and D Mon–Fri, D only Sat. **$$–$$$** *www.frenchculinary.com*

On a good night, L'Ecole offers one of the greatest gourmet bargains in New York with its $30, 5-course, prix-fixe menu. This is where pupils at the French Culinary Institute *(see page 119)* try out their new skills, but they're not all A-grade students, so quality is not guaranteed.

Félix

340 W. Broadway (at Grand St) [B2]. Tel: 212-431-0021. Open: L and D daily. **$$–$$$** *www.felixnyc.com*

At weekends, art and fashion types line the block for hours waiting for brunch in this classic, tin-ceilinged bistro. Dinners or weekday lunches are less frenzied, and it can be a joy to sit at the prized window seats. The atmosphere is lively-going-on-rowdy, and while the menu seldom strays from the standard bistro list (escargots, coq au vin, steak frites, etc.), it's reliable and decent value.

Le Jardin Bistro

25 Cleveland Pl. (bet. Kenmare and Spring sts) [C2]. Tel: 212-343-9599. Open: L and D daily. **$$** *www.lejardinbistro.com*

Le Jardin Bistro has one of the most romantic gardens in Manhattan. The trellised walls, French street signs, and comical stone frogs make you feel as if it's springtime in Paris, even when it's autumn in New York. The specials, notably salade niçoise, bouillabaisse, and cassoulet, occasionally have the power to transport.

Jean Claude

137 Sullivan St (bet. Prince and Houston sts) [B2]. Tel: 212-475 9232. Open: L and D daily. **$$**

New York is chock full of places trying to emulate the Parisian bistro, but few get as close as Jean Claude. A murmur of French echoes round the room, everyone at the table rises to kiss newcomers twice on the cheek, and there's even the option of playing 'baby-foot' (table football), so popular in Gallic student cafes. The food is also very close to authentic; starters and desserts are excellent, the main courses slightly less reliable but still much better than you'd expect at these prices.

Lucky Strike

59 Grand St (bet. W. Broadway and Wooster St) [B2]. Tel: 212-941-0772. Open: daily, Fri –Sat to 4am. **$$** *www.luckystrikeny.com*

The scene is set with French movie posters, nicotine-stained walls, distressed mirrors, and a menu scrawled on the wall. The food is a predictable list of bistro standards, plus American classics, and seldom rises above good-to-satisfying; however, the crowd is above-average attractive, and the Lucky Martinis (Absolut, grapefruit juice, and cherry herring) are fabulous.

Le Pescadou

18 King St (at Sixth Ave) [A1]. Tel: 212-924-3434. Open: L and D Mon–Fri, D Sat–Sun. **$$$**

Le Pescadou leans toward classic seafood dishes such as soupe de poisson, which can, at times, be underwhelming. The same can't be said for the marvelous pastries, near-perfect crème brûlées, and creamy, fruity clafoutis. It's also worth a visit for the scene: this corner, where SoHo meets the West Village, is part of a very hip neighborhood, and Pescadou is its favored watering hole.

Raoul's

180 Prince St (bet. Sullivan and Thompson sts) [B1]. Tel: 212-966-3518. Open: D only, daily. **$$$** *www.raouls.com*

There's something enormously sexy about Raoul's with its dark red banquettes. Ask for a table in the back room, if only for the hot walk through the middle of the kitchen. Raoul's is pricey, but worth it for the great food, buzz, and chance of being seated near a celebrity.

SoHo Steak

90 Thompson St (bet. Spring and Broome sts) [B2]. Tel: 212-226-0602. Open: D only Mon–Fri, Br and D Sat–Sun. **$$**

Despite the name, this isn't a steakhouse but a neat little French restaurant that happens to do a good, juicy steak. Among other notables are gorgeous grilled foie gras and carpaccio drawn from filet mignon. The tiramisu and pear tart are knockouts, as is the clientele.

Global

Rice

277 Mott St (bet. Prince and Spring sts) [C2]. Tel: 212-226-5775. Open: L and D daily. **$** *www.riceny.com*

The menu at Rice consists of around ten varieties of the grain (including Bhutanese red, Thai black, and Japanese short), which are topped with a variety of accompaniments, from ratatouille to curries and Vietnamese lemongrass-chicken salad. There are also occasional specials such as a great paella. Finish with rice-crispy treats or pudding (no prizes for guessing what kind).

Greek

Snack

105 Thompson St (bet. Prince and Spring sts) [B2]. Tel: 212-925-1040. Open: L and D daily. **$**

This tiny jewel of a restaurant is something of a misnomer, since all the food is either too hearty, too messy, or too delicious to be treated as a mere snack. Gorgeous Greek dishes including boureki, stifado, and honey yoghurt with halvah caused such lines that there is now the larger Snack Taverna *(63 Bedford St)* in the West Village.

Lucky Strike offers satisfying bistro standards

TIP

The Guggenheim Museum SoHo *(575 Broadway, at Prince St)* is a beautiful loft space with modern art by Andy Warhol and other famous Downtown artists. It also has the nicest, cleanest, most freely available bathroom in this corner of SoHo.

Indian

Hampton Chutney Co.
68 Prince St (bet. Lafayette and Crosby sts) [C2]. Tel: 212-226-9996. Open: 11am–9pm daily. **$**
You often have to duck the yoga mats beneath customer's arms to get to the counter of this chilled-out vegetarian Indian restaurant, where fast food meets upscale and healthy. There's a daily, great-value thali tray of one soup, one curry, plus rice, naan bread, raita, and chutneys. Most of the SoHo yogi, however, opt for the house specialty of dosas – lacy pancakes with a delicious variety of fillings.

Italian

Bread
20 Spring St (bet. Elizabeth and Mott sts) [C2]. Tel: 212-334-1015. Open: L and D daily. **$**
This tiny café-wine bar is devoted to bread and all that can go between it. Hot sarnies come filled with everything from pesto chicken and avocado to goat's cheese and shiitakes, and fresh sardines and tomatoes to the more traditional Parma ham, mozarella, and taleggio. Bread also has an anti-pasti plate of unusual variety and deliciousness and some pasta dishes.

Back to basics at Peasant

Cipriani Downtown
376 W. Broadway (bet. Broome and Spring sts) [B2]. Tel: 212-343-0999. Open: L and D daily. **$$$**
Long-time denizens of SoHo scoff that this Downtown outpost of the distinctly uptown Cipriani mini-chain is nothing but dash, flash, and eurotrash. It's true that it is a little pricey – and there is a distinctly 'foreign' flavor to the suited-and-booted crowd – but the food is actually rather good and it is served in a lovely room.

Fiamma Osteria
206 Spring St (bet. Sullivan St and Sixth Ave) [A2]. Tel: 212-653-0100. Open: L and D Mon–Fri, D only Sat, Sun. **$$$**
Everything about this three-story SoHo brownstone reeks of sophistication. A glass elevator glides between the two bars and dining rooms, thc staff are courtly, and the clientele grown-up and glam. Nothing, however, can out-sparkle the seemingly simple but exceptionally subtle food. Pastas are especially good, as is the veal chop with sage, the grilled orata in clam broth, and the heavenly gianduja, – chocolate-hazelnut ice cream.

Lombardi's
32 Spring St (bet. Mott and Mulberry sts) [C2]. Tel: 212-941-7994. Open: L and D daily. **$**
The thin-crusted pizzas with lightly charred edges coming out of the venerable coal-oven are legendary. There's a wide choice of toppings, but you'd be mad not to try one of

Tuscan trattoria, Savore

Lombardi's two most popular ones – the farm fresh mozzarella and tomato or the white clam.

Peasant

194 Elizabeth St (bet. Prince and Spring sts) [C2] Tel: 212-965-9511. Open: D Tues–Sun. **$$$**

With its brick walls, spare decor, and achingly hip patrons, this place could only be in downtown Manhattan. But breathe in, and you'll feel you're in Italy, as the open-fire oven releases such heady aromas of garlic, olive oil, and herbs. A little bowl of ricotta and crusty Pugliese bread arrives with the menu: delicious but try not to overdo it, as there are *molto* good things to come.

Pepe Rosso to Go

149 Sullivan St (bet. Houston and Prince sts) [B1]. Tel: 212-677-4555. Open: L and D daily. **$**

You've got to love any place with the motto: No Diet Coke/No Skim Milk/No Decaf Coffee/Only Good Food. Pepe Rosso does take out, but you're also welcome to have a meal at one of their small tables.

Savore

200 Spring St (at Sullivan St) [B2]. Tel: 212-431-1212. Open: L and D Mon–Fri, Br and D Sat, Sun. **$$**

This attractive garden restaurant has mostly Tuscan dishes in an authentic trattoria setting. The pasta comes with gutsy rich sauces, but those going on to primi piatti won't be disappointed: the game and roasted meats are particularly good.

Japanese

Blue Ribbon Sushi

119 Sullivan St (bet. Prince and Spring sts) [B2]. Tel: 212-343-0404. Open: L and D daily. **$$$**

The sense of Zen at Blue Ribbon Sushi may owe more to *Wallpaper* magazine than to anything classically Japanese, but this beautiful basement restaurant consistently wins readers' polls and visitors' hearts for its delicious sushi and sashimi. It can be a long wait for a table at dinner, so it may be best to treat yourself to lunch when they're less pressed.

Honmura An

170 Mercer St (bet. Houston and Prince sts) [B1]. Tel: 212-334-5253. Open: L and D Wed–Sat, D only Tues and Sun. **$$$**

Honmura An is credited with introducing the joys of soba (buckwheat noodles) to New York. Watch the 'dough wrangler' pounding and shaping the noodles in a glassed-off area, then choose from hot or cold soba in fragrant broths with delicious accompaniments.

TIP

Visit **Eileen's Special Cheesecake** *(17 Cleveland Pl.).* Eileen Avezzana started making cheesecakes in her kitchen 40 years ago and now bakes 19 varieties that she FedExes to customers all over the US. Frank Sinatra used to have them delivered and Robert Redford and Peter Falk are still keen customers.

Dos Caminos for Mexican chic

TIP
All-you-can-eat buffets are not the exclusive preserve of Vegas – there are many in New York including a great Indian one at Karahi (508 Broome St) every lunchtime: $7.95 weekdays; $8.95 at weekends.

Kitchen Club
30 Prince St (at Mott St) [C2]. Tel: 212-274-0025. Open: L and D Tues–Sat, D only Sun. **$$**
www.thekitchenclub.com
The Dutch chef-owner lived in Japan for six years during which time she learned to cook like a native. Her seasonal interpretation of the bento box, with small portions showcasing contrasting flavors and textures, is masterly. For good measure she adds some French and Dutch dishes. Attached is a tiny sake bar named Chibi, after her French bulldog.

Omen
113 Thompson St (bet. Prince and Spring sts) [B2]. Tel: 212-925-8923. Open: D daily. **$$$**
Omen is like no Japanese restaurant you've been to before – it's dark and cozy and promises home-style cooking. Unlike the dainty dishes served in most other Japanese restaurants, the dishes at Omen appear rustic and, well, a little rough. But appearances can be deceptive, and the food is very refined, refreshing, and delicious.

Latin American

Café Habana
17 Prince St (at Elizabeth St) [C1]. Tel: 212-625-2001. Open: B, L, and D daily. **$**
Every bit as vibrant and hip as the city from which it takes its name, Café Habana, lovingly styled like a 1950s' luncheonette, seethes with a beautiful young crowd, especially for weekend brunches. The nuevo cubano menu is hearty and good.

Café el Portal
174 Elizabeth St (bet. Spring and Kenmare sts) [C2]. Tel: 212-226-4642. Open: L and D Mon–Sat. **$**
El Portal's ultra-authentic Mexican fare is so cheap you can afford to order bravely. Ever wondered what cactus tasted like? Wonder no more – try one in a burrito at this brightly colored little Mexican joint. It's so tasty, you'll be amazed you've never had it before. Another pleasant surprise is the refreshing cucumber water, spiked with lime.

Dos Caminos SoHo
475 W. Broadway (at Houston St) [B1]. Tel: 212-277-4300. Open: L and D Mon–Fri, Br and D Sat–Sun. **$$$**
www.beourguestrestaurants.com
If you expect sombreros, Sancho Panza waiters, and 54 varieties of refried bean from your Mexican restaurants, this chic, sleek Mejicano will surprise. The trendy design is 'warm modern,' and (unlike at the original Dos Caminos on Park Ave) there's a

nightclub-style vibe. The food, with its emphasis on ceviche, fish, and salads, remains at the lighter end of Mexican cuisine.

Ideya

349 W. Broadway (bet. Broome and Grand sts) [B2]. Tel: 212-625-1441. Open: L and D Mon–Fri, Br and D Sat–Sun. **$$**
www.ideya.net
This laid-back Pan-Latin pleasure house has waiters in traditional attire, tropical murals, bent-cane chairs, gentle salsa, and summery cocktails. The food is slightly less reliable, but the Caribbean plaintain chips, Argentine steaks, and Mexican seafood tacos are crowd-pleasers.

Mediterranean

Alma Blu

179 Prince St (bet. Sullivan and Thompson sts) [B1]. Tel: 212-471-2345. Open: L and D Mon–Sat, Br and D Sun. **$$**
Anything goes in this bright and breezy haven, in which dishes from Italy, Spain, Greece, and North Africa co-exist happily. The welcoming staff encourage you to mix and match crostini with cous-cous, pasta and paella, and meze and merguez.

Spanish

Ñ

33 Crosby St (bet. Broome and Grand sts) [B2]. Tel: 212-219-8856. Open: D daily. No credit cards. **$**
An arty, 30-something crowd squashes into this sexy little tapas bar, which specializes in sherries from Andalusia. And if you still think that sherry is for vicars and the blue-rinse brigade, try the sangria or rioja instead. No matter which, it all partners wonderfully well with the luscious little bowls of olives, fish, shrimp, sausage, salads, and vegetables.

Cafes and Bars

SoHo is one of the best places in New York – and arguably in the world – to hang out and to people-watch. At **Housing Works Used Book Café** *(126 Crosby St)* you can see penurious writers nibbling cakes and scribbling furiously into battered notebooks. There are frequent readings here from famous writers and poets and these bring in the local artists, academics, and literature students. Across the street in the global enemy **Starbucks** *(Prince and Crosby sts)*, wannabe scriptwriters can be seen tapping just as furiously into their laptops.

The area's three luxury hotels – **SoHo Grand Hotel** *(310 W. Broadway, at Canal and Grand sts)*, **The Mercer** *(99 Prince St, at Mercer St)* and **60 Thompson** *(60 Thompson St)* – all have great bars and lounges that award insight into the international media, music, and fashion spheres. Most of their celebrity guests are either doing some kind of business Downtown or are escaping the dreary Midtown hotels.

The art-world doesn't really convene in SoHo any more, but you see the occasional paint-spattered type in **Palacinka** *(see page 91)* or try the 200-year-old **The Ear Inn** *(see page 88)*, which is always a good place to relax over a pint of beer.

To watch NoLita hipsters in action, try the wonderfully named **Sweet & Vicious** *(5 Spring St)* or **Spring Lounge** *(48 Spring St)*. **Bar 89** *(89 Mercer St)* is worth a visit for its SoHo chic – and for the gimmicky bathrooms with transparent doors that turn opaque when locked. **The MercBar** *(151 Mercer St)* is quintessentially SoHo, and in summer, when the doors are open, it's a great place from which to watch the designer-clad world slink by.

Pizza goes Pop

This Italian staple is currently undergoing a gourmification in New York – and the transformation is causing something of a stir

Pizza is taken so seriously in the US that it's even enshrined in the constitution – the House of Representatives has a 'pizza rule' that allows lobbyists to provide the nation's favorite take-out to congress members working late or at weekends. But nowhere is pizza taken as seriously as in New York, the city in which immigrants first introduced the cheesy-tomatoey pie to the Americas in the 1880s.

The metropolitan area of New York currently has some 2,750 pizzerias, and its 'paper of record,' *The New York Times*, has been known to run earnest articles on who is the true claimant to New York's original pizza. Among parlors adhering rigidly to traditional methods are **John's** in the West Village, **Ottimo**, and the dimly lit **Patsy's**, an ancient pizza joint in Harlem (plus newer outposts at Union Square, Murray Hill, and the Upper West Side). Then there's **Lil' Frankies**, in the East Village, the Upper West Side's **Celeste**, and **Naples 45**, in the Flatiron district.

A new breed of pizza

And yet, in a city where the history and authenticity of its pizzas and toppings are treated with such gravitas, something extremely odd is happening: pizza has come over all trendy. Chefs have started – horror of horrors – putting pizzas on a grill. Even worse, they have also been using toppings as wild as wasabi with tuna, peking duck, and tandoori chicken. And, to top it all, pizza has started to appear on the menus of restaurants that aren't even Italian, such as the up-market Indian, **Tabla** *(see page 37)* near Union Square, which has a 'pizza' of naan bread topped with paneer and cilantro.

This gourmification of pizza has stirred the sort of impassioned arguments among New Yorkers that are usually reserved for discussing the Yankees and the Mets. Despite the furore, there's no turning back the flow of dough, and pizza in the five boroughs is transmogrifying into something very cosmopolitan, drawing from New York's melting pot of culinary cultures.

The new griddled pizza is incredibly light, paper-thin, and delectably crisp, with a deeply smoky crust sparingly topped with Bel Paese and Romano

cheeses. Unsurprisingly perhaps, its advent is as shrouded in controversy as its traditional forebear: some swear their Uncle Frank has been slinging pizza on the backyard barbecue since the 1960s, others claim it was invented by a chef in Providence, Rhode Island, in the 1980s.

The heavyweights

Whichever, it slowly made its way into NYC's restaurants until it finally reached full-blown trend status in 2002 when three restaurants specializing in it – **Crispo**, **Gonzo**, and **Otto** – opened to much ado. Other places for a trendy gourmet pizza are Flatiron's **Scopa**, **Scopa to Go**, and Midtown's **Fresco by Scotto**. The 800-pound gorilla among them is Otto. Headed by the mega-famous TV chef Mario Batali, who is responsible for the incredibly successful trio of restaurants, Esca, Babbo, and Lupa, it grabs all the headlines. And not undeservedly so: Otto's lardo (pork fat) and rosemary pizza has brought normally stern traditionalists to the brink of tears and compulsive obsession.

Meanwhile, Otto's more modest neighbors quietly churn out exceptional confections on crispy bases. Gonzo has 50 variations, 12 of which are available at any one time, while Crispo does rounder, thicker, slightly smokier versions, thanks to cherry- and apple-wood chips added to the gas grill.

ADDRESSES

Celeste 502 Amsterdam Ave (at 85th St), tel: 212-874-4559
Crispo 240 W. 14th St (bet. Seventh and Eighth aves), tel: 212-229-1818
Fresco by Scotto 34 E. 52nd St (bet. Madison and Park aves), tel: 212-935-3434 and **Fresco on the Go** 40 E. 52nd St, tel: 212-754-2700
Gonzo 140 W. 13th St (bet. Sixth and Seventh aves), tel: 212-645-4606
John's 278 Bleecker St (at Jones St), tel: 212-243-1680
Lil' Frankies 19 First Ave (bet. First and Second sts), tel: 212-420-4900
Naples 45 Met Life Building, 200 Park Ave (at 45th St), tel: 212-972-7001
Ottimo 6 W. 24th St (at Fifth Ave); tel: 212-337-0074
Otto 1 Fifth Ave (at Eighth St); tel. 212-995-9559
Patsy's 2287 First Ave (bet. 117th and 118th sts), tel: 212-534-9783
Scopa 79 Madison Ave (at 28th St), tel: 212-686-8787 and **Scopa to Go** 27 E. 28th St (bet. Madison and Park Ave S.); tel: 212-213-2424
Tabla 11 Madison Ave (at 25th St), tel 212-889-0667

Danube
30 Hudson

TRIBECA, THE FINANCIAL DISTRICT, AND CHINATOWN

Lower Manhattan has risen from the ashes of 9/11 with new determination, new intentions and new businesses

New York has always been typified as a feisty, fighting sort of town with plenty of attitude. The kind of place that if knocked down, gets back up, dusts itself off, and gets right back to business. And in recent years Lower Manhattan has really been put to the test on that score. The terrorist attacks of 9/11 affected Tribeca (TRIangle BElow CAnal), the Financial District, and Chinatown more than they did any other part of New York. Personal losses were greatest among those living and working in Lower Manhattan, and the damage to local businesses was immediate and long-lasting, if not terminal. For months, the whole area was cordoned off, while rescue workers set about the grim task of cleaning up Ground Zero. So even if stores and restaurants escaped broken windows, shattered structures, and smoke damage, their trade was severely hit by the fact that few people could get beneath Canal Street; moreover, many of those that did were not really in the mood for enjoying themselves. By summer 2002, hundreds of businesses had gone under. However, by then the checkpoints had gone, the flow of traffic was restored, the atmosphere was almost smoke-free again, and people were cautiously venturing Downtown. Since then, the district, particularly Tribeca, has really shown its mettle: more restaurants and other businesses have started up in Lower Manhattan than were forced to close.

Standing the test of time

Perhaps Tribeca's ability to rise out of the ashes shouldn't have come as too big a surprise. The district had, after all, been born from a blasted industrial wasteland in the first place. When pioneer restaurants Odeon *(see page 105)* and Montrachet *(see page 108)* opened their doors more than 20 years ago, NYC's culinary community thought it was a case of madness or severe delusion. Tribeca, formerly New York's dairy district, was a rundown and deserted scene of dereliction into which even the city's most hardened cabbie refused to venture. Somehow, though, the gamble paid off, the punters took a risk and went down to see what all the fuss was about and, to this day, Odeon and Montrachet are doing a fine business. Not only that, but their example was followed by scores of restaurateurs moving in to beautiful big spaces with, at the same time, almost give-away rents. Also in the late 1970s and early 1980s residents cottoned on to the fact that there were some fabulous loft spaces going for a song down in this area. The most famous speculator was Robert De Niro, who not only started living in Tribeca in 1976, but set up his film company there, invested in Montrachet (and later Nobu, *see page 111*, and the Tribeca Grill, *see page 105*), and started promoting his chosen 'hood as a cool area in which to hang out. Tribeca's boom continued unabated until 9/11 caused it to bust in spectacular fashion.

Opposite: David Bouley's elegant Austrian restaurant, Danube

The Harrison *(see page 105)* was due to open on September 17, 2001, and in the weeks and days around it, the owners were constantly being asked, 'Are you going ahead? It's such a terrible time. Why open now?' At first they were unsure what to do but each time their unbidden, unconscious response was: 'Well, when is a good time?' And that's the tough-minded mantra that has saved Downtown. The Harrison opened six weeks later than originally

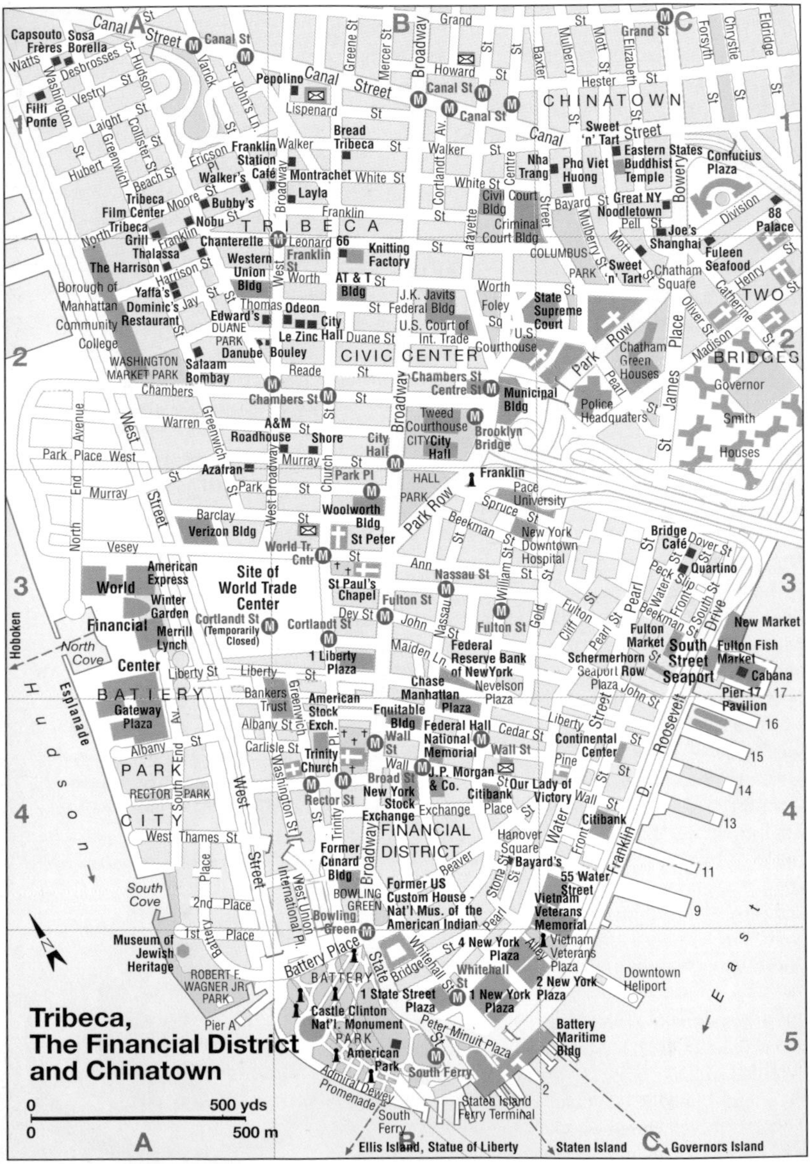

Tribeca, The Financial District and Chinatown

planned, and other new restaurants began springing up all over, like poppies after a shower.

FIVE OF THE BEST

Bouley: one of the city's best-loved destinations for special occasions
Bubby's: great place for brunch
Nha Trang: lovely fresh Vietnamese food
Nobu: world-famous Japanese restaurant
Odeon: the original Downtown hot-spot

A pared-down approach

This is not to underestimate how hard restaurants in the area have had to work to stay afloat. The older establishments that managed to keep their doors open and their stoves burning throughout have had to re-adjust and modify themselves in ways that make them even stronger. Prior to 9/11, local restaurants worked on business plans that depended heavily on the World Trade Center's pool of 100,000 workers and the million more business-related workers who were said to pass through it each day. But now, instead of looking to high-earning, expense-accounted 'suits' for the majority of their business, Downtown restaurants are having to turn themselves into neighborhood places designed to serve the locals.

Tribeca's gourmet restaurants such as Bouley, Montrachet, and Chanterelle had been accused of a certain high-handed snootiness in dealing with their clientele. That attitude has long gone. Downtown's highest profile celebrity chef, David Bouley, had been planning an empire including a cooking school, a bakery, and a casual restaurant. On September 12, 2001, he shelved his ambitious plans, re-opened his original restaurant Bouley *(see page 108)*, got back into the kitchen, and concentrated on doing what he does best – cooking.

A similar paring down has worked for the rest of Tribeca and the Financial District's restaurants. For example, the ambitious Pico won three stars and high praise from the critics. However, in the new subdued climate, its young star chef, John Villa, found his clientele balking at the (possibly justified but undeniably) high prices of haute cuisine and has reopened in the same space as Dominic's Restaurant/Social Club *(see page 110)*, a much more relaxed and informal Italian spot.

Chinatown has more than 200 restaurants

All the big new success stories of the region, such as Fresh, Thalassa *(see page 109)*, and the Wall Street branch of Les Halles *(see page 36)*, are very welcoming places where good, unfussy food and your comfort come first.

Once Tribeca and Wall Street were all about fancy food, high-end service, and opulent surroundings, and there was very little in between Nobu, where dinner could set you back $100 a head, and Bubby's where it can be as little as $15. Nowadays, there is a growing number of inexpensive and mid-range places on offer – something that makes it a very good time to visit Lower Manhattan, where, now more than ever before, the customer rules.

Chinatown

Meanwhile, across in Chinatown – the largest Chinatown in the US – little has changed in recent years. The aftermath of 9/11 and the recession that followed it temporarily blocked the area's growth, but has had little, if any, longer-term impact. Chinatown, and the smaller Little Vietnam within it, currently has more than 200 restaurants, and the count grows almost weekly. Also in the neighborhood are booming fruit and fish markets and stores with sticky buns and sweets that you can chew on while taking in the sights on the fascinating, winding, and overcrowded streets.

Bubby's, a home from home

American

A&M Roadhouse

57 Murray St (at West Broadway) [B2]. Tel: 212-385-9005. Open: L and D daily. $$ www.aandmroadhouse.com

This is a chunk of Americana that you might expect to find somewhere along Route 66 between ranches and truck stops, rather than in the heart of downtown New York. A&M Roadhouse has all the hearty American favorites – Georgia white bean soup or Cobb salad to start; ribs, wings, crab cakes and chilis next up, and brownies and cakes to follow. It's cheap, cheerful, and most nights there's live music too.

Bayard's

1 Hanover Square (bet. Pearl and Stone sts [B4]. Tel: 212-514-9454. Open: D only Mon–Sat. $$$ www.bayards.com

To enter Bayard's 1851 Federal-style building is to be transported into an Edith Wharton novel or Merchant Ivory film. The setting is extremely romantic – so much so, that it's a popular place for men to go down on bended knee. The food is classy (duck is popular) and very fresh, as most of the produce comes from the chef's Long Island farm. Prices are reasonable, but the wine list is pretty steep.

Bridge Café

279 Water St (corner of Dover St) [C3]. Tel: 212-227-3344. Open: L and D Sun–Fri, D only Sat. $$

The three most important things about this bistro? Location, location, location, and in order of importance they are: beneath the Brooklyn Bridge; in a former brothel; and in the oldest surviving wooden building on Manhattan. Despite the olden-days longshoreman feel about it, the Bridge Café does food that is upscale, light, creative, and modern.

Bubby's

120 Hudson St (at North Moore St) [A1]. Tel: 212-219-0666. Open: B, L, and D daily. $ www.bubbys.com

Harvey Keitel and Ed Norton are said to be regulars at Bubby's. Local nobility aside, this place is a farmhouse kitchen transplanted into Tribeca. Every order comes with a basket of wonderful buttermilk biscuits (more like scones than cookies), and the menu boasts 'food like Mom would make if she only knew how.' Kids under three eat free at Sunday lunchtime; however, it's most mobbed by everybody, three and up, at weekend

Did you know?

Fraunces Tavern (54 Pearl Street) is where a tearful George Washington bid farewell to his troops in 1873. The pub and restaurant is now one of the few watering holes to share a building with a museum.

brunch. If there isn't room, nip over to their new Brooklyn branch (1 Main St, DUMBO) and get seated there in the time it would have taken to work your name down the list here.

City Hall

131 Duane St (bet. Church St and West Broadway) [B2]. Tel: 212-227-7777. Open: L and D Mon–Fri, D only Sat. ***$$$***
www.cityhallnewyork.com

City Hall is a big, boisterous kind of a place, with a bustling dining room and an even busier bar. It's a steakhouse, which ages all its own meat, but it also does excellent seafood, a mean burger, and a justifiably famous chocolate soufflé. It's also a great place for people-watching, especially at lunchtime, when the law-makers and power-brokers of the real City Hall across Broadway flock in.

Edward's

136 West Broadway (bet. Duane and Thomas sts). Tel: 212-233-6436. [A2] Open: L and D daily; Fri and Sat until 3am. ***$$***

Until autumn 2001, this cozy spot was Bar Odeon – overspill for its more-famous neighbor across the street. Odeon sold in the difficult months after 9/11 and Edward's was born. The rebirth changed remarkably little; it's still a reliable, tasty, and cheap alternative to the starry destination opposite. On Tuesdays, those starving in garrets (no proof needed) can choose from a limited 'artist's menu,' on which everything is $3.

The Harrison

355 Greenwich St (at Harrison St) [A2]. Tel: 212-274-9319. Open: L and D daily. ***$$$***
www.theharrison.com

The Harrison is a neighborhood haunt with white, wainscoated walls, a warm welcome, and a strong aura of comfort – something that is echoed by the food. But the Harrison has stripped 'comfort' of its dull and, heaven forbid, stodgy connotations. Dishes such as wood-smoked pork chop, chicken crisped in the pan, and day-boat cod may sound bland, but they are exceptional: beautifully executed and bursting with character and flavor.

Odeon

145 West Broadway (bet. Duane and Thomas sts) [B2]. Tel: 212-233-0507. Open: L and D daily until 2am. ***$$$***
www.theodeonrestaurant.com

Odeon is the archetypal New York restaurant – a beautiful, big, glittering room, full to bursting with beautiful, thin, gliterrati. The place is a marvel: it's managed to maintain high heat and hipness levels for over two decades while not changing a thing and remaining totally unpretentious. You may have to wait, but no hurry – its open late and the bar has excellent Martini's.

Tribeca Grill

375 Greenwich St (at Franklin St) [A1]. Tel: 212-941-3900. Open: L and D Sun–Fri, D only Sat. ***$$$***
www.myriadrestaurantgroup.com

The Harrison

Acclaimed chef David Bouley works his magic on Austrian classics at Danube

Many come to the Tribeca Grill in the hope of seeing co-owner Robert DeNiro or film biz luminaries from his Tribeca Film Center upstairs. The closest you'll get to a DeNiro sighting is one of his dad's paintings that decorate the walls, and while you do occasionally see people talking 'back-end' and reading scripts, most of the clientele are regular business types and star-struck tourists. The food, however, rarely disappoints.

Walker's

16 North Moore St (at Varick St) [A1]. Tel: 212-941-0142. Open: B, L, and D daily until 4am, food served until 12.30/1am. **$**

Walker's is Tribeca's comfort station and has been since 1890. It's been a local to Downtown residents through riots, fiscal crises, blackouts, and recessions from the Great Depression up. Unsurprisingly, this solid, three-roomed pub was a vital focal point during the World Trade Center disaster – where people went to be together, hear the latest, and forget their troubles awhile. The American diner fare is heartening too.

Austrian

Danube

30 Hudson St (at Duane St) [A2]. Tel: 212-791-3771. Open: D only Mon–Sat **$$$$**
www.bouleyrestaurant.com

This is David Bouley's Viennese waltz and very charming it is too, with its high-ceilinged room decorated with glittering Klimt paintings. The menu is anchored with Austrian classics in the Monarchie section, but for the rest of the menu, called Impression, Bouley lets his imagination take over and uses a lighter touch than tradition would dictate. Imperial desserts.

Caribbean

Cabana

89 South St Seaport (Pier 17, third floor) [C3]. Tel: 212-406-1155. Open: L and D daily. **$$**
www.cabanarestaurant.com

Most of the restaurants down on South Street Seaport are shameless tourist traps and/or soulless theme places. Cabana is a rare exception; its rainbow-hued decor and hot Jamaican jerk can revive even the most extorted of sightseers. The ceviches are refreshing, the fritters surprisingly good, and the jerk pork kicks just like it should.

Chinese

66

241 Church St (at Leonard St) [B2]. Tel: 212-925-0202. Open: L and D daily. **$$$$**
www.jean-georges.com

The waiters look like movie stars, and the decor is sleek white-on-white furnished with mid-century Eames and Knoll. And you're in a Chinese restaurant? The only clues are the red banners with golden

Did you know?

Locals refer to the restaurant-laden stretch of Greenwich Street between Franklin and Murray streets as 'Bob Row,' after Robert DeNiro who pioneered the then unexplored and empty industrial area of Tribeca as the place to be.

Cantonese script floating from the ceilings and the chopsticks beside your porcelain plate. But this is gourmet chef, Jean-Georges Vongerichten's version of Shanghainese – scrupulously authentic and elevated by the use of fresh ingredients of the highest quality.

88 Palace

88 East Broadway (bet. Forsyth and Market sts [C1]. Tel: 212-941-8886. Open: L and D daily. **$**

Eight is a lucky number in China, and you'll feel pretty fortunate to have found this handsome big restaurant beneath the Manhattan Bridge. It's widely known as one of the best places for dim sum in Chinatown; the little carts of small plates just keep coming, and you keep grabbing them even when you feel you couldn't even manage the steam off a dumpling.

Fuleen Seafood

11 Division St (bet. Confucius Place and East Broadway) [C2]. Tel: 212-941-6888. Open: L and D daily. **$$**

Chefs as celebrated as David Bouley visit for high-quality seafood specials including the highly prized shark's-fin soup that goes for around $38 (most dishes are around $10). The menu is daunting, but ask the staff as they're very helpful. Look at what your neighbors are eating, too, in case you want to copy them.

Great NY Noodletown

281/2 Bowery (at Bayard St) [C1]. Tel: 212-349-0923. Open: L and D daily, until 3.30am. **$**

Despite the restaurant's name, the roasted meats, especially the signature roast duck with flowering chive, are the real treat here. This is another Chinatown favorite where decor takes second place to the food, and chefs are said to flock after kitchen hours.

Joe's Shanghai

9 Pell St (bet. Bowery and Mott sts) [C1]. Tel: 212- 233-8888. Open: L and D daily. **$$**

Joe's Shanghai is a very convivial experience; everyone gets seated together, sharing in the single goal of working out what's best on the long menu. They have the best steamed buns west of the Yangtze: crab-soup dumplings, lion's heads (a sort of Sino-meat loaf made of pork belly), and turnip pancakes. The Chinese believe fish, cooked whole, symbolize abundance, and they're not kidding – the one at Joe's comes in a luscious, garlicky black-bean sauce.

Sweet 'n' Tart

20 and 76 Mott St [C1]. Tel: 212-964-0380 and 212-334-8088. Open: L and D daily. **$**
www.sweetntart.com

Sweet 'n' Tart is renowned for its tong shui – drinks and juices designed to restore your body's

TIP

Heard of the Chinese rice soup, Congee, and want to try it? Go to **Congee** *(98 Bowery St)*, an unthreatening Chinatown joint specializing in what traditionally is a breakfast food. Try it with duck, meatballs, squid, chicken, whatever you want, garnished with flakes of toasted garlic and scallions.

Opposite: Chanterelle, sophisticated cuisine in a serene setting

ying and yang. However, Chinatown residents also come here to eat; the menu includes Chinese sausage, baked chicken with ginger, and hotpots. Not much English is spoken, but the staff deals with you with the utmost patience.

French

Bouley (🍴)

120 W. Broadway (at Duane St) [A2]. Tel: 212-964-2525. Open: L and D daily. ***$$$$*** *www.bouleyrestaurants.com*

Truly inspired cuisine from a chef universally praised as one of today's best, plus elegant surroundings and immaculate service. If Bouley is beginning to sound intimidating, don't despair – it may have four stars from the notoriously hard-to-please *New York Times*, but there is nothing elitist or forbidding about it. Yes, it costs a lot, but you'll leave feeling it was money extremely well spent.

Capsouto Frères

451 Washington St (at Watts St) [A1]. Tel: 212-966-4900. Open: L and D Tues–Sun, L only Mon. ***$$$*** *www.capsoutofreres.com*

A handsome big room, presided over by the three brothers Capsouto with true flair. The restaurant manages to be both very romantic and the perfect place to introduce kids, who are made very welcome, to good cuisine. The country French cooking is the heart of the place, so resist the lure of pasta or the more 'creative' options. The tarte tatin is absolutely fabulous.

Chanterelle

2 Harrison St (at Hudson St) [A2]. Tel: 212-966-6960. Open: L and D Tues–Sat, D only Mon. ***$$$$*** *www.chanterellenyc.com*

Everything about Chanterelle is exquisite – the stunning flower arrangements, the covers of the menu created by a bi-annually changing artist, the spare but warm room, the attentive, informed, but never intrusive service. Everything, that is – except the classic French food, which goes one step further, to exceptional. The ideal place for a proposal, an anniversary, or a splurge.

Montrachet

239 West Broadway (near White St) [B1]. Tel: 212-219-2777. Open: D only Mon–Thurs, Sat L and D Fri. ***$$$$*** *www.myriadrestaurantgroup.com*

Named, as it is, for a wine region, it is perhaps unsurprising to learn that Montrachet has not one, not two, but three sommeliers and a wine list with some Burgundy vintages reaching $2,400. It's more surprising to learn, then, that Mondays is BYOB day, when Montrachet fans uncork their own vintages to sample with the timeless, exquisite, and excellently executed French food.

Le Zinc

139 Duane St (bet. Church St and West Broadway) [B2]. Tel: 212-513-0001. Open: L and D daily. ***$$*** *www.lezincnyc.com*

Le Zinc shares ownership and an executive chef, David Waltuck, with Chanterelle *(see left)*, so it's little wonder that this bistro's basics come with a twist. The story goes that Waltuck cooked *en famille* for Chanterelle's staff and enjoyed rustling up the stews, roasts, and basic fare so much he decided to open a restaurant dedicated specifically to that kind of food. Mostly French, the menu also has burgers, Hungarian highlights from Waltuck's family recipe trove, and a fine saké list.

Shopping for a picnic? Go to Bazzini's (339 Greenwich St). This former nut importer and roaster is now an upscale grocery with a salad bar, sandwiches, and baked goods. There are also a few tables so you can eat in, if you want, or if the weather dictates.

Global

Franklin Station Café
222 West Broadway (at Franklin St) [B1]. Tel: 212-274-8525. Open: L and D daily. **$**
www.franklinstationcafe.com
There aren't many places you get to choose between a steak sandwich and a mango shrimp curry, but this French-Malaysian café offers precisely such an eclectic mix. A friendly spot for good, cheap salads, sandwiches, stir fries, and curries.

Yaffa's
353 Greenwich St (at Harrison St) [A2]. Tel: 212-274-9403. Open: L and D daily, kitchen open until 11pm and bar until 2am at weekends. **$**
A colorful, shabby-chic restaurant that is good for a reinvigorating stop-by at any time of day and late into the night. The eclectic menu includes breakfasts, burgers, soups, salads, and heavier dishes, all with a Middle-Eastern accent.

Greek

Thalassa
179 Franklin St (bet. Greenwich and Hudson sts [A2]. Tel: 212-941-7661. Open: L and D Mon–Fri, D only Sat, Sun. **$$$$**
www.thalassanyc.com
This beautiful space with its white columns and attractively tiled bar is owned by a family of Greek food importers. It serves top-of-the-line Greek cuisine and wines (those raised on holiday retsina will be shocked at the high quality). Thalassa is Greek for 'the sea,' and fish is the house specialty – the day's catch is displayed over ice – but everything here is tasty, even the land-lubber lamb shanks. Delicious fig ice cream.

Indian

Salaam Bombay
317 Greenwich St (at Duane St) [A2]. Tel: 212-226-9400. Open: L and D daily. **$$**

Dishes from every corner of the former Raj crowd the menu at this upscale Indian restaurant, but some of the best dishes are Gujerati including the signature dish, a rich coconut-tinged vegetable curry. Tandoori lobster and lamb are recommended, as are the Goan shrimp and fish dishes.

Italian

Bread Tribeca

301 Church St (at Walker St) [B1]. Tel: 212-334-8282. Open: L and D daily. **$$**

www.breadtribeca.com

The younger, but bigger and bolder, sister of NoLita's tiny panini bar Bread *(see page 94)* this Tribeca branch has a brick oven and a menu that goes far beyond the confines of the sandwich. The traditional Ligurian fare features a wonderfully strong-flavored, handmade pesto, and the joyous capon magro, a colorful block of layered squares of seafood and vegetables that is reserved for feast days back home in Liguria.

Dominic

349 Greenwich St (bet. Jay and Harrison sts) [A2]. Tel: 212-343-0700. Open: L and D Mon–Fri, D only Sat, Sun. **$$**

This may look like regular Italian fare – bucatini with tomato sauce, tomatoes with buffalo mozzarella, strozzapretti alla carbonara, linguine with clams – albeit with some exotic additions such as quail and suckling pig. But at Dominic, even the most standard dish is exceptional: the flavors have a strength and purity rare in moderately priced establishments. The zeppole, hot little donuts, served in a brown paper bag with powdered sugar for shaking, are a special treat.

Filli Ponte

39 Desbrosses St (bet. Washington St and West Side Highway) [A1]. Tel: 212-226-4621. Open: L and D Mon–Fri, D only Sat, Sun. **$$$$**

Try for a window table, so you can add fabulous views of the Hudson to the pleasures of eating in this beautiful old room. Ponte's has Italian-American, rather than mother-country-Italian, cuisine; it's sometimes overwhelming in its enormity but is always of high quality. It verges on overpriced but, for most people the utter coolness of this venue and the river views more than compensate for the size of the check.

Pepolino

281 West Broadway (bet. Canal and Lispenard sts) [B1]. Tel: 212-966-9983. Open: L and D daily. **$**

Pepolino is a very friendly restaurant with a warm welcome, a cozy dining room, and delicious hearty food. The gnocchi are a knockout, the pappa al pomodoro is strong and subtle, the pasta dishes are all good, and the meatballs are deeply satisfying. The desserts get the prizes though – particularly the light ricotta cheesecake and the rich, dense chocolate cake.

***Opposite:* room with a view at Filli Ponte *Below:* Upscale Indian restaurant, Salaam Bombay**

Quartino

21 Peck Slip (at Water St) [C3]. Tel: 212-349-4433. Open: L and D daily. $$

This rustic osteria and wine bar has super fresh ingredients, almost all of which are organic, even the flour used in the pizza and pasta. The fish is always wild, never farmed, and great attention is given to the flavorsome details, whether it's the use of good olive oil, the inclusion of excellent imported cheeses, or the production of a nice strong espresso. This isn't just about the good life, but a healthy one, as the four owners of the title are all qualified doctors.

Japanese

Nobu

105 Hudson St (at Franklin St) [A1]. Tel: 212-219-0500. Open: L and D Mon–Fri, D only Sat, Sun. $$$$

www.myriadrestaurantgroup.com

One of the most successful and lavishly praised chefs in the world, Nobuyiku Matsuhisa re-works traditional Japanese recipes to incorporate new ingredients and modern inflections. His tasting menu is widely thought to include the best sushi in the world – the chances are, you'll never know unless you're prepared to plan your visit years ahead, have the patience of a saint, or the notoriously difficult-to obtain-hotline number. Thankfully, however, there's also **Next Door Nobu** *(105 Hudson St, at Franklin St, tel: 212-334-4445. Open: D daily. $$$$)* It looks like Nobu, it tastes like Nobu but, unlike the real thing, you can get in. Next Door was opened to appease those who couldn't get into Nobu, and has a no-reservations policy. If you arrive early (dinner begins at 5.45pm), you can just walk in and take a seat; later, your name goes on a waiting list (expect a wait of two or more hours).

Latin American

Sosa Borella

460 Greenwich St (at Debrosses St) [A1]. Tel: 212-431-5093. Open: L and D daily. $$

Unusually for an Argentine, Sosa Borella is not unmitigated meat madness. There's a delectable bife,

For real, old-fashioned New York ice cream go to Custard Beach in the World Financial Center, where the 'frozen custards' come in regular flavors such as vanilla and chocolate, plus a special of the day. It could be creme caramel, peach cobbler, or pretzel; yes, you read correctly.

Layla's for Middle Eastern meze and performing midriffs

which comes drenched in chimichurri, but luckily for vegetarians, the herb and oil sauce also comes in a little bowl with bread for dipping. The house special is parillada – a threesome of grilled meats, but the seafood version is every bit as good, and all fish and vegetable dishes are given as much loving attention.

Middle Eastern

Layla

211 W. Broadway (at Franklin St) [B1]. Tel: 212-431-0700. Open: daily. **$$**

Layla was almost rendered extinct after 9/11, when the owners felt New Yorkers might shy away from Middle-Eastern food. They decided eventually, however, that nobody could blame a whole culinary culture, and Layla remains as lovely (and well-loved) as ever. The menu has been extended to include Mediterranean dishes, so risottos now compete with the flavorful tagines (and nightly belly dancers) for your attention.

Seafood

American Park

Battery Park (near State St at Pearl St) [B5]. Tel: 212-809-5508. Open: Sun–Fri L and D. **$$**

Even if the food were dire – and thankfully it's far from that – American Park at the Battery would be worth a mention for its spectacular view of the Statue of Liberty. The menu calls itself American Continental but there's a heavy emphasis on seafood. If you want to slum it in the summer months, the Battery Gardens cafe, called The Wave, has all-American favorites such as burgers, BLTs, and grilled chicken caesars on the outdoor patio.

Shore

41 Murray St (bet. W. Broadway and Church St) [B2]. Tel: 212-962-3750. Open: L and D Sun–Fri, D only Sat. **$$**

A New England-style chowderhouse in a dark-paneled tavern that'll remind you of the bar Mark Wahlberg and John C. Reilly got drunk in before setting sail into *The Perfect Storm*. Like them, you can eat off the boat – Shore is co-owned by Morning Seafood, supplier to some of the city's top chefs, so Shore's chef gets the best

Did you know?

An empanada is a South American-style Cornish pasty with a variety of fillings such as Argentine sausage, spicy chicken, tomato, tuna, or vegetables. A couple make a great, and quick, take-out lunch. Grab them at Ruben's Empanadas (64 Fulton St and 15 Bridge St).

of the daily catch. Choose from baked, stuffed, and battered fish.

Spanish

Azafran

77 Warren St (bet. W. Broadway and Greenwich sts) [A2]. Tel: 212-284-0577. Open: D only Tues–Sun. **$$**
www.myazafran.com
This sleek Tribeca tapas bar cannily went to Spain's Basque country to procure a brace of promising young chefs from San Sebastián's cooking school. They now produce a trove of inventive tapas, plus plates of Spanish cured hams, sausages, and cheeses and artfully piled saffron-yellow paella.

Vietnamese

Nha Trang (🍴)

87 Baxter St (bet. White and Walker sts) [C1], Tel: 212-233-5948. Open: L and D daily. **$**
A very plain storefront belies a restaurant that is always packed with people sampling excellent Vietnamese food. The crisp fried squid – muc chien don – has to rate among NYC's best, and the condensed milk desserts are an acquired – but deliciously addictive – taste. There's now a second restaurant at 148 Centre Street, near Walker Street *(tel: 212-941-9292).*

Pho Viet Huong

73 Mulberry St (bet. Bayard and Canal sts [C1]. Tel: 212-233-8988. Open: L and D daily. **$**
In the back there's a little shrine to the Buddha, with incense and fake banana trees, all of which make for a peaceful meal. And the DIY dishes – a fondu and the table-grilled specials – invoke calm too. There's also a phenomenal pho (noodle soup) and an excellent green papaya and grilled beef salad.

Cafes and Bars

Lower Manhattan is badly served for cafes and decent places for a quick snack. However the Winter Gardens in the World Financial Center has a **Cosí** – one of the better coffee and sandwich bar chains – and the **Elixir Juice Bar**, which has wonderful fruit and vegetable juices, designed to put the pep back in your step. **The Financier** *(62 Stone St)* is an oasis, not only for its delicious patisserie, such as the namesake financier, a heart-shaped, buttery cookie, but for its lunchtime panini, salads, and soups.

Champagne Charlies should head for the **Bubble Lounge** *(228 West Broadway),* where you can choose from 350 bottles of bubbly. A slightly more down-home drinking atmosphere can be found in the funky **Liquor Store Bar** *(235 West Broadway).* And for a distinctly no-frills working man's saloon feel go to: **Walker's** *(see page 106),* **Puffy's Tavern** *(81 Hudson St),* and the **Tribeca Tavern** *(247 West Broadway).*

Fans of the film 25th Hour can drink in **Happy Ending** *(302 Broome St),* in which Edward Norton sank a few the night before his departure to an upstate prison. Rumor has it that this basement space was once a Chinese-run massage parlor and takes its name from one of their unadvertised practices. Round the corner is its sister bar, the equally hip Double Happiness (713 Mott St).

The steak restaurant **Dylan Prime** *(62 Laight St)* has a lovely bar next door, called Dylan. It faces on to Greenwich and is a great place to sip a Martini and watch all the celebrities and onlookers traipsing up and down 'Bob Row.'

The bar at **Vine** *(25 Broad St, at Exchange Place),* set in a former bank vault, is an impressive place for a drink. As soon as the afternoon bell rings in the Stock Exchange across the street, it fills with throngs of money men.

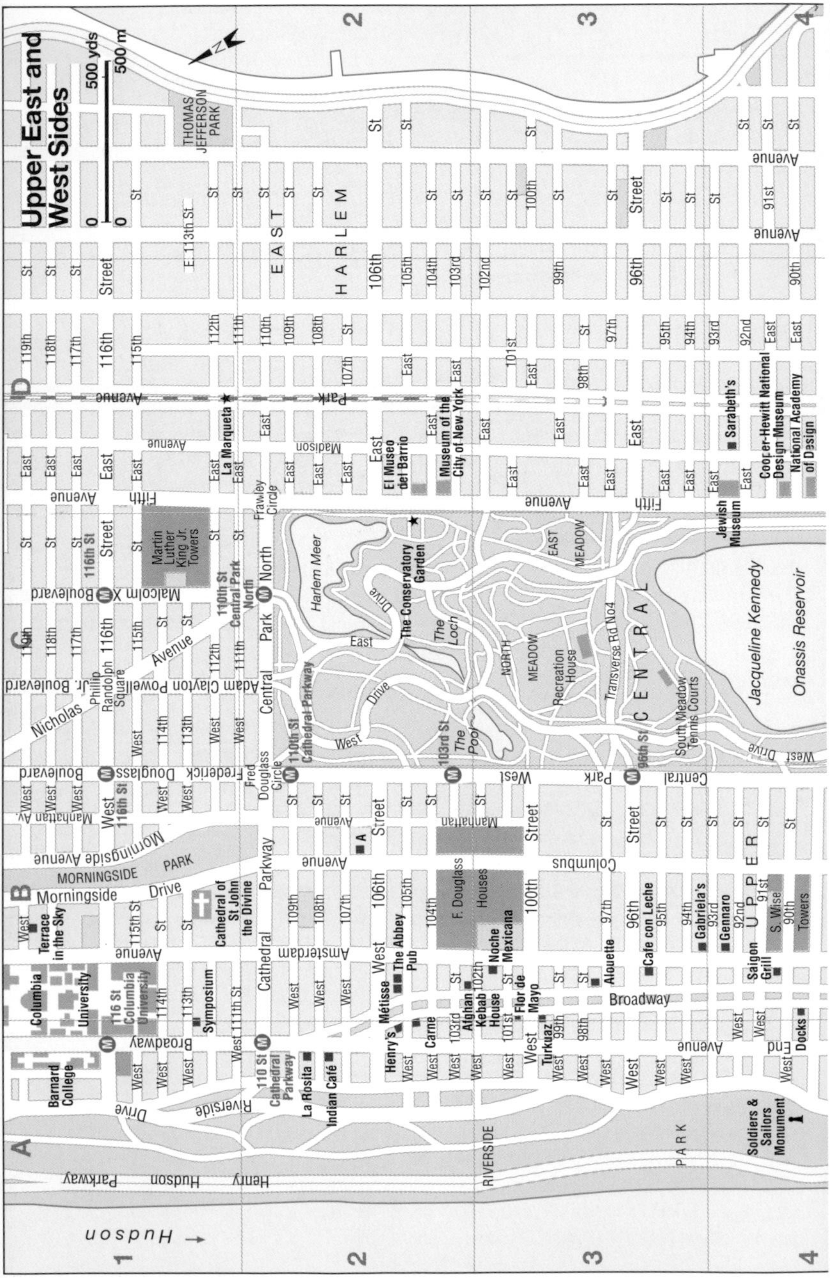
Upper East and West Sides
0 500 yds
0 500 m
N
Hudson
Henry Hudson Parkway
RIVERSIDE PARK
Riverside Drive
Barnard College
Columbia University
116 St Columbia University
Broadway
Amsterdam Avenue
Terrace in the Sky
Symposium
Cathedral of St John the Divine
Morningside Drive
MORNINGSIDE PARK
Morningside Avenue
Manhattan Av.
Frederick Douglass Boulevard
Fred Douglass Circle
110 St Cathedral Parkway
110th St Cathedral Parkway
Cathedral Parkway
La Rosita
Indian Café
Henry's
Métisse
The Abbey Pub
Carne
Afghan Kebab House
Noche Mexicana
Flor de Mayo
Turkuaz
Alouette
Cafe con Leche
Gabriela's
Gennaro
Saigon Grill
Docks
Soldiers & Sailors Monument
F. Douglass Houses
S. Wise Towers
West End Avenue
Columbus Avenue
Manhattan Avenue
103rd St
96th St
Central Park West
UPPER
Nicholas Avenue
St Nicholas Jr. Boulevard
Adam Clayton Powell Jr. Boulevard
Phillip Randolph Square
Malcolm X Boulevard
116th St
110th St Central Park North
Central Park North
Martin Luther King Jr. Towers
Frawley Circle
Harlem Meer
The Conservatory Garden
The Loch
The Pool
NORTH MEADOW
EAST MEADOW
Recreation House
Transverse Rd No4
CENTRAL
South Meadow Tennis Courts
Jacqueline Kennedy Onassis Reservoir
West Drive
East Drive
Fifth Avenue
Madison Avenue
Park Avenue
La Marqueta
El Museo del Barrio
Museum of the City of New York
Jewish Museum
Sarabeth's
Cooper-Hewitt National Design Museum
National Academy of Design
EAST HARLEM
THOMAS JEFFERSON PARK
E. 113th St
116th Street
106th Street
96th Street
A
B
C
D
1
2
3
4

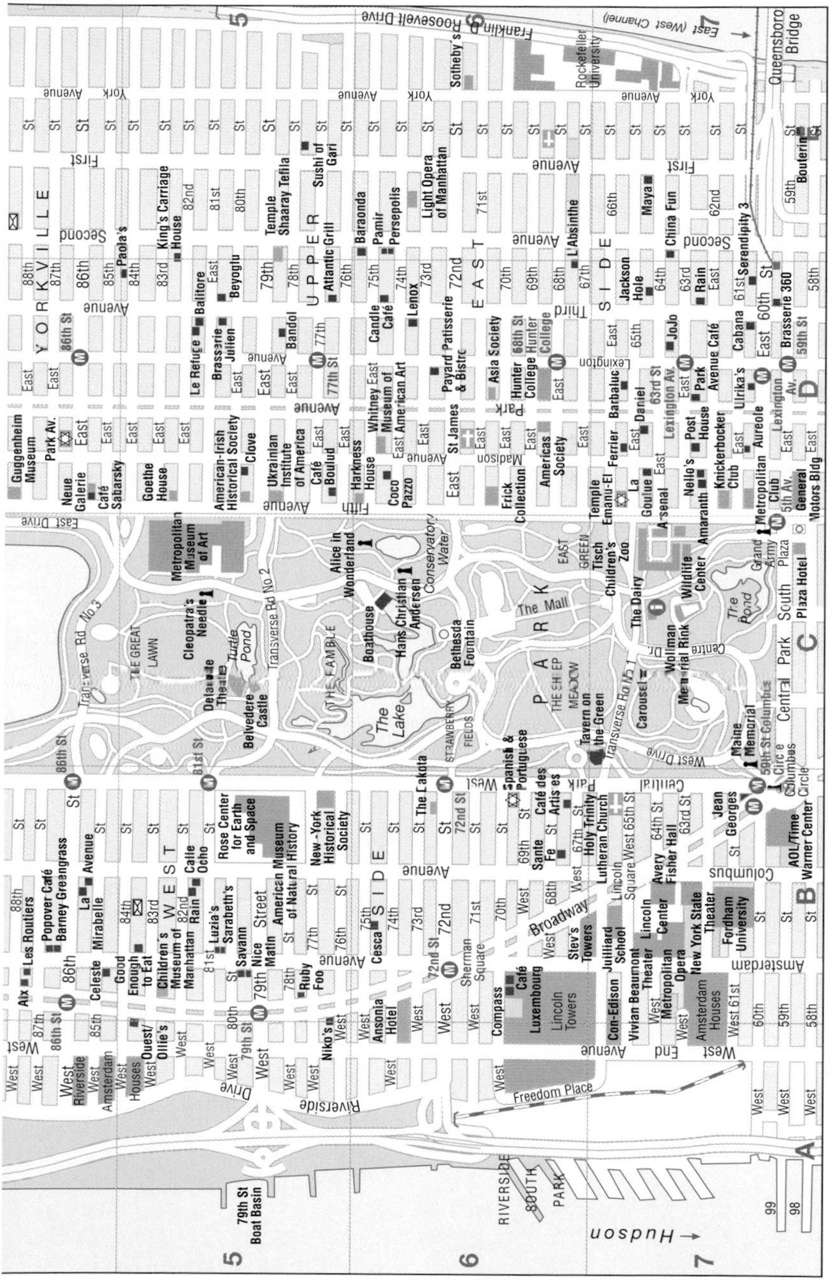
YORKVILLE
UPPER EAST SIDE
UPPER WEST SIDE
CENTRAL PARK
Guggenheim Museum
Neue Galerie
Café Sabarsky
Goethe House
American-Irish Historical Society
Clove
Ukrainian Institute of America
Café Boulud
Harkness House
Coco Pazzo
Whitney Museum of American Art
Candle Café
Lenox
Payard Patisserie & Bistro
St James
Asia Society
Hunter College
Frick Collection
Americas Society
Temple Emanu-El
La Goulue
Ferrier
Barbaluc
Daniel
Post House
Nello's
Knickerbocker Club
Amaranth
Park Avenue Café
Ulrika's
Aureole
Metropolitan Club
General Motors Bldg
Plaza Hotel
Grand Army Plaza
Cabana
Brasserie 360
Serendipity 3
JoJo
Rain
China Fun
Maya
Jackson Hole
L'Absinthe
Light Opera of Manhattan
Barbaonda
Pamir
Persepolis
Atlantic Grill
Sushi of Gari
Temple Shaaray Tefila
Bandol
Brasserie Julien
Le Refuge
Balitore
Beyoglu
King's Carriage House
Paola's
Sotheby's
Rockefeller University
Bouterin
Queensboro Bridge
Franklin D. Roosevelt Drive
East (West Channel)
Metropolitan Museum of Art
Cleopatra's Needle
The Great Lawn
Turtle Pond
Delacorte Theatre
Belvedere Castle
Transverse Rd No 3
Transverse Rd No 2
Transverse Rd No 1
The Ramble
The Lake
Boathouse
Hans Christian Andersen
Alice in Wonderland
Conservatory Water
Bethesda Fountain
Strawberry Fields
The Mall
East Green
The Sheep Meadow
Tavern on the Green
Carousel
Wollman Memorial Rink
The Dairy
Tisch Children's Zoo
Arsenal
Wildlife Center
The Pond
Central Park South
Maine Memorial
59th St Columbus Circle
Columbus Circle
Jean Georges
AOL/Time Warner Center
Spanish & Portuguese
Café des Artistes
Sante Fe
Holy Trinity Lutheran Church
The Dakota
New-York Historical Society
American Museum of Natural History
Rose Center for Earth and Space
Calle Ocho
Sarabeth's
Luzia's
Rain
Children's Museum of Manhattan
Enough to Eat
Good
Mirabelle
La Avenue
Popover Café
Barney Greengrass
Les Routiers
Aix
Celeste
Ouest/Ollie's
Savann
Nice Matin
Ruby Foo
Cesca
Niko's
Ansonia Hotel
Café Luxembourg
Compass
Lincoln Towers
Con-Edison
Vivian Beaumont Theater
Juilliard School
Lincoln Center
Metropolitan Opera
New York State Theater
Avery Fisher Hall
Lincoln Square
Fordham University
Amsterdam Houses
Stev's Towers
Sherman Square
Broadway
Freedom Place
Riverside Drive
Riverside South Park
79th St Boat Basin
Hudson
West End Avenue
Amsterdam Avenue
Columbus Avenue
Central Park West
Fifth Avenue
Madison Avenue
Park Avenue
Lexington Avenue
Third Avenue
Second Avenue
First Avenue
York Avenue
A
B
C
D
E
5
6
7

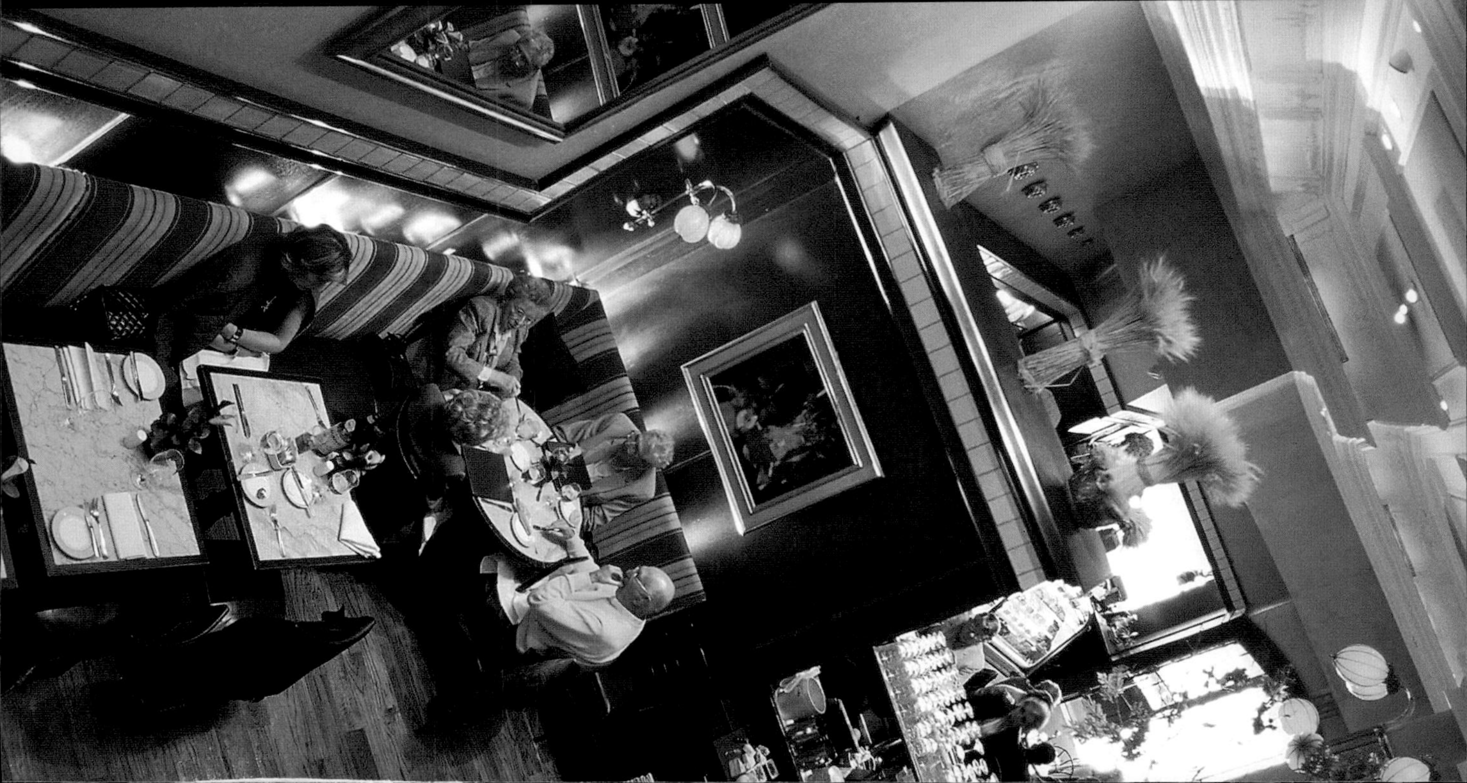

UPPER EAST SIDE

Map on pages 114–115

With sky-high real-estate prices and shops to match, the upscale Upper East Side is where ladies of leisure like to lunch

The Upper East Side was once undisputedly the most fashionable and expensive address in the city – the place to come for a high-toned New York dining experience. To a degree, this is still the case. The blocks between 59th and 96th streets and Fifth Avenue and the East River continue to house the rich and famous; in fact, the so-called Silk Stocking District, as the blocks from Fifth to Park avenues are known, is one of the wealthiest residential enclaves in the world. Movie stars, business executives, and exiled royalty call the Upper East Side home, as does the city's mayor, who lives in Gracie Mansion, on the East River at 89th Street.

What's changed over recent decades is not the Upper East Side but the rest of the city. Other neighborhoods are not only hipper than this classic part of town, they're also just as expensive and desirable; superb restaurants are opening all the time in parts of town that many New Yorkers find to be more exciting and a lot less stuffy than the Upper East Side.

You can, however, dine very well indeed on the Upper East Side. The neighborhood demographics supply the sort of crowd that appreciates a good meal, and you only need to step into Daniel *(see page 123)* or Aureole *(see page 120)* to enjoy the kind of food and ambiance that epitomize fine dining. Many of the neighborhood's best restaurants are old standbys that seem tailor-made for special occasions, or to wine and dine a client or a visiting in-law. The neighborhood attracts chefs in search of customers with refined tastebuds and big dining budgets – it's no accident that Jean-Georges Vongerichten opened his much-lauded Jo Jo *(see page 124)* up here, and Philippe Bertineau has found ready takers for his patisserie/bistro combo, Payard *(see page 124)*.

Culture and classy consumerism

Many visitors come to the Upper East Side not to dine but to partake of a vast array of high-brow activities – to wander through museum galleries, shop for antiques, or peruse racks of European couture. Fifth Avenue is graced with a string of institutions, including nine major museums – from the Frick Collection (70th Street) and the Metropolitan Museum of Art (82nd Street) to the Solomon R. Guggenheim Museum (89th Street). Smaller but worthy collections such as the Goethe Institut (82nd Street), the Neue Galerie (86th Street), Cooper-Hewitt National Design Museum (91st Street), the Jewish Museum (92nd Street), El Museo del Barrio (104th Street), and the Museum of the City of New York (103rd Street) also line this stretch of Fifth Avenue. These bastions of culture have earned for the street the well-deserved moniker "Museum Mile."

A block east, on Madison Avenue, the emphasis switches from culture to consumerism. Art and antiques collectors step in and out of galleries and auction houses, and fashionistas are treated

Opposite and below: tarts to suit every taste at Payard Patisserie & Bistro

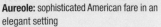

FIVE OF THE BEST

Aureole: sophisticated American fare in an elegant setting
Boathouse: a memorable lakeside brunch
Daniel: a gastronomic heaven serving stellar French cuisine
Park Avenue Café: inventive American creations amid a soothing hush
Sushi of Gari: ultra-fresh fish in a minimalist setting

Pack a tasty picnic or eat brunch in Central Park

to block after block of beautifully arrayed shop windows. Madison is a fantasy come true for the fashion-aware, housing the outposts of designers from Armani to Hermès to Valentino.

Yet the Upper East Side is not all about glitz and glamour. It is also home to upwardly mobile middle-class New Yorkers, especially east of Third Avenue. If there's an ethnic edge to the Upper East Side, it's of the old-fashioned variety: Yorkville, as blocks at the eastern end of 86th Street are known, is a former German neighborhood, with the occasional wurst (sausage) shop and butcher to prove it. Catering to the non-millionaire segment of the neighborhood populace are innumerable bars, pubs, and restaurants that, while not extraordinary, often serve commendable meals at middle-of-the-road prices.

Where to eat

For the most part, the best restaurants are concentrated in the western part of the neighborhood, on leafy streets lined with palatial townhouses and white-glove apartment houses – between gastro-temple Daniel, just off Madison Avenue, and the soothing, club-like Lenox *(see page 121)* on Third Avenue. The farther east you go, the younger the restaurant crowd bcomes – Second Avenue, especially, is noted for its noisy bars and eateries catering to restless singles on the prowl.

If you are making the excursion to the Upper East Side to visit museums, you won't even need to leave the premises to dine, because in most you can grab a bite at cafes and cafeterias. An especially pleasant place to satisfy your hunger is the roof garden at the Metropolitan Museum, where from May through October you can enjoy sandwiches and beverages on a perch overlooking Central Park. For a memorable indoor experience, settle into Café Sabarsky at the Neue Gallery, where the mood of fin-de-siècle Vienna infuses everything from the elegant wood-paneled decor to the goulash, pastry, and coffee.

The Upper East Side is an especially good place to lunch. Many of the neighborhood restaurants cater to well-heeled shoppers in need of sustenance, and restaurants near the southern edge of the area (adjacent to Midtown) open at midday to serve the expense-account crowd.

Whether you are lunching or dining on the Upper East Side, you can avoid disappointment and a lot of walking by making reservations, especially on weekends. The most fashionable restaurants can be booked up weeks in advance. You'll probably want to dress well, too, just as the locals do.

Cooking Schools

A fun alternative to dining out in a restaurant is to spend an evening with other food enthusiasts learning how to prepare a gourmet meal

There are many schools in New York offering one-night cooking courses, averaging at about $95 a class. The **Institute of Culinary Education** *(50 W. 23rd St, bet. Fifth and Sixth Aves, tel: 212-847-0700, www.iceculinary.com)*, one of the nation's most important cooking schools, holds classes in all types of cuisine, including Italian, French, Thai, and vegetarian. These are taught throughout the day and evening in the institute's recreational division. Here, ten or twelve students gather around work tables, chopping and dicing, while others fry and stir at the professional stoves, under the guidance of chefs such as Rati Lohtia who teaches south Indian classic dishes, or Heather Carlucci, the pastry chef at the acclaimed Midtown restaurant L'Impero, who teaches pastry techniques as well as classes in Cuban and German cooking.

The New School *(various locations, tel: 212-225-4141, www.nsu.newschool.edu/culinary)* has a culinary arts division which offers many one-night or one-afternoon classes, as well as tours of some of the city's best restaurants including Chanterelle *(see page 108)*, Aquavit *(see page 25)*, and 66 *(see page 106)*. There, students chat with the chef, tour the kitchens, occasionally get a short cooking demonstration, then sit down and enjoy a full meal. The school also organises food-oriented walking tours of Chinatown, Little India, and the Union Square farmers' market, all ending with cooking instruction and a meal. Be sure to register well in advance.

For a more casual approach, Chef Paul Vandewoude (formerly of Tartine and Le Zinc) holds friendly but informative classes at the **Miette Cooking School** *(109 MacDougal, bet. Bleecker and W. 3rd Sts., tel. 212-460-9322, www.cookingwithmiette.com)*, located in a charming 19th-century townhouse. Students gather in the kitchen to learn about techniques and dishes, then enjoy the food they've made in the adjoining dining room. At about $75 for the class and meal, it's great value. Chris Fisk of nearby **Culinary Explorers** *(85 MacDougal St. bet. Houston and Bleecker Sts., tel: 212-673-8184)* offers a wide variety of entertaining and interesting classes ranging from knife skills to authentic Mexican cuisine and wine tastings held at different downtown locations.

For Italian-food lovers, it's a treat to spend the evening at **Micol Negrin's Rustico Cooking at Grace's** *(1237 Third Ave at 71st St., tel: 917-602-1519)* where cookery writer Micol Negrin demonstrates rustic Italian cooking in the kitchen of an Upper East Side trattoria. In one evening, for example, you'll learn how to make seafood risotto, lamb chops with mint sauce, endive salad, and tiramisu, and enjoy it with a selection of Italian wines.

For those who simply want to sit down and enjoy the work of professional cooking students at a fraction of the cost of a three- or four-star restaurant, there is one outstanding choice: **L'Ecole at the French Culinary Institute** *(462 Broadway at Grand St., tel: 212-219-3300, www. Frenchculinary.com)*, which offers a four- or five-course meal for just $29.95.

Budding chefs at the French Culinary Institute

Boathouse: the perfect spot for a warm-weather brunch

American

Aureole 🍴
34 E. 61st St (bet. Madison and Park aves) [D2]. Tel: 212-319-1660. Open: Mon–Fri L and D. **$$** *(set l)* **$$$$**
www.aureolerestaurant.com
A two-level dining room in Orson Wells's former townhouse is a suitable showcase for inspired and luxurious fare. Salmon is crusted with truffles, quail is boneless for easy eating, service is flawless, and only the lunchtime prix fixe is really affordable. Indeed, founding chef Charlie Parker has created a dining experience so theatrical that he's opened an Aureole in Las Vegas, too, the only city to rival New York for showy extravagance.

Boathouse 🍴
Central Park, enter on E. 72nd St [C6] Tel: 212-517-2233. Open: L and D daily April–Oct, Br Sat, Sun. **$$$$** *www.thecentralpark boathouse.com*
The lake and surrounding greenery of Central Park are the most memorable part of a meal in this airy, glass-fronted dining room and waterside terrace (the perfect spot for a warm-weather brunch). True to the watery surroundings, the kitchen sends out such nautically inspired flourishes as sea urchin and caviar in a scallop shell and pan-roasted monkfish and seared wild striped sea bass. Meanwhile, surefire brunchtime hits of the French toast and omelet variety satisfy the hungry weekend crowds.

Clove
24 E. 80th St (bet. Fifth and Madison aves) [D5]. Tel: 212-249-6500. Open: L and D daily.
$$$$
With its smart address and elegant townhouse setting, Clove attracts a well-dressed, well-mannered crowd – and museum-goers in the know. Chef-owner Jennifer Handler does not disappoint, with a menu of classics that doesn't get much riskier than a lavender-infused chicken. Service is white-glove.

Jackson Hole
232 E. 64th St (bet. Second and Third aves) [D7]. Tel: 212-371-7187. Open: L and D daily. **$**
www.jacksonholeburgers.com
The city's favored canteen for true carnivores has several brightly lit, basically decorated, minimally staffed outlets. They all grill up a mean 7oz burger, piled high with cheese, bacon, onions, and all the other trimmings, and served with

steak-fries and other full-fat accompaniments. This branch provides quick and inexpensive sustenance in a neighborhood where such fare is hard to find.

King's Carriage House

251 E. 82nd St (bet. Second and Third aves) [E5]. Tel: 212-734-5490. Open: L only Mon–Sat, T and D Sun. ***$$$***

You'll forget you're in Manhattan, or even in the 21st century amid the highly polished colonial surroundings and snooty wait staff here. The teatime extravaganza appropriately harkens back to more genteel times, and the well-prepared, steak-and-potatoes-style prix-fixe dinner is accompanied by a hefty dose of candlelit romance.

Lenox

1278 Third Ave (at 73rd St) [D6]. Tel: 212-772-0404. Open: L and D Mon–Sat, D only Sun. ***$$$$*** *www.lenoxroom.com*

Come well dressed and well groomed and you'll fit right in with the local burghers who mix and mingle in the lounge and the plush, clubby, wood-paneled dining room. While the predictable array of meat and fish dishes is reliable, what you might remember most is your meal-time conversation – you can actually hear your tablemates in the blessedly hushed dining room.

Park Avenue Café

100 E. 63rd St (at Park Ave) [D7]. Tel: 212-644-1900. Open: L and D Mon–Fri, D only Sat, Sun. ***$$$$*** *www.parkavenuecafe.com*

The name and address demand some notable cuisine, and the kitchen delivers the goods. Salmon pastrami, morels, and other luxurious ingredients infuse dishes that are served with aplomb by a pampering wait staff, against a countrified backdrop. Best enjoyed on a generous expense account.

Post House

28 E. 63rd St (bet. Madison and Park aves) [D7]. Tel: 212-935-2888. Open: L and D Mon–Fri, D only Sat. ***$$$$*** *www.posthouse.com*

Unlike in most Manhattan steak houses, the testosterone level is kept to a minimum here, in the elegant dining room of the sublimely subdued Lowell Hotel. Lunching ladies are as much at home here as the business-suit brigade, and all are well attended by a staff that's friendly but as seasoned as the aged rib eye.

Sarabeth's

1295 Madison Ave (bet. 92nd and 93rd sts) [D4]. Tel: 212-410-7335. Open: B, L, T, and D Mon–Fri, Br and D Sun. ***$$*** *www.sarabeths.com*

Waffles, fluffy eggs, and other brunch favorites keep the neighborhood lining up, while succulent roasts and other serious and well-prepared dishes come out at dinner time. Child-friendly environs and homey decor. Also a branch in the Upper West Side *(423 Amsterdam Ave, tel: 212-496-6280).*

TIP

The sign offering delivery to the Hamptons is indicative of the upmarket clientele who shop at **Sherry-Lehmann** *(679 Madison Ave),* purveyors of fine wines and spirits since 1934. The expert staff really know their grain from their grape.

Sarabeth's, top tip for an uptown brunch

Serendipity 3

225 E. 60th St (bet. 2nd and 3rd aves) [D7]. Tel: 212-838-3531. Open: L and D daily. ***$$*** *www.serendipity3.com*

The frozen hot chocolate and huge banana splits are legendary, and soups, sandwiches, and pasta add protein to the mix. Kids and shoppers from nearby Bloomingdale's crowd in by day, clubbers stop by at night; and no one seems to mind the cranky service or grown-up tabs.

Austrian

Café Sabarsky: irresistible Viennese treats in a Beaux Arts mansion

Café Sabarsky

1048 Fifth Ave (at 86th St) [D4]. Tel: 212-288-0665. Open: L and D Thur–Sun, L only Mon, Wed. ***$$$*** *www.wallserestaurant.com*

Enter this wood-paneled salon of the Beaux Arts mansion that houses the Neue Gallerie of German and Austrian art, and you'll think you're on Vienna's Ringstrasse. Chef Kurt Gutenbrunner lives up to the surroundings, and the beef goulash, cod strudel, linzer torte, and other fare from the banks of the Danube take museum food to new heights.

French

L'Absinthe

227 E. 67th St (bet. Second and Third aves) [D6]. Tel: 212-794-4950. Open: L and D Tues–Sat, D only Sun, Mon, closed Sun July, Aug. ***$$$*** *www.labsinthe.com*

The etched mirrors, polished brass, and French waiters in white aprons are as authentic as the poached sausages with potatoes and lentils and other classic brasserie fare. Add the prosperous-looking locals who find the place as addictive as its namesake aperitif, and you can easily imagine you are in the genteel 16th arrondissement in Paris.

Bandol

181 E. 78th St (bet. Lexington and Third aves) [D5]. Tel: 212-744-1800. Open: L and D Mon–Fri, D only Sat, Sun. ***$$*** *www.bandolbistro.com*
The wonderfully aromatic Provençal wine lends its name to a little wine bar as sunny and welcoming as a Mediterranean vineyard in July. Accompanying a long list of mostly French and reasonably priced vintages is a simple menu of such favorites as coq au vin and fish soup.

Bouterin

420 E. 59th St (bet. First and York aves) [E7]. Tel: 212-758-0323. Open: D daily. ***$$$$*** *www.bouterin.com*
Chef-owner Antoine Bouterin claims to take his inspiration for food and decor from his *chère grandmère*, a restaurateur in St-Rémy-de-Provençe, in southern France, and he does her memory proud. Flowers scent the air, antiques and mementos crowd every surface, and the menu delves into such calorie-rich, pre-nouvelle cuisine favorites as duck à l'orange and lamb stew.

Brasserie 360

200 E. 60th St (at 3rd Ave) [D7]. Tel: 212-688-8688. Open: L and D daily. ***$$$***
The ground level of this airy and sunny Art Deco space is given over to a Parisian brasserie, where moules-frites and other brasserie classics hold sway. Upstairs, you cross continents to Tokyo. Here, the Japanese chefs at the sushi bar work wonders with denizens of the deep that seldom surface in New York. Both offer respite for weary shoppers from nearby Bloomingdale's.

Brasserie Julien

1422 Third Ave (bet. 80th and 81st sts) [D5]. Tel: 212-744-6327. Open: D daily. ***$$*** *www.brasseriejulien.com*
Julien does not trade solely in tradition – you'll hear some North American voices among the wait staff, and new-fangled foods of the ostrich-burger variety make an appearance on the menu. Then again, so do choucroute, thick onion soup, and other old-fashioned bistro favorites.

Café Boulud

20 E. 76th St (bet. 5th and Madison aves) [D5]. Tel: 212-772-2600. Open: L and D Tues–Sat, D only Sun, Mon. ***$$$$*** *www.danielnyc.com*
Though it could never be said that haute restaurateur Daniel Boulud takes a casual approach to his exquisite food, the environs and offerings in this wonderfully comfortable khaki-colored room are a little less formal than at Daniel *(see below)*. Andrew Carmellini does the cooking, and he lets his guests mix and match from four tempting menus that range from traditional dishes to market-fresh vegetarian choices to the cuisines of faraway lands.

Daniel

60 E. 65th St (bet. Park and Madison aves) [D7]. Tel: 212-288-0033. Open: D only Mon–Sat. ***$$$$*** *www.danielnyc.com*
Welcome to the magical world of Daniel Boulud – the flower arrangements and candlelit table settings are sumptuous, the service unhurried and pampering, the food, from the caviar to the cheese course, an absolute work of art. Dish after dish provides an amazing revelation of flavors and textures. The price tag will bring you back to the real world, but for a memorable flight of dining fantasy you can't do any better. Reserve well ahead.

TIP

On Friday or Saturday evenings in the summer, the rooftop sculpture garden of the **Metropolitan Museum of Art** (1000 Fifth Ave, tel: 212-879-5500) often has live jazz music. This is a great place to sip champagne and take in a glorious view of the Manhattan skyline.

Ferrier

29 E. 65th St (bet. Madison and Park aves) [D7]. Tel: 212-772-9000. Open: L and D daily. **$$$**

The pencil-thin clientele is distractingly gorgeous, the noise level distractingly loud, the Gallic wait staff distractingly charming. Even so, your attention might not be so easily diverted when the food arrives – the cassoulet, steak frites, and other French bistro fare is actually very good, hence the popularity of this place.

La Goulue

746 Madison Ave (bet. 64th and 65th sts) [D7]. Tel: 212-988-8169. Open: L and D daily. **$$$** *www.lagouluerestaurant.com*

Madison Avenue meets the Riviera in a darkened room where a well-dressed clientele chatter on cell phones, blow air kisses across the room, and tuck into salad with black-truffle vinaigrette, lamb shank with gnocchi, steak au poivre, and the restaurant's trademark lunchtime cheese soufflé. The atmosphere is always buzzing, and there are sidewalk tables in fine weather.

JoJo

160 E. 64th St (bet. Lexington and Third aves) [D7]. Tel: 212-223-5656. Open: L and D daily. **$$$$** *www.jean-georges.com*

A recent makeover has endowed these hallowed premises with a rich, emerald-and-burgundy color scheme, luxurious fabrics, and warm-hued tiles that are all as inviting as a menu that includes such delicacies as foie gras with quince and lobster in herb broth. All told, this outpost of chef Jean-Georges Vongerichten's ever-expanding worldwide empire continues to serve up one of Manhattan's best French food extravaganzas.

Payard Patisserie and Bistro

1032 Lexington Ave (bet. 73rd and 74th sts) [D6]. Tel: 212-717-5252. Open: L and D Mon–Sat. **$$** *www.payard.com*

You may not make it beyond the cafe-style tables in the front room, where glass cases are filled with delicate pastries, ice creams, and rich chocolates. But if you're hungry for protein, press on to the back room for a full menu of dependable bistro classics.

Le Refuge

166 E. 82nd St (bet. Lexington and Third aves) [D5]. Tel: 212-861-4505. Open: L and D Tues–Sun, D only Mon. **$$$** *www.lerefugeinn.com*

Jackie O, who knew a good French country meal when it was placed in front of her, was a regular here, and Pierre St. Denis continues to feed an appreciative crowd of well-heeled locals in three simple rooms that seem to have been air-lifted intact from the French countryside. You can enjoy the gratineed oysters, roasted duck, and other classics on the good-value prix-fixe menu or à la carte.

Italian

Baraonda

1439 Second Ave (at 75th St) [E6]. Tel: 212-288-8555. Open: D only Mon–Fri, L and D Sat, Sun. **$$$** *www.baraonda.com*

A gorgeous crowd packs into this high-energy Euro club nightly, mostly for self-admiration, and, as the evening wears on, table dancing and other dolce-vita-style antics. If you want to add some sustenance to your people-watching, pasta is the way to go.

Barbaluc

135 E. 65th St (bet. Lexington and Park aves) [D7]. Tel: 212-

Did you know?

From the Whitney Museum to 59th Street, Madison Avenue turns into a veritable orgy of conspicuous consumption. The names on the storefronts read like a roster of the fashion elite: Ralph Lauren, Yves Saint Laurent, Kenzo, Giorgio Armani, Prada, Calvin Klein, to name but a few. Needless to say, unless you're packing a king-size bankroll, most of these stores are more for browsing than buying.

774-1999. Open: L and D Mon–Sat. ***$$$***

The minimalist decor makes it all the easier to pay attention to the foods and wines of the Friuli region (northeastern Italy) at Barbaluc, and they well deserve the spotlight. Fried montasio cheese, goose tarts, venison stews, and other satisfying dishes rarely offered elsewhere in New York are nicely complimented by the wine list, which includes 20 vintages by the glass (the restaurant, incidentally, takes its name from the sprite that lives in your wineglass).

Coco Pazzo

23 E. 74th St (bet Fifth and Madison aves) [D6]. Tel: 212-794-0205. Open: L and D daily. ***$$$$***

Movers and shakers strike their deals here, celebrities float in and out, and an attentive staff is as beautiful as the patrons. Despite the hype, the kitchen keeps its focus on the real business at hand to ensure that rabbit stewed in red wine, rigatoni with sweet sausage, Florentine steak, and other hearty Tuscan staples are the real stars in this galaxy.

Nello's

696 Madison Ave (bet. 62nd and 63rd sts) [D7]. Tel: 212-980-9099. Open: L and D daily. ***$$$***

Pasta is pricey and the picatas predictable, but no one at this little slice of Rome on the Upper East Side seems to mind. A designer-clad neighborhood crowd feels right at home, proving that even the most urbane sophisticates appreciate friendly service and down-to-earth cooking.

Paola's

245 E. 84th St (bet. Second and Third aves) [D5]. Tel: 212-794-1890. Open: L and D Tues–Sun. ***$$$***

Barbaluc, a minimalist setting for Friulian food and wine

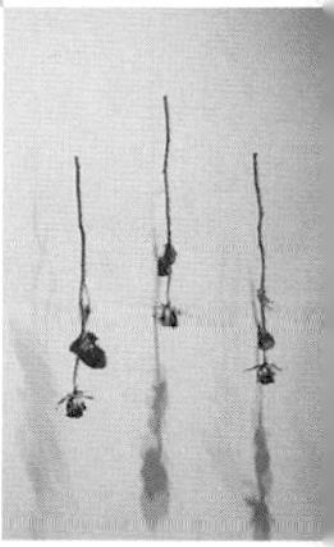

Neighborhood high-rise dwellers love this little hidey-hole, where two intimate rooms supply the perfect setting for a proposal, or at least a seduction. A lengthy menu includes dishes such as beet and ricotta ravioli that manage to be comforting and sophisticated at the same time.

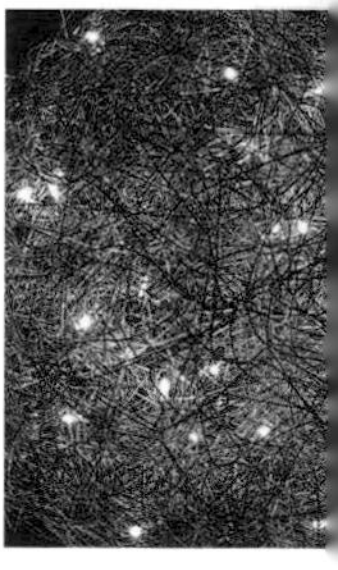

Japanese

Sushi of Gari 🍴

402 E. 78th St (bet. 1st and York aves) [E5]. Tel: 212-517-5340. Open: D only Tues–Sun. ***$$$***

When a tasting menu tops $50, you expect the raw fish to be mighty tasty, and Gari (Japanese for pickled ginger) doesn't disappoint. Indeed, price doesn't deter legions of loyal fans who wait patiently for a table or place at the sushi bar, swearing all the while that the inventive creations here are the best in town.

Smorgasbord art at Ulrika's

TIP

If time is short during a shopping session, consider taking advantage of one of the department-store eateries: Le Train Bleu or Forty Carrots in Bloomingdale's, and Fred's in Barney's.

Latin American

Cabana

1022 Third Ave (bet. 60th and 61st sts) [D7]. Tel: 212-980-5678. Open: L and D daily. **$$**

Neighborhood stockbrokers love to kick back at what is essentially an indoor beach party, with tropical colors, spicy ceviches, and rum-laced blender potions. Drink enough of the latter and you may believe that the rush of traffic on Third Avenue is the sound of waves on a sandy beach.

Maya

1191 First Ave (bet. 64th and 65th sts) [E7]. Tel: 212-585-1818. Open: L and D daily. **$$$**

Gourmets whose tastes run south of the border relish such flavorful Mayan-inspired creations as red snapper with cactus relish and seafood-stuffed roasted poblano pepper, served in cheery and classy surroundings. The potent margaritas help even the most stressed-out executive wind down.

Mediterranean

Amaranth

21 E. 62nd St (near Madison Ave) [D7]. Tel: 212-980-6700. Open: L and D daily. **$$$$**

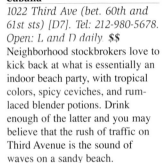

This chic restaurant is a magnet to Manhattan's Euro set, but the simple Mediterranean fare is no afterthought. Find your place amid the swirl of the tanned and the toned and enjoy the seafood carpaccios, pasta, and excellent wines.

Middle Eastern

Beyoglu

1431 Third Ave (at 81st St), 2nd floor [D5]. Tel: 212-650-0850. Open: D daily. **$$**

All the flavors of the Middle East seem to explode from the array of dishes on offer, from minty yogurt rice soup, to the lamb or beef doner kebabs, and experiencing them can be as exciting as a walk through the Istanbul neighborhood for which this Turkish tapas house is named. Since the portions are ideal for sharing, come with a group and explore the entire menu.

Pamir

1437 Second Ave (bet. 74th and 75th sts) [E6]. Tel: 212-734-3791. Open: D daily. **$$**

Wall hangings provide an exotic backdrop for kebabs, grilled lamb, and other excellent Afghan dishes. Add the gracious service and reasonable tabs, and it's easy to see why this place is so popular.

Persepolis

1423 Second Ave (bet. 74th and 75th sts) [E6]. Tel: 212-535-1100. Open: L and D daily. ***$$***

One of the few Persian eateries in New York provides an exotic alternative to the often ho-hum options on this stretch of the Upper East Side. Coal-grilled salmon, filet mignon, creamy spreads, and kebabs seem fit for a shah, and are served in pleasantly subdued surroundings.

Scandinavian

Ulrika's

115 E. 60th St (bet. Lexington and Park aves) [D7]. Tel: 212-355-7069. Open: L and D Mon–Fri, Br and D Sat, Sun. ***$$$$***

Ulrika Bengtsson, former chef to the Swedish consul general, has filled her pretty restaurant with crystal, art, and knick-knacks from her Scandinavian homeland. In the kitchen she uses market-fresh ingredients to prepare a roster of national dishes that include, of course, pickled herring and meatballs, which can be sampled on a satisfying tasting menu.

Seafood

Atlantic Grill

1341 Third Ave (bet. 76th and 77th sts) [D6]. Tel: 212-988-9200. Open: L and D daily. Br on Sun ***$$$***
www.brguestrestaurants.com

When the urge for seafood hits, the neighborhood heads to this big, boisterous, stylish fish house, and you'd have to throw out a line yourself to haul in a catch any fresher. Waits can be long, but start with a sesame-crusted lobster roll, and you'll be glad you stuck it out.

Vegetarian

Candle Café

1307 Third Ave (bet. 74th and 75th sts) [D5]. Tel: 212-472-0970. Open: L and D daily. ***$***
www.candlecafe.com

The staff at this small bastion of health serve up innovative, tasty vegan fare. Even carnivores might be tempted by the stir-fried tempeh with peanut sauce and casseroles of sweet potatoes and steamed greens, not to mention the carrot cake with tofu frosting.

Cafes and Bars

The 20-block stretch of Second Avenue between approximately 72nd–92nd streets has a conspicuous number of Irish pubs including **Kinsale Tavern** *(1672 Third Ave, tel: 212-348-4370)* and **O'Flanagan's Ale House** *(1591 Second Ave, tel: 212-472-2800)*, frequented mostly by students who live in the vicinity. Most of them don't serve anything more complicated than beers and simple wines, and easy, home-style dishes. There are a handful of noteworthy wine bars that tend to attract an older, more sophisticated clientele. Two of the best are **Bandol** *(181 E. 78th St, tel: 212-744-1800)* and **Lexington Bar and Books** *(1020 Lexington Ave, tel: 212-717-3902)*. Apart from the delightful Viennese **Café Sabarsky** *(see page 122)*, most of the best cafes in the neighborhood are attached to French or Italian restaurants. **Barbaluc** *(135 E. 65th St, tel: 212-774-1999)* and **Brasserie Julien** *(1422 Third Ave, tel: 212-744-6327)* both have fine cafes. Though part of a chain, **Le Pain Quotidien** *(1131 Madison Ave, tel: 212-327-4900)* is a good place to sit and rest your feet if you're experiencing culture overload at the nearby museums; or head over to **Melrose**, across from the Met, for an aperitif and people-watching from their sidewalk cafe.

Area 9: Upper West Side

Upper West Side

This part of town, home to Lincoln Center and the focal point of the New York Jewish community, is good for chic, understated dining

Map on pages 114–115

For years it's been claimed that the Upper West Side is a dining wasteland and it's best to satisfy your hunger before venturing north of Columbus Circle. This has never been true – no one has ever gone hungry on the Upper West Side for lack of a place to dine. Admittedly, the dining scene in the neighborhood is less lively than in say Midtown or Greenwich Village, but in recent years, exciting new restaurants such as Jean Georges *(see page 135)*, Aix *(see page 134)*, and Ouest *(see page 133)* are putting the Upper West Side firmly on the dining map.

Ethnic neighborhood

Despite the naysaying, the West Side, a long, narrow strip of Manhattan between 59th Street and 116th Street, bounded by Riverside Park and the Hudson River on the west and Central Park for most of its eastern flank, has always been home to some very good and idiosyncratic restaurants. Barney Greengrass is the last of a breed of restaurants that began opening in the early 20th century to serve solidly middle-class Jewish immigrants who moved up, literally and figuratively, into the neighborhood from the Lower East Side; the neighborhood is still largely Jewish. Puerto Ricans, Dominicans, and other Spanish-speaking immigrants began arriving in the 1960s, and with them came such standbys as Flor de Mayo *(see page 137)* and La Rosita *(see page 138)*. Young urban professionals discovered the neighborhood in the late 1970s and 1980s, and they began renovating old apartments and brownstones with a vengeance, and demanding their own brand of comfort food. While many of the restaurants serving this brand of cuisine are just too bland to warrant reviews, places such as the Popover Café, Good Enough to Eat, Henry's *(all page 133)*, and Sarabeth's *(see page 121)* are noteworthy for their solid American cooking.

Area attractions

With some notable exceptions, it's unlikely that restaurants alone will lure you to the Upper West Side. You'll probably wander into the neighborhood to do something else. Lincoln Center, New York's largest performing arts complex, is located off Broadway, between 62nd and 66th streets. The monumental American Museum of Natural History presides over Central Park West between 77th and 81st streets; this august institution, with its dinosaur-filled galleries and adjoining planetarium, provides many hours' worth of interest for visitors, old and young alike, and you can feed gnawing appetites in any number of on-site cafeterias. Columbia University (established 1754) is at the northern edge of the neighborhood, centered on Broadway and 116th Street. Here, around the gates to one of the USA's oldest centers of learning, you'll find a pleasant community of coffee shops, markets, and other student-oriented businesses.

Opposite: Ouest on Broadway – be sure to book first

Five of the Best

Aix: hearty, heart-warming fare and a taste of Provence
Gennaro: superb Italian food served in friendly surroundings at reasonable prices
Jean-Georges: innovative French cuisine in elegant surroundings
Ouest: innovative interpretations of chops, ribs, and other American classics
Les Routiers: one of the most welcoming neighborhood bistros in New York

While the Upper West Side is not particularly known for its restaurants, the neighborhood counts among its major attractions some of the city's finest and most entertaining markets. To do the rounds of these vast, well-stocked food emporia, walk up the west side of Broadway and step into Fairway, at 74th Street, then Citarella, at 75th Street, and, finally, Zabar's, at 80th Street *(see also page 42)*.

Exploring the neighborhood

Aside from seeing the big sights, you might also want to take some time just to poke around the neighborhood's streets and avenues, which are lined with old brownstones and grand apartment houses. Here, you can see a typical Manhattan residential neighborhood and catch New Yorkers in their native habitats. You should also come to the neighborhood to walk in Central Park (the walking trail around the reservoir, reached via an entrance at West 86th Street, is especially appealing) or along the Hudson River on the waterside promenade in Riverside Park, which stretches the length of the neighborhood.

If you plan on keeping an eye out for an appealing restaurant as you wander, work Amsterdam Avenue between 86th and 96th streets into your route. Along this rather drab urban thoroughfare are some of our favorite choices; see the reviews for Les Routiers, Genarro, Gabriela's, and Cafe con Leche *(see pages 134–138)*. Avoid, for the most part, Columbus Avenue, which has morphed over the years from a low-key neighborhood shopping street to a chic boutique-and-club strip in the 1980s and has now been homogenized into suburban blandness, with chain stores and some truly unexciting restaurants. Of course, there are a few exceptions, notably Calle Ocho *(see page 137)* and Avenue *(see page 132)*, and the Sunday market at Columbus Avenue and 77th Street is a good place to pick up fresh fruit, baked goods, and other delicacies. Oddly, the area around Lincoln Center also seems to be resilient to good, affordable restaurants. (With a few exceptions, such as Sante Fe, you're better advised to head farther north into the Upper West Side or to travel to a different neighborhood for a post- or pre-performance meal.)

Finally, keep a few things in mind. If you don't feel like wandering, plan ahead: the neighborhood is almost 3 miles (5 km) long, so you can save yourself a lot of walking if you look at our reviews and get an idea of where you might want to dine before you set out. The number 1, 2, 3, and 9 subways run up the length of the Upper West Side and, since it's so narrow, all restaurants are within an easy walk of the stops along this line. There's no need to dress up to dine at most Upper West Side restaurants, and in all but a few places jeans are standard (if you want to stand out from the crowd, dare to wear a color other than black). While plenty of restaurants are open at midday, many are not (this part of town is not a haunt of the expense-account crowd), so be sure to check opening times if you want to lunch in a particular place. Reservations are required in only the most expensive restaurants.

New York Experiences

Experience authentic New York, whether at a humble deli counter or in the glitziest of celebrity haunts

Where better to bite off an authentic slice of Big Apple life than the city's famous delicatessens. Foremost among these is the **Carnegie Deli** *(see page 16)*, where smart waiters serve huge sandwiches that can be enjoyed in the presence of hundreds of famous patrons, who look down from photos plastering the walls. **Katz's** *(see page 73)*, although far less slick, is such a long-standing presence on the Lower East Side that signs dating from World War II still proclaim, 'Buy a Salami for your Boy in the Army.' Uptown, **Barney Greengrass** *(see page 132)* serves lox, smoked sturgeon, and other Jewish standards in surroundings that have not changed since the 1950s.

Then there's the glamorous side to New York, as depicted in numerous movies. If you believe hundreds of film images, this is the elegant metropolis where glam couples sit sipping champagne against a backdrop of twinkling lights. And if that's how you see yourself, climb aboard the **River Cafe** *(see page 142)*; this barge floating beneath the Brooklyn Bridge is a veritable love boat, going on the number of marriage proposals the killer views and superb cuisine have facilitated. **The Four Seasons** *(see page 17)*, meanwhile, surrounds you with such style that you won't feel the need for a view.

Want to partake of that quintessential New York experience and hang out with celebrities – or at least sit across a room from one? Hunting grounds change with the wind, but **Balthazar** *(see page 91)*, **Asia de Cuba** *(Morgans Hotel, 237 Madison Ave, between 37th and 38th sts, tel: 212-726-7755)*, and **Tribeca Grill** *(see page 105)* remain ripe, even though they date all the way back to the end of the last century (20th, that is). Celeb spotting may be the only reason to visit **Sardi's** *(234 West 44th St, tel: 212-221-8440)*, a legendary 80-year-old showbiz hangout that still counts a legend or two among its patrons. Or do you prefer past legends? The spirits of writer Dorothy Parker and her silver-tongued lunch pals still seem to float around the dining room of the **Algonquin Hotel** *(59 W. 44th St, tel: 212-840-6800)*, while the arched **Grand Central Oyster Bar** *(see page 25)* still echoes with the clamor of the travelers who have dined on fresh oysters and creamy chowders over the years. To sip a cocktail in classic New York style head for the **King Cole Bar** at the St. Regis Hotel *(see page 26)* and while you're there ask the bartender to explain what's happening in the Maxfield Parrish murals behind the bar.

Finally, for a New York experience that brings home the melting-pot character of the city, stop in for lunch at the United Nations **Delegates' Dining Room** *(see page 22)*. The food and crowd are global, and the security's tight – how much more 21st-century New York can you get than that?

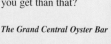

The Grand Central Oyster Bar

American

The Abbey Pub

237 W. 105th St (bet. Broadway and Amsterdam Ave) [B2]. Tel: 212-222-8713. Open: daily, D only. **$**

Find a snug wooden booth and chow down on a juicy burger and fries. The menu pulls no punches, but for an authentic, neighborhood experience, linger here a while and watch the Columbia students mingle with gravely voiced, boozy regulars.

Avenue

520 Columbus Ave (at 85th St) [B4]. Tel: 212-579-3194. Open: B, L, and D Mon–Fri, Br and D Sat, Sun. **$$** *www.therestaurantgroup.com*

A neighborhood hot spot that serves salads and sandwiches by day, then lights the candles and brings on basics such as grilled fish and steak with a French twist by night. The good news for grazers is that you can order most dishes as small appetizers. Wine is half price on Monday.

Barney Greengrass

541 Amsterdam Ave (bet. 86th and 87th sts) [B4]. Tel: 212-724-4707. Open: B and L Tues–Sun. **$** *www.barenygreengrass.com*

The faded murals and formica tables are deceptively downbeat, but New Yorkers continue to herald this West Side institution as the best place in town for lox, smoked sturgeon, chopped liver, and other Jewish fare. Weekend lines are long, and in them you might spot Bill Murray, Woody Allen, and other celebrity regulars.

Carne

2737 Broadway (105th St) [A2]. Tel: 212-663-7010. Open: L and D Mon–Fri, Br and D Sat, Sun. **$$**

One of few steakhouses on the Upper West Side, Carne's retro cafeteria decor and well-prepared, nicely priced steaks and burgers are a winning combination.

Barney Greengrass, the well-known local deli

Students from nearby Columbia University and neighborhood locals keep the place hopping most nights, and in good weather the crowd spills on to the sidewalk tables.

Compass

208 W. 70th St (bet. Amsterdam and West End aves) [B6]. Tel: 212-875-8600. Open: L and D Sun–Fri, D only Sat. **$$–$$$**

Downtown chic arrives uptown in this muted gray dining room that is very stylish, if a little austere. The New American menu brings together the freshest fish and choicest cuts of meat in innovative preparations. You can keep the tab from heading too far north with the $30 prix-fixe bistro menu, accompanied by a daily selection of US wines in the $20 a bottle range. Reservations advisable.

Good Enough to Eat

483 Amsterdam Ave (bet. 83rd and 84th sts) [B5]. Tel: 212-496-0163. Open: B, L, and D Mon–Fri, Br and D Sat, Sun. **$**

Meat loaf, pork roast, home-baked pies – the gamut of Betty Crocker favorites are prepared to perfection and served in rustic, Americana-filled surroundings. Join the weekend morning rush for muffins and pancakes that are worth the wait.

Henry's

2745 Broadway (105th St) [A2]. Tel: 212-866-0600. Open: L and D daily, B Sat, Sun. **$–$$**

A jeans-clad Upper West Side crowd, often with kids in tow, packs into this large, softly lit space that opens to Broadway through a long row of French doors. The American bistro fare doesn't get much fancier than grilled fish and chops, but it's reliably good, and you'll be left to relax and linger as long as you like – a rarity in New York.

Ouest

2315 Broadway (bet. 83rd and 84th sts) [A5]. Tel: 212-580-8700. Open: D daily, Br Sun. **$$$**

In a jazzy interior of round red booths, chef Tom Valenti serves his own version of American classics such as lamb shank and short ribs, concentrating on solid flavors rather than showiness. The place is loved by West Side gastronomes, so reservations are essential.

Popover Café

551 Amsterdam Ave (bet. 86th and 87th sts) [B4]. Tel: 212-595-8555. Open: B, L, and D daily. **$** *www.popovercafe.com*

You'd think folks would have better things to do with their precious weekends than wait in the brunch lines at this cozy neighborhood haunt with a penchant for teddy bears. But wait they do, to be rewarded with fluffy omelets, hearty soups, and other comfort food.

Tavern on the Green

Off Central Park West and 67th St. [C7]. Tel. 212-873-3200. Open: L and D Mon–Fri, Br and D Sat, Sun. **$$$** *www.tavernonthegreen.com*

Even native New Yorkers feel like tourists out for a big night at this Central Park lair, bedecked with fairy lights. The fact that the Tavern's steak and fish fare is run-of-the-mill is more than compensated for by the festive atmosphere and setting, which is all the more magical if you manage to nab a table on the summertime terrace. Reservations recommended.

Asian

Rain

100 W. 82nd St (bet. Columbus and Amsterdam aves) [B5]. Tel: 212-501-0776. Open: L and D daily. **$$**

TIP

Grab a sandwich at **Zabar's** *(Broadway and 80th St)*, **Barney Greengrass** *(see opposite)*, or any of the neighborhood's other delis, then find a spot on the Great Lawn in Central Park or on a grassy slope above the river in Riverside Park.

Thai, Vietnamese, Malaysian – all the cuisines of Southeast Asia seem to show up here, amid rattan-filled, jungle-themed environs that make you feel like you're trapped inside a travel poster. While the food can be as forgettable as the setting, the green papaya salad, stir-fried peanut beef, and other spicy fare keep a hopping crowd of young Janes and Tarzans happy.

Ruby Foo
2182 Broadway (at 77th St) [B5]. Tel: 212-724-6700. Open: L and D Mon–Sat, Br and D Sun. **$$** *www.brguestrestaurants.com*
Until not so long ago, the Upper West Side was well endowed with cavernous, darkly exotic lairs serving mediocre Chinese food. Consider this cheerfully dramatic, always lively room to be the current incarnation. The blends of Asian cuisine at Ruby's can be as exciting as the atmosphere: you can go wild and pair sushi with tamarind-glazed baby back ribs and follow it up with a chocolate sundae. Reservations essential.

TIP

Papaya King, at the busy intersection of Broadway and 72nd Street, serves the cheapest meal in the neighborhood – just over $2 for two hot dogs and the beverage of your choice. 'Dining' here is a good way to offset the cost of a ticket at nearby Lincoln Center.

Caribbean

A
947 Columbus Ave (bet. 106th and 107th sts) [B2]. Tel: 212-531-1643. Open: D Tues–Sat. **$**
Jerk chicken and other Caribbean fare so authentic they more than warrant the trek up to this small, spartan room. Try to come early or late if you don't want to wait for one of the few tables, and even then you might have to. Cash only.

Cafe con Leche
726 Amsterdam Ave (bet. 95th and 96th sts) [B5]. Tel: 212-595-7000. Open: L and D daily. **$**
The eponymous brew is the best you're going to find in Manhattan, while the generous portions of roast pork and other Dominican dishes, served in lively surroundings never fail to add a spice to an evening. Another location at 424 Amsterdam.

Rain offers a Southeast Asian pick-and-mix menu

Chinese

Ollie's
2315 Broadway (at 84th St) [A5]. Tel: 212-362-3111. Open: L and D daily. **$**
Upper West Siders save the subway fare to Chinatown and flock instead to this clamorous space. Service is brusque, and the decor nothing to write home about, but the noodles, dumplings, and other Cantonese fare is more authentic than at most other Uptown equivalents.

French

Aix
2398 Broadway (at 88th St) [B4]. Tel: 212-874-7400. Open: D daily, Br Sun. **$–$$$** *www.aixnyc.com*
A Provençal air infuses the lush, mellow-hued rooms of this spacious restaurant, and acclaimed chef Didier Virot brings the same southern French spirit to such inspired creations as pistou and broiled squab. You may be tempted to abandon your budget and indulge in the five-course tasting menu ($78), and why not accompany each course with a different selection from the excellent wine list? Reservations essential.

Alouette
2588 Broadway (bet. 97th and 98th sts) [B3]. Tel: 212-222-6808. Open: D daily. **$–$$** *www.alouette.com*
It comes as a surprise to find such a lovely, elegant French bistro on this workaday stretch of Broadway. Hanger steak, roasted monkfish, and other bistro classics are well

Aix

turned out, occasionally with an Oriental twist. The staff work hard to ensure a meal here is an experience to remember. Best to reserve.

Café des Artistes

1 W. 67th St (bet. Central Park W. and Columbus aves) [B6]. Tel: 212-877-3500. Open: L and D Mon–Fri; Br and D Sat, Sun. ***$$$*** *www.cafenyc.com*

It's been a long time since these mural-lined rooms were a home away from home for the bohemians who lived and worked in the studios – now posh apartments – upstairs, but legend lives on in the old place. You'll find better French fare in the neighborhood, but not in surroundings as appealing as these.

Café Luxembourg

200 W. 70th St (bet. Amsterdam and West End aves) [A6]. Tel: 212-873-7411. Open: B, L, and D daily. ***$$***

This buzzing Art Deco bistro has been a hot spot for decades, and red banquettes and tiled walls still provide just the right ambiance for steak-frites or a 'Luxembourger' – ideal for late-night cravings.

Jean-Georges (🍴)

Trump International Hotel, 1 Central Park West [B7]. Tel: 212-299-3900. Open: L and D Mon–Sat, Br Sun. ***$$–$$$$***

The ungainly skyscraper on chaotic Columbus Circle is an unlikely location for one of the city's most sophisticated and relaxing retreats. Here, chef Jean-Georges Vongerichten surprises diners with dazzling versions of French classics. While the bill can soar as high as the eyesore in which the restaurant is housed, the $20 lunchtime prix-fixe in the less formal Nougatine Room brings these gastronomic heights within earthly reach. Reservations essential.

Métisse

239 W. 105th St (bet. Broadway and Amsterdam Ave) [B2]. Tel. 212-666-8825. Open: D daily. ***$$***

A comfortable, small, brick-walled room is just the right, easy-going setting for comfort food of the roast lamb, roast chicken, and duck confit variety. If you find this combination as appealing as the regulars do, pay your compliments to the chef-owner, Claude Waryniak, who circulates among the tables to make sure everyone is happy.

La Mirabelle

102 W. 86th St (bet. Columbus and Amsterdam aves) [B4]. Tel: 212-496-0458. Open: D daily. ***$$***

Francophiles delight in this homey cafe that is thoroughly Gallic. Wisecracking waitresses of a

Did you know?

Riv vus: that's Manhattanese for river views, and you'll get your fill of them, along with burgers and sandwiches, at two informal eateries in Riverside Park – the Boat Basin Café, at 79th Street off Riverside Drive, and the Dog Run Café (so called for its proximity to a fun playground for four-legged New Yorkers), 104th Street off Riverside Drive.

The cheery terrace of Indian Café

certain age hum along with the Edith Piaf soundtrack (sometimes they break into a full-voiced song), and the menu is packed with onion soup, escargots, kidneys, lamb chops, and other caloric pleasures.

Nice Matin

201 West 79th St (at Amsterdam Ave) [B5]. Tel: 212-873-6423. Open: L and D daily. **$$**

Traffic noise and the cacophony bouncing off the 1970s' mod decor lays waste to the attempt to re-create the Riviera, but the inspired fare will whisk you away to the shores of the Mediterranean. Grilled sardines, poached mussels, pissaladière, and other delectable starters ease the way into such memorable entrées as a rosemary-infused leg of lamb, all served with haughty indifference that seems a lot more French than the surroundings.

Les Routiers 🍴

568 Amsterdam Ave (bet. 87th and 88th sts) [B4]. Tel: 212-874-2742. Open: D Mon–Sat. **$$**

The name means 'truck drivers' in French, and the maps on the wall of the comfy booths and old-fashioned, robust French fare are nods to that profession. After a hearty meal of lamb shank or pork roast at this pleasant wayside spot, you'll hit the road feeling satisfied.

TIP

Where to find the best bagels – Upper West Siders are divided on the issue, splitting their loyalties between **H & H**, Broadway and 80th Street, and **Absolute**, Broadway, located between 107th and 108th streets.

Savann

414 Amsterdam Ave (bet. 79th and 80th sts) [B5]. Tel: 212-580-0202. Open: D Mon–Fri, Br and D Sat,Sun. **$$**

You'll probably be more impressed with the cozy, bistro atmosphere than anything you eat here, but at least this neighborhood favorite gets half the equation right. You'll be happiest if you keep your choices to grilled chicken breast and other simple fare, or one of the best weekend brunches around.

Terrace in the Sky

400 W. 119th St (bet. Morningside Dr. and Amsterdam Ave) [B1]. Tel: 212-666-9490. Open: L and D Tues–Fri, D only Sat. **$$$** *www.terraceinthesky.com*

New Yorkers tend to forget about this sky-high room at the northern, unfashionable edge of the city. But when they do wander in, they're impressed anew with elegant French classics of the foie gras and lobster-tail variety that are as sparkling as the city lights below.

Greek

Niko's Mediterranean Grill

2161 Broadway (at 76th St) [B5]. Tel: 212-873-7000. Open: L and D daily. **$$** *www.nikosgrill.com*

In cramped surroundings little fancier than a coffee shop, the only nods to decor are the colorful travelogues of the Greek isles that run on the big-screen TVs. "So what?" the devoted regulars seem to say. The authentic Greek appetizers, grilled fish, and delicious lamb dishes, chosen off an encyclopedic menu, more than compensate.

Symposium

544 W. 113th St (bet. Broadway and Amsterdam Ave) [B1]. Tel: 212-865-1011. Open: L and D daily. **$**

It's almost impossible to read the comic-book menu, but most of the customers have been coming to this secret hideaway in a brownstone basement for so long that they don't need to look. It's worth the effort, though, for the Greek salad, authentic appetizers, and excellent grilled meats and fish.

Indian

Indian Café
2791 Broadway (at 108th St) [A2]. Tel: 212-749-9200. Open: L and D daily. ***$***
Stumble into the neighborhood's favorite Indian spot and you'll probably be surprised by the quality of the tandooris and the selection of expertly baked breads. Plus, unlike many a dim Indian lair (bringing the black hole of Calcutta to mind), this colorfully painted room faces Broadway from a cheery, glassed-in terrace.

Italian

Celeste
502 Amsterdam Ave (bet. 84th and 85th sts) [B4]. Tel: 212-874-4559. Open: D daily, Br Sat, Sun. ***$***
Upper West Siders are always hungry for homey food in comfy surroundings, and judging by the eager crowds lining up on the sidewalk, this snug brick-walled room fits the bill. Thin-crusted pizzas and pasta with clams and other southern Italian classics are near perfect in their simplicity and are just rewards for the uncomfortably crowded seating and long waits.

Cesca
164 West 75th St (bet. Amsterdam and Columbus aves) [B6]. Tel: 212-787-6300. Open: D Tues–Sun. ***$$–$$$***
Rustic Italian has long been the rage in Manhattan, and this Tom Valenti outpost *(see Ouest, page 133)* overflows with Tuscan earthiness. Farmhouse furnishings and bold Tuscan colors set the stage for an encyclopedic range of *cuccina rustica* that includes antipasti (great Parmesan fritters), rich pasta, and no-nonsense meat dishes (from grilled chops to tripe stew). Panini and lighter fare are on offer at refectory-style tables by the bar.

Gennaro
665 Amsterdam Ave (bet. 92nd and 93rd sts) [B4]. Tel: 212-665-5348. Open: D daily. ***$–$$***
The huge antipasto platters, heavenly homemade gnocchi, succulent osso buco, and other delights from Gennaro Picone's kitchen more than justify the wait you're likely to have to get in here – in fact, they earn this little place kudos as one of Manhattan's best Italian restaurants. Cash only, no reservations.

Latin American

Calle Ocho
446 Columbus Ave (bet. 81st and 82nd sts) [B5]. Tel: 212 873-5025. Open: D Mon–Sat, Br and D Sun. ***$$***
The multicolored lights in the bar up front signal the scene that prevails in a cavernous dining room that is like a second home to the neighborhood's successful young professionals. Regulars dine well on grilled pork and other innovative version of Latin classics, washed down with what many claim are New York's best mojitos.

Flor de Mayo
2651 Broadway (bet. 100th and 101st sts) [B3]. Tel: 212-787-3388. Open: L and D daily. ***$***
New York's melting-pot image comes to life in this animated

Calle Ocho, masters of the mojito

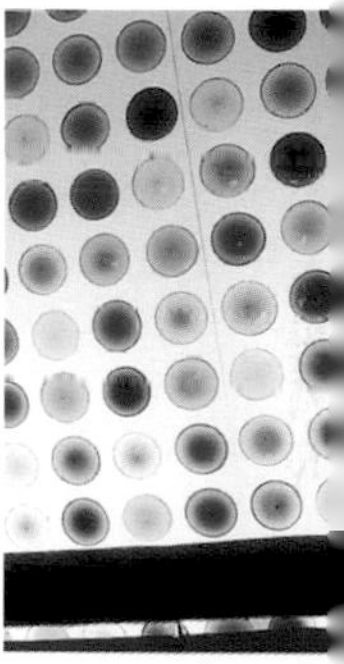

Luzia's, a corner of Portugal located on Amsterdam Avenue

room, where Chinese-Peruvian immigrants serve a fuss-free version of fusion cuisine. Pass on the mediocre Asian dishes, though, and try such Latin standbys as *secco de res*, a hearty beef stew.

Gabriela's

685 Amsterdam Ave (at 93rd St) [B3]. Tel: 212-961-0574. Open: L and D daily. **$**
www.gabrielas.com

Don't fall sway to the sublime margaritas until you've had a chance to enjoy the offerings from the kitchen, including such basics as an addictive herb-laced roast chicken. The setting is festive but far more grown up than that in many Manhattan Mexican eateries.

La Rosita

2809 Broadway (bet. 108th and 109th sts) [A2]. Tel: 212-663-7804. Open: B, L, and D daily. **$**

It's good to know that there are still comfy, no-nonsense but exotic places like this on the Upper West Side. Huge platters of *huevos rancheros* come out at breakfast, while chicken with rice and beans and other old-fashioned Latin fare provide a hearty lunch or dinner.

Noche Mexicana

852 Amsterdam Ave (bet. 101st and 102nd sts) [B3]. Tel: 212-662-6900. Open: B, L, and D daily. **$**

Neighborhood professionals share this tiny storefront space with Mexican lads who linger over their beers while listening to Latin tunes on the jukebox. The latter are rendered homesick by the hearty chalupas, homey pozole, and other simple and satisfying fare, served without fuss at crazily low prices.

Sante Fe

72 W. 69th St (bet. Columbus Ave and Central Park W.) [B6]. Tel: 212-724-0822. Open: L and D daily. **$$**

The years have not taken the simmer out of this old hot spot, just steps from Lincoln Center and a nice option for a pre- or post-performance meal. The mesquite-grilled meats, enchiladas, and other southwestern offerings are reliably good, and they are served in a series of elegant, desert-hued rooms. It's best to reserve for dinner.

Middle Eastern

Afghan Kebab House

2680 Broadway (at 102nd St) [B2]. Tel: 212-280-3500. Open: L and D daily. **$**

While there are several outlets of this authentic Afghan eatery in

Manhattan, this one seems especially well suited to its comfortably funky, somewhat studenty neighborhood not far from Columbia University. A nice assortment of vegetable dumplings and fish and meat kebabs are served in a cramped room charmingly bedecked with kilims.

Turkuaz
2637 Broadway (at 100th St) [B3]. Tel: 212-665-9541. Open: L and D daily. ***$–$$***
www.turkazrestaurant.com
Aside from the occasional kebab, Turkish food is relatively scarce in New York. Still, it's plentiful enough in this lavish, striped tent of an interior, where the spicy eggplant purees, grilled chops, and yes, kebabs, are memorable, as are the costumed waiters and belly dancers (on Fri and Sat evenings).

Portuguese

Luzia's
429 Amsterdam Ave (bet. 80th and 81st sts) [B5]. Tel: 212-595-2000. Open: L and D Tues–Fri, Br and D Mon–Sat, Br and D Sat, Sun. ***$–$$***
If the tiles and brickwork make you feel that you've found a little piece of Portugal on busy Amsterdam Avenue, you're quite right. You'll really be in a holiday mood when the exotic shrimp and pork dishes emerge from the kitchen and you've partaken of a few glasses of the house's vinho verde.

Seafood

Docks
2427 Broadway (bet. 89th and 90th sts) [B4]. Tel: 212-724-5588. Open: L and D daily. ***$$***
Noise levels in this tiled room can amplify into the danger zone and the wait staff tends to make it clear they'd rather be elsewhere. But you'll probably forgo at least some of your qualms when a superb selection of ocean-fresh oysters on the half shell and simply prepared fish dishes arrive on the table. Best to reserve for dinner.

Did you know?
Much of the film *West Side Story* was shot on blocks off Broadway between 62nd and 66th streets – they were about to be demolished for the construction of Lincoln Center.

Cafes and Bars

Lounge lizards, of whom there are many on the Upper West Side, have their pick of a range of watering holes. The less discriminating among them go directly to a stretch of noisy bars on Amsterdam Avenue between 79th and 86th streets; here, at dark hidey holes such as the **Raccoon Lodge** *(480 Amsterdam Ave, tel: 212-874-9984)*, they join a bunch of inebriated youngsters in rooms where the floors are wet with what you can only pray is spilled beer.

On the other side of the spectrum are retro cocktail lounges where Mr And Ms Young Stockbroker sip Cosmos and talk about their portfolios; the best of these is the lounge at **Calle Ocho** *(see page 137)*, bathed in murky green light, which gives it the impression of an underground grotto.

Then there's the old guard – the mellow, friendly lairs filled with neighborhood regulars, students, and older folks. To join them, check out **Dublin House** *(225 W. 79th St, tel: 212-874-9528)* or **Cannon's** *(2794 Broadway, tel: 212-678-9738)*. If you want a caffeine fix in surroundings a little more exotic than the ubiquitous Starbuck's, make your way to Gothic-looking **Edgar's Café** *(255 W. 84th St, tel: 212-496-6126)*, named for the writer Edgar Allan Poe, who lived on the block, or **Café Lalo** *(201 W. 82nd St, tel: 212-496-6093)*, where the huge selection of cakes seems to keep the crowds satisfied. Another popular place to assuage carb cravings is the **Silver Moon Bakery** *(2740 Broadway, tel: 212-866-4717)*, whose freshly baked goodies fly off the shelves.

HOT COFFEE
PIZZA
FRENCH FRIES ° KNISHES
Grill
HOUSE
Shish Kebabs
Hot Sausage
Cold Beer
Cold Soda
FRIED CHICKEN
°ICE CREAM
°COTTON CAN
°POP CORN
°KNISHES
COTTON CANDY · ICE CREAM · GRILL HOUS
PRETZEL
FRYED CHICKEN
WITH F.F.
CORN DOGS
ICE COLD SODA
HAMBURGER
FRYED SHRIMP
LOLLYPOP
HOT COFFEE
PIZZA
SHRIMP
FRENCH FRIES
SODA
BEER

BROOKLYN

Out of all four 'outer' boroughs, Brooklyn is the most happening. So much so that different parts of it keep being twinned with bits of Manhattan, New York's one and only 'inner' borough. Williamsburg, with its proliferation of galleries, performance spaces, edgy bars, and cafes, is the new Lower East Side, while Park Slope, which has a preponderance of laid-back, child-friendly cafes and restaurants, is the new Upper West Side. And the incredibly high-concentration of ambitious new restaurants on Smith Street has made it the new SoHo. Still, we haven't scratched the surface of Brooklyn's more than two-dozen districts. DUMBO (for Down Under Manhattan Bridge Overpass) is becoming the 'new, new Lower East Side,' or the 'new Williamsburg.' Newly trendy districts aside, there are also many old, unreconstructed neighborhoods, such as Redhook with its great old Irish bars including Sonny's, where there are regular Sunday readings. Fort Greene has been home to the Brooklyn Academy of Music since 1908, but only in the past several years have the culture vultures stayed around to enjoy the long-established African-American neighborhood and its newer lounges and restaurants, such as the Garden Café, Butta Cup Lounge, or Loulou. Coney Island is great for an old-fashioned pizza at DiFaros or a hotdog and ice cream from the stalls along the boardwalk. A little farther along is Brighton Beach, where a thriving Russian community comes to hang out in Gambrinus, National, Rasputin, and Gina, most of which have weekend entertainment and dancing, as well as good Russian food and lakes of vodka.

Brooklyn Heights, Carroll Gardens, and Boerum Hill

Banania Café

241 Smith St, near Butler St, Carrol Gardens. Tel: 718-237-9100. Open: D daily. **$$**

Banania is the buzzing bistro that pioneered Smith Street, Brooklyn's restaurant row, as a dining location in 1999. The name comes from a French brand of milkshake, and while the menu's broadly French, influences from the Americas, Asia, and the Middle East have been shaken in too. Those used to Manhattan prices will be pleasantly surprised at how well you can eat for around $25 and impressed by the very reasonable wine list.

The Grocery

288 Smith St (bet. Sackett and Union sts). Tel: 718-596-3335. Open: D Mon–Sat. **$$$**

In summer, you can sit in the Grocery's gracious garden. Otherwise, the fresh sage-green rooms are a touch of spring and a serene backdrop to American bistro food of the highest quality. Prices are slightly higher than at most of its neighbors, but the chowders, salads, and entrées are all imaginative and good. Carrot sorbet may sound a little too imaginative, but is actually delicate, sweet, and delicious.

Opposite: Seaside snacks at Coney Island. Below: Banania pancakes

Patois

255 Smith St (bet. DeGraw and Douglass sts). Tel: 718-855-1535. Open: D Tues–Sat, Br and D Sun. **$**

Satisfyingly traditional French bistro fare – escargots, steak-frites, etc. – in a funky, fashionable setting that makes you want to speak this patois's language. It's consistently voted one of the best neighborhood restaurants in New York, and the weekend lines outside (there's a no-reservations policy) bear testimony to its popularity.

The River Café

1 Water St (at Old Fulton St). Tel: 718-522-5200. Open: L and D Mon–Sat, Br and D Sun. **$$$$** *www.therivercafe.com*

You often have to weave through wedding crowds assembled outside The River Café, and countless questions have been popped at this ritzy romantic restaurant with truly breathtaking views across to Manhattan. The mostly classic American menu is good (although the Brooklyn Bridge rendered in chocolate is perhaps a lapse in taste); the service from tuxedoed waiters rather formal; and the wine list highly priced. But, really, with that great view to look at, everything else becomes water under the bridge.

Robin des Bois

195 Smith St (bet. Baltic and Warren sts). Tel: 718-596-1609. Open: L and D Tues–Sun, L only Mon. **$** *www.sherwoodcafe.com*

An original red Michelin man welcomes you in to a kitsch jumble of 1950s' tables, chairs, memorabilia, and artifacts. You may feel you've walked into a junk shop, and you're not entirely wrong – by day, Robin des Bois doubles as a gallery and antiques store. The best part of this rustic French cafe is the patio out back; next best are the very reasonable prices.

Sur

232 Smith St (bet. Butler and Douglass sts). Tel: 718-875-1716. Open: D Mon–Fri, L and D Sat, Sun. **$$**

Sur is a real head-turner. Even if you're heading somewhere else you can't help looking in at the sophisticated room with exposed beams, brick walls, and glass doors, while grinning at huge plates of deliciously grilled meat. Empanadas and salads to start are good, but keep room for the special – a mixed grill that includes steak, short ribs, half a chicken, and various sausages.

Zaytoons

283 Smith St (at Sackett St). Tel: 718-875-1880. Open: L and D daily. **$**

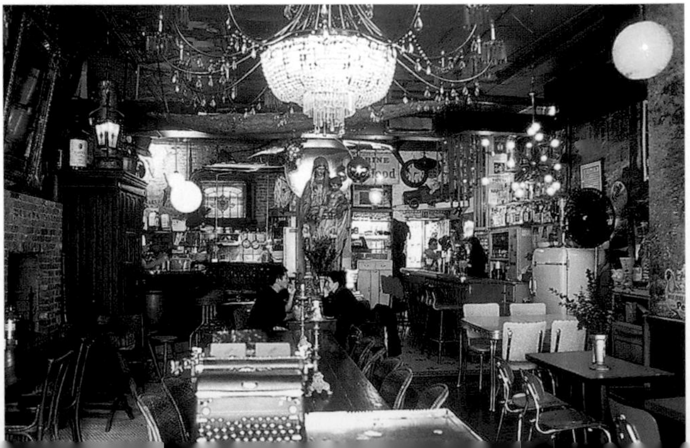

Robin des Bois: antiques store, gallery, and cafe in one

A totally unprepossessing, unadorned restaurant, where no attempt at design or decoration have been made. But that's fine, because once the fluffy pitta bread comes and the rest of the tangy, meticulously prepared food follows it, you won't have eyes for anything else. And when the check arrives, you'll be delighted they didn't pass the cost of swish decor on. Basbousa, a semolina caked with honey and almonds, is a pleasing lighter alternative to the similarly delicious baklava.

Park Slope

Al di La

248 Fifth Ave (at Carroll St). Tel: 718-783-4565. Open: D Wed–Mon. $$

Plan ahead, as the combined excellence, compact size, and no-reservations policy of Al di La means a possible long wait. The northern Italian specials change almost daily and all live up to their name, but the pasta, such as large diaphanous ravioli stuffed with beets, are especially special.

Blue Ribbon Brooklyn

280 Fifth Ave (bet. Garfield Pl. and First St). Tel: 718-840-0404. Open: D Mon–Sat (until 2am Mon–Thur, until 4am Fri, Sat), Br and D Sun (until midnight). $$

Park Slope knew it had definitely arrived as a serious foodie location once the highly regarded Blue Ribbon chainlet turned its attention here. Blue Ribbon Brooklyn tries to be all things to all men – saloon, oyster bar, deli, bistro, and somewhere you feel equally at home with just a dish of olives as you would doing some serious dining – and succeeds. Blue Ribbon Sushi (278 Fifth Ave.) is just next door.

Brooklyn trattoria, Al di Là

Bistro St. Mark's

76 St. Mark's Ave (bet. Flatbush and Sixth aves). Tel: 718-857-8600. Open: L and D daily. $$

Fifth Avenue is to Park Slope what Smith Street is to Cobble Hill: foodie central. And Bistro St. Mark's, although hidden away nearer to Sixth Avenue, is the area's star. It's run by two chefs who've worked with David Bouley. Seafood, including a remarkable scallop carpaccio, is particularly recommended. Monday night's $25 tasting menu is a delight and a bargain to boot.

Coco Roco

392 Fifth Ave (bet. Sixth and Seventh sts). Tel: 718-965-3376. Open: L and D daily. $

A bowl of roasted corn kernels is brought while you chew over the menu. Take your time, the traditional Peruvian snack is very moreish and there's a lot to choose from. Zingy, fresh ceviche, roast chicken, steak stir-fry, grilled snapper, and tropical-fruit ice creams are among the favorites that won Coco Roco such a large following.

Convivium Osteria

68 Fifth Ave (bet. Bergen St and St. Mark's Pl.). Tel: 718-857-1833. Open: D daily. $$

There's nothing like a rusty old farm implement for giving off olde-worlde charm; add communal tables, candlelight, and soft

Did you know

A *knish* is a potato and onion dumpling that's long been a staple of the Eastern European kosher table and Mrs Stahl's Knishes (10001 Brighton Beach Ave, Coney Island) is acknowledged as among the world's best, and most authentic, purveyors.

Right and opposite: Lovingly restored Miss Williamsburg Diner

Spanish music and it gets pretty romantic. The menu, drawn from the rustic reaches of Italy, Spain, and Portugal, starts with tapas-style appetizers and follows with great grilled fish, a steak for two, seafood couscous, and pasta.

Cucina

256 Fifth Ave (bet. Carroll St and Garfield Pl.). Tel: 718-230 0711. Open: D Tues–Sun. **$$**
www.cucinarestaurant.com

Cucina is an elegant, white-table-clothed Italian restaurant, whose pasta frutta di mare has justifiably won a fervent following. The chef also has a winning touch with vegetables, especially artichokes.

Locanda Vini I Olii

129 Gates Ave (at Cambridge Pl.). Tel: 718-622-9202. Open: D Tues–Sun. **$$**
www.locandaviniiiolii.com

Set in a lovingly restored 130-year-old pharmacy complete with wooden apothecary drawers and rolling library ladders, this Italian trattoria is a tonic. Fresh ingredients and loving preparation raise the fairly standard list of crostini, pastas, and *primi piatti* way above what you'd expect at these prices. Try to keep room for the traditional baked ricotta cheesecake flavored with rosewater.

Williamsburg

Bean

172 North 8th St (at Bedford Ave). Tel: 718-387-8222. Open: D daily. **$**

There's a laid-back southwestern vibe at this trendy Billy'burg haunt where the home-made blueberry lemonade is very popular and not just for those who forgot (or didn't realise they had to) bring their own beer. Other favorites are the plates of corn chips smothered in melted cheese, the juicy mussels in spicy garlic and tomato broth, and the nachos with pinto beans and guacamole sauce.

Chickenbone Café

177 South 4th St (bet. Driggs and Roebling sts). Tel: 718-302 2663. Open: D Tues–Sun. **$**

The founder chef dubbed Chickenbone's cuisine as: 'Global Brooklyn.' It sounds facetious but isn't. You can have smoked fish prepared locally by Hasidim; kielbasa and potato-dill bread from Sikorski's, a long-established Brooklyn/Polish supplier; mozzarella, handmade by an 84-year-old neighborhood Italian woman; and salads grown on the North Fork of Long Island. Soups and vegetables change daily and reflect a blend of Asian, Italian, and French influences.

Diner

85 Broadway (at Berry St). Tel: 718-486-3077. Open: L and D daily. **$$**

In a lovingly restored but rundown-looking 1927 dining car, a hip, crowd of musicians, actors, pho-

Did you know?

The Riegelman Boardwalk which runs through Coney Island and Brighton Beach was the inspiration for the Drifters' song *Under the Boardwalk*. It's also home to the original Nathan's and scene of their annual July 4 hot-dog eating contest.

tographers, designers, models, etc., gather for breakfast, lunch, brunch, cocktails, and dinner – in fact, it's impossible to pick a time of day when people aren't gathered here for something. The plain-sounding menu of soup, burger, roast chicken, and salads, belies a talented and generous chef behind the scenes.

Miss Williamsburg Diner

206 Kent Ave (bet. Metropolitan Ave and North Third St). Tel: 718-963-0802. Open: D Tues–Sun. **$$**

Miss W. is a lovingly restored old diner that was once a greasy spoon. At last renovation, it was turned into a fine Italian restaurant with bruschetta and branzino where there were once only hash and fries. The seafood and pasta are fabulous, desserts are less reliable except the black-chocolate soufflé, which can cause serious cravings. In warmer months, you can sit outside in the pretty garden (formerly a truck-weighing station). Cash only.

Oznot's Dish

79 Berry St (at North Ninth St) Tel: 718-599-6596. Open: L and D daily. **$**

Oznot has a very wide dish indeed, encompassing foods from the stretch between Persia and Morocco and back to the Caucasus. The decor is equally wide-reaching, incorporating mosaics, mismatched furniture, and jumbled artworks. Stylistically, the resulting fusion stops just short of confusion. And sometimes the food doesn't quite live up to the full scope promised. But Oznot has plenty of allure nonetheless.

Peter Luger

178 Broadway (bet. Bedford and Driggs aves). Tel: 718-387-7400. Open: L and D daily. **$$$$** *www.peterluger.com*

Brooklyn's most famous restaurant, and arguably New York's best-loved steakhouse, Peter Luger opened as a German beer hall in 1887. It's barely changed since, and of late its owners have been accused of resting on their laurels. Peter Luger doesn't go out of its way to please, with bare wooden tables, gruff wisecracking waiters, an uncompromising menu (they only have one cut of steak – the porterhouse), but still people come back again and again.

Relish

225 Wythe Ave (at North Third St). Tel: 718-963-4546. Open: L and D daily. **$$** *www.relish.com*

Relish is set in a gleaming, chrome-and-leather, railcar-style diner with comfy booths and a mellow, back-room annex. The menu offers a 'classic-with-a-twist' take on traditional American food, resulting in roast chicken with pecan waffles, and hanger steak with sun-dried tomato sauce. The brunch menu's cheddar grits

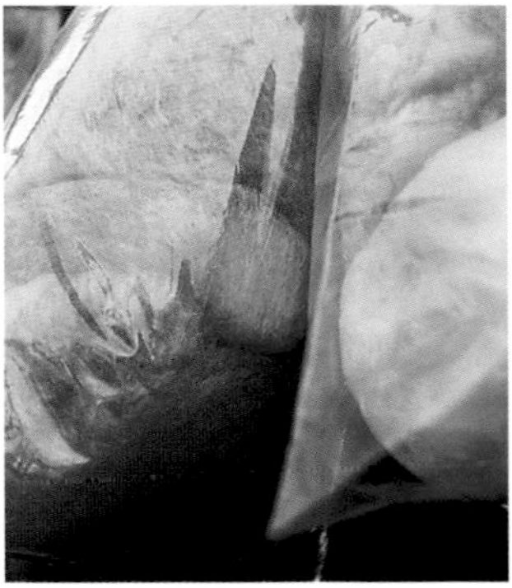

and ham is a lovely high-class take on an old standard.

SEA Thai Restaurant and Bar

114 North Sixth St (at Berry St) Tel: 718-384 8850. Open: L and D Tues–Sun. $

The 75,000 sq-foot (7,000 sq-meter) former industrial premises keeps winning awards for its stunning Asian-modern design. And no wonder: there's a Buddha statue floating above a reflecting pool, a 1970s-style lounge with bubble chairs, a state of the art sound system, and a rose-lit circular bar with swings. It may sound very 'bells and whistles,' but is actually very beautiful and serene. The food is exquisite, traditional Thai and very cheap.

Coney Island

Nathan's

1310 Surf Ave. Tel: 718-946-2202. Open: B, L, and D daily. $ www.nathansfamous.com

Eating a Nathan's hot dog is a very New York experience (they're served from most of the city's hot-dog stands). However, they taste better here, in the original Nathan's restaurant, with a breath of sea air added and the sounds of the nearby amusement park as garnish. On July 4 this is the stage for the Hot-Dog Eating contest – one of the nation's first eating competitions.

Totonno Pizza

1524 Neptune Ave. Tel 718-372 8606. Open: noon–8.30pm. Closed Mon–Tues. $

This very traditional pizzeria (one of the first in New York City to have a coal-fired oven) has untraditional hours (it closes early) and a very fine thin-crusted pie. Totonno's opened in 1924, when working-class Italians would head to Coney Island for weekend fun, and is still feeding up the seaside visitors before they take a stroll on the boardwalk.

Harlem

For the past five years, New York's magazines and newspapers have been running articles on the 'new' Harlem. And judging by the proliferating numbers of dumpsters outside soon-to-be-gentrified townhouses, and the soaring prices of once unsaleable brownstones above 110th Street, something of a revival is going on. In 2000, Bill Clinton rented office space on 125th Street, and Michael Jordan opened the area's first multiplex cinema. Corporations such as Gap and Starbuck's followed suit, finally starting to pay attention to the markets north of Central Park and opening debut branches in Harlem. All of which has given a fillip to the local economy. Slowly, local entrepreneurs are opening high-wattage restaurants and bars more familiar to a Downtown location. So, things are definitely changing. However, don't expect to emerge from the subway at 125th and see anything very different than you would have done 10 years ago. There's still a lot of poverty here, and Harlem still has a run-down, but not threatening or dangerous, air about it. It may be wise to travel with a couple of mini-cab numbers in your pocket, as taxis are seldom spotted this far north. Some of the best new places are casual cafes and lunch spots such as Native *(161 Malcolm X Blvd)*, Home Sweet Harlem *(270 West 135th St)*, and Settepani *(196 Malcolm X Blvd)*, which also has great buns, cookies, and sandwiches to take away. And despite all the bright new venues in Harlem, a major reason for visiting is the lovely old Lenox Lounge *(288 Malcolm X Blvd)*, where Billie (Holiday), Miles (Davis) and Sarah (Vaughan) once spent time; here, you can enjoy top-notch jazz in recently renovated Art-Deco surroundings.

TIP

Some of the avenues in Harlem have been renamed for local figureheads. When navigating above 110th, it helps to know which avenues are which: Frederick Douglass Boulevard is 8th; Adam Clayton Powell Jr Boulevard is 7th, and Malcolm X Boulevard (aka Lenox Avenue) is 6th Avenue.

Amy Ruth's

113 West 116th St (bet. Lenox and Seventh aves).
Tel: 212-280-8779.
Open: L and D daily. $
www.amyruthsrestaurant.com

The owner was driver to local politician, the Reverend Al Sharpton (memorably portrayed in Tom Wolfe's *Bonfire of the Vanities*) for eight years, before opening Amy Ruth's. Partly

The ever-popular Amy Ruth's

because of that, the restaurant attracts political, sporting, and entertainment luminaries. However, the big attraction is mostly down to the fantastic southern food available here – from crispy yet fluffy waffles to tender short ribs, smoked ham hocks, and delicious pineapple-coconut cake.

Bayou

308 Lenox Ave (bet. 125th and 126th sts). Tel: 212-426-3800. Open: L and D Mon–Fri, D only Sat, Br and D Sun. **$$**

Bayou (fairly hard to find, as it's above pizzeria *A Slice of Harlem*) is a classy bistro with bare brick walls and spacious window seats. It is a deliciously big slice of New Orleans in New York. Creole classics – crawfish etouffee, turtle soup, fried oysters, and a rich, smoky jambalaya – would do anyone from the Big Easy proud. It's also apparently good enough for Bill Clinton, whose office parties are catered to from here.

Charles's Southern-Style Kitchen

2839 Frederick Douglass Blvd (bet. 151st and 152nd sts). Tel: 212-926-4313. Open: L and D Tues–Sun until 8pm. **$**

Charles really puts the soul into southern food. The fried chicken is juicy, the salmon cakes floaty, the pork ribs sweet, and even the sides – black-eyed peas, collard greens, and molasses-sweetened yams – provoke soulful feelings. The only drawback is Charles's gets so crowded, you're politely asked not to take more than 30 minutes over your meal at peak times.

El Rincón Boricua

158 East 119th St (bet. Third and Lexington aves). Tel: 212-534-9400. Open: L daily. **$**

If for any reason pork is not in your diet, steer clear of El Rincón, as this tiny lunch counter is a hive of activity all centered around hacking, chopping, and snipping various bits of tender barbecued pig and dishing it up with rice, beans, and plaintains. This is Puerto-Rican home cooking at its most succulent and powerfully flavored, and is likely to turn you temporarily into a, yes, sorry, pig.

La Marmite

2264 Frederick Douglass Blvd (bet. 121st and 122nd sts). Tel: 212-666-0653. Open: daily. **$**

This is a very basic restaurant with formica tables and paper napkins, and you could be the only non-Senegalese party not joining in the cross-table chatter, but it would be a shame to let that deter you. The specialty is *dibi* – a pile of sizzling little lamb chops in onion sauce, and everything's around the $10 mark.

Miss Maude's Spoonbread Too

547 Lenox Ave (bet. 137th and 138th sts). Tel: 212-690-3100. Open: L and D daily. **$**
www.spoonbreadinc.com

Miss Maude's is one of Harlem's most inviting restaurants – the cheerful check cloths, roses in jam jars, and family photographs lining the walls could almost have you thinking Miss Maude was one of your relatives too. Most diners come for the southern fried chicken, which has a crisp oniony crust, but the pork chops smothered in peppery gravy, cornmeal fried shrimp, and hot seafood gumbo are hard to pass by.

Mo-Bay Uptown

17 West 125th St (bet. Fifth and Lenox aves). Tel: 212-876-9300. Open: L and D daily. **$$**
www.mobayrestaurant.com

A Caribbean soul restaurant with a delightful dining room through the fringed curtain, a welcoming

TIP

Perched high above the Hudson River in Upper Manhattan, **The Cloisters Museum** *(Fort Tryon Park, tel: 212-923-3700, www.metmuseum.org)* isn't just for culture, it also has a great restaurant on its grounds. The **New Leaf Café** is run by Bette Midler's New York Restoration Project and profits go to the upkeep of Fort Tryon Park, so you can feel you are not just selfishly satisfying yourself with the good, fresh food in beautiful surroundings.

thatched bar out front, and a bakery next door. Whatever you eat – BBQ, jerk, fried fish, try to keep room for the giddying rummy-rum cake. At time of going to press Mo-Bay had not been granted a liquor license (call ahead to check current situation), but you can bring your own bottle. However, the fumes off this potent dessert more than make up for it.

Revival

2367 Frederick Douglass Blvd (at 127th St). Tel: 212-222-8338. Open: L and D daily. ***$$***
www.harlemrevival.com
This upscale diner is as smooth as its R&B soundtrack: votive candles give soft lighting, high-backed booths offer seductive seating, and the staff are very friendly. The food doesn't always live up to the imaginative promise of the fusion menu, but the portions are huge, prices are low, and the apple pie is absolutely delicious. While the name speaks hopefully of Harlem's renaissance, the somewhat desolate streets outside belie it.

Sugar Hill Bistro

458 West 145th St (bet. Convent and Amsterdam aves). Tel: 212-491-5505. Open: D daily. ***$$***
www.sugarhillbistro.com
This beautifully restored four-story brownstone has a ground-floor bar with live jazz (Thursday to Saturday nights) and displays of work by African-American artists. The restaurant on the second floor is elegantly situated and does blessedly light-on-the-fat, defter-than-usual southern food. Saturday's R&B brunch and the Sunday gospel brunch are big crowd-pullers.

Sylvia's Soul Food Restaurant

328 Malcolm X Blvd (bet. 126th and 127th sts). Tel: 212-996-0660. Open: L and D daily. ***$$***
www.sylviasrestaurant.com
In 1962 Sylvia's was a lunch counter with 35 seats; nowadays, it can seat 450, and tour buses arrive almost hourly – it's a must for politicians courting the Harlem vote. Miss Sylvia Woods still labors over the stove, but the southern cooking has inevitably lost that personal touch. The cakes and banana pudding however are still enough to make a southerner weep for home.

El Rincón Boricua, Puerto-Rican home cooking at its most succulent

QUEENS

Queens is the largest of NYC's five boroughs and has many vibrant immigrant neighborhoods where you can eat authentically and very cheaply. Flushing has the city's second biggest Chinatown and a burgeoning Little Korea, where you can shop for exotic snacks in massive Asian supermarkets or dip into Dumpling House with its astonishing 100+ choice of dumplings. Sunnyside and Woodside are home to older Italian and Irish communities. Astoria is almost exclusively Greek and is a good location for the kebab-obsessed who shouldn't miss Kabab Café or Uncle George's Greek Tavern. Jackson Heights is home to a large Indian community, and you can go for fabulous, extra-hot and spicy curries (to American tastes) at the Delhi Palace and great samosas, bhajis, and Naan bread at Jackson Diner. There's a lot to explore in Queens, but a good first stop is Long Island City, where you can eat your way around the world in one small district. The population is around 11,000 and the area is a melting pot of Greeks, Irish, Italians, Indians, Thai, Latinos, and Eastern Europeans. In addition, the temporary residence of the Museum of Modern Art (while its Midtown Manhattan premises are being revamped from 2001–4) has brought in busloads of visitors and given the whole area something of a facelift.

TIP

Discover the only pit barbecue restaurant in New York at **Pearson's Texas Barbecue** *(71-04 35th Ave, Jackson Heights)*, where the pork ribs, the sausages, the chicken, and the steak all get turned a glorious chestnut brown by the smoke.

Bella Via

47/46 Vernon Blvd (at Tenth Ave). Tel: 718-361-7510. Open: L and D Mon–Sat, D only Sun. **$$**

Vernon Boulevard is trying to market itself as New York's Left Bank, which may seem far-fetched, given that it isn't exactly the 'lovely way' its name might give you to believe. However, with the Brasilian Coffee Shop buzzing all-day long, and French, Mexican, and American bistros opening up all around, this stretch is reminiscent of Williamsburg *(see page 144)* five years ago. A wood-burning oven and the delicious crispy-based pizzas coming out of it are the centerpiece of Bella Via.

Cornel's Garden Restaurant

46-04 Skillman Ave (at 46th St). Tel: 718-786-7894. Open: L and D daily. **$$**

This is not a garden restaurant in that it doesn't have a garden; it does, however, have indoor trellises bedecked with plastic roses. And it is a strong magnet for New York's Romanians who flock here for *mamaliga-brinza-smintina* – a delicious mouthful of warm polenta covered with Romanian ewe's

Bella Via's wood-burning oven turns out delicious crispy-based pizzas

cheese and sour cream – plus *mititei* (sausages), donuts smothered in sour cream and strawberry preserves, and vast quantities of Romanian wine.

Kum Gang San

138-28 Northern Blvd, Flushing. Tel: 718-461-0909. Open: daily, 24 hours. $

The specialty here is Korean barbeque – the pre-marinated meats are brought to the table so that you can cook them to your own liking and bathe in their smoky aromas before eating them.

Ping's Seafood

83-02 Queens Blvd, Elmhurst. Tel: 718-396-1238. Open: 8am–2am daily. $

The outer boroughs outpost of the more famous Ping's Seafood on Mott Street in Manhattan's Chinatown is actually the original. It's a quiet haven where you can get fresh fish and seafood with a delectably light touch. People who normally run screaming from gooey sweet-and-sour dishes should be forced to try them here where the seasoning is delicate and most unlike the more familiar, heavy, and overly sweet fare.

Telly's Taverna

28-13 23rd Ave, Astoria. Tel: 718-728-9056. Open: Mon–Sat 4pm–midnight, Sun noon–midnight. $$

Telly's is a very popular spot for Astoria's Greek community and for non-Greeks from all over the city who flock in to enjoy good plain cooking. There are excellent fresh gilled meats and fish sprinkled with little more than a few drops of olive oil and a few grains of sea salt to surprisingly delicious effect.

Tournesol

50-12 Vernon Blvd (at 50th Ave). Tel: 718-472-4355. Open: L and D Mon–Sat. $$

This French bistro with its cheery yellow walls is a little splash of sunshine near the drab, gray mouth of the Queens-Midtown tunnel. The chefs at Tournesol make all their own terrines and pâtés; the foie gras and rabbit terrines would be remarkable eaten anywhere but seem more so tucked away here, at these prices. The plats du jours, such as cassoulet and coq au vin, are reliably good, and the prices are remarkably kind.

La Vuelta Bistro Latino

10-43 44th Drive at 11th St. Tel: 718-361-1858. Open: L and D Mon–Fri, D only Sat. $

You always get such a cheery ¡Hola! at La Vuelta that once you've closed the door and entered the Cubano vibe you could almost be in old Havana – especially if it's summer, and you can nurse a mojito in the pretty patio outback. The menu is pan-Latin, and while the Mexican dishes are fine, the highlights are the Cuban specials such as pulled pork and *arroz con camarones* (saffron rice with grilled shrimp).

Water's Edge

East River at 44th Drive. Tel: 718-482-0033. Open: L and D Mon–Fri, D only Sat. $$$ www.watersedgenyc.com

If approached from the road, this seafood restaurant looks more like "Industrial Estate's Edge," so the most canny diners get the ferry over from 34th Street. Approached this way, Water's Edge is a romantic riverside restaurant with breathtaking views of the Chrysler Building and an intriguing roster of seafood and fish specials. The white-jacketed waiters give it a formal look, but it is actually a very relaxed and comfortable place from which to watch the lights of Manhattan twinkling.

TIP

Mostly when restaurants have adjectives in their names it is at best an exaggeration, but believe in **Spicy and Tasty** *(133-43 Roosevelt Ave, Flushing)*. The Sichuan specialties are very spicy and they're not fibbing about the tasty either, especially when it comes to the delicate tea-smoked duck.

The Bronx

Most visitors to NYC only venture to the Bronx for the airports, or maybe a trip to the Yankee Stadium, but there are other compelling attractions here, not least the Bronx Zoo. There's also Riverdale Park, a preserved forest where you can hike and bike all day, getting a feel for what New York was like before it was inhabited – plus the odd glimpse of the mighty Hudson. The Bronx, however, has a reputation as a wilderness of a more urban kind, and you are not advised to wander about, particularly in the South Bronx, after dark. In Belmont, there is a thriving Little Italy satellite town, where you'll find Arthur Avenue, a street full of stores bursting with every delicacy you'd find in a Roman supermarket. At the southernmost tip of the Bronx is Hunts Point, where artists are starting to move for cheap rents and huge, formerly industrial spaces; this is also home to Terminal Market, the largest wholesale food market in the Americas. At the northernmost point is City Island, once a prosperous shipbuilding center, now a slice of the seaside within city limits.

Did you know

The Bronx has a large Jamaican community and they all like to go to **Vernon's New Jerk House** *(987 233rd St, Eastchester)* for rice and peas or curried goat. And, of course, the fantastic jerk pork and chicken in which you can discern not just heat but all the flavors – ginger, allspice, thyme, soy and Scotch bonnet peppers.

Dominick's

2335 Arthur Ave (at 187th St). Tel: 718-733-2807. Open: L and D daily. ***$$***

Fans of Dominick's, and they are legion, claim that this is the real Little Italy. There's no menu, so listen up, your waiter will tell you what there is today. You sit at long benches, and the atmosphere is relaxed and convivial. There's no check either – they just take a look at you and pronounce a figure, so don't dress too fancy.

Jimmy's Bronx Café

281 West Fordham Rd (bet. Cedar Ave and Major Deegan Expressway). Tel: 718-329 2000. Open: D daily. ***$$***

When Fidel Castro was in town for the UN anniversary celebrations, the only place he visited was Jimmy's, now the center of Hispanic life in the Bronx. It's a fabulous, sizzling salsa supper club where baseball fans can spot some of the Yankee players on a good night. Dine early if you're not interested in entering the salsa frenzy; the Caribbean seafood (like the cilantro-sautéed shrimp) and yucca fries are yummy.

Johnny's Reef Restaurant

2 City Island Ave. Tel: 718-885-2086. Open: L and D Wed–Sun, closed Dec–Feb. ***$$***

City Island's waterfront has more seafood restaurants than you can shake a stick at; most, sadly, are mediocre and/or overpriced. This one, though, is the real deal, where you can get a good, old-fashioned Long Island 'fish fry' (deep-fried battered fish) in fabulous 1950s' surroundings with incredible views. As you make your way down the cafeteria line, make sure you get plenty of the fantastic home-made cocktail sauce to dip your fries into.

Roberto's

632 Crescent Ave (at 186th St and Belmont Ave). Tel: 718-733-9503. Open: L and D Tues–Sun. ***$*** *www.robertorestaurant.com*

Two blocks over from Arthur Avenue, this quiet Belmont restaurant is a true slice of Italian life. Roberto will glide out of the kitchen in his whites to greet you, and you may even get to meet his floury-handed Mama if she takes a break from her daily round of making the pasta.

Staten Island

Mention dining on Staten Island to the average New Yorker and you'll provoke a laugh as big as if you'd said 'English food' or 'Canadian cricket.' They know there's a free ferry going over to Staten Island for residents returning home, and for tourists to get an eyeful of the Manhattan harbor views, but the idea of actually getting off and dallying awhile on Staten Island would be a big old joke to most Manhattaners, Brooklynites, et al. Staten Island is a series of quiet residential communities, and there are obviously restaurants catering to them. Most are chain restaurants and moderate family places, but some compete with what's on offer across the water for a fraction of the price.

Aesop's Tables

1233 Bay St (at Maryland Ave). Tel: 718-720-2005. Open: D only Tues–Sat. ***$$***

The focus is on fresh seasonal food – even the ketchup is home-made – and contemporary American cooking in this warm, country-style restaurant. The garden, open to diners in the summer, is a delight and one of the best places to eat brunch-time Swedish pancakes imaginable.

Killmeyer's Old Bavaria Inn

4254 Arthur Kill Rd. Tel: 718-984-1202. Open: L and D daily. ***$***

Killmeyer's is in an 18th century building set in a nature reserve, and it's a scene so unchanged by passing years that you almost expect to see people arrive by horse-drawn carriage. The time-machine feeling is compounded by the Lederhosen-clad barmen and cobblestone Biergarten. The food comprises enormous portions of bratwurst, veal or roast pork with dumplings, potato pancakes, and sauerkraut on the side. Strudels and liquor ice creams are suitably rich and starchy to finish.

Lento's

289 New Dorp Lane (bet. Clawson and Edison sts). Tel: 718-980-7725. Open: L and D daily. ***$$***

This is the Staten Island outpost of an Italian mini-chain that started with the original Lento's *(7003 Third Ave at Ovington Ave)* in Bay Ridge, Brooklyn, in 1933. The southern Italian cooking – most notably a subtle, spicy marinara sauce, home-made pasta, and the crisp-crust pizzas – have not suffered at all from their translation into new surroundings.

For great Manhattan harbor views, take a ride on the Staten Island ferry

Directory

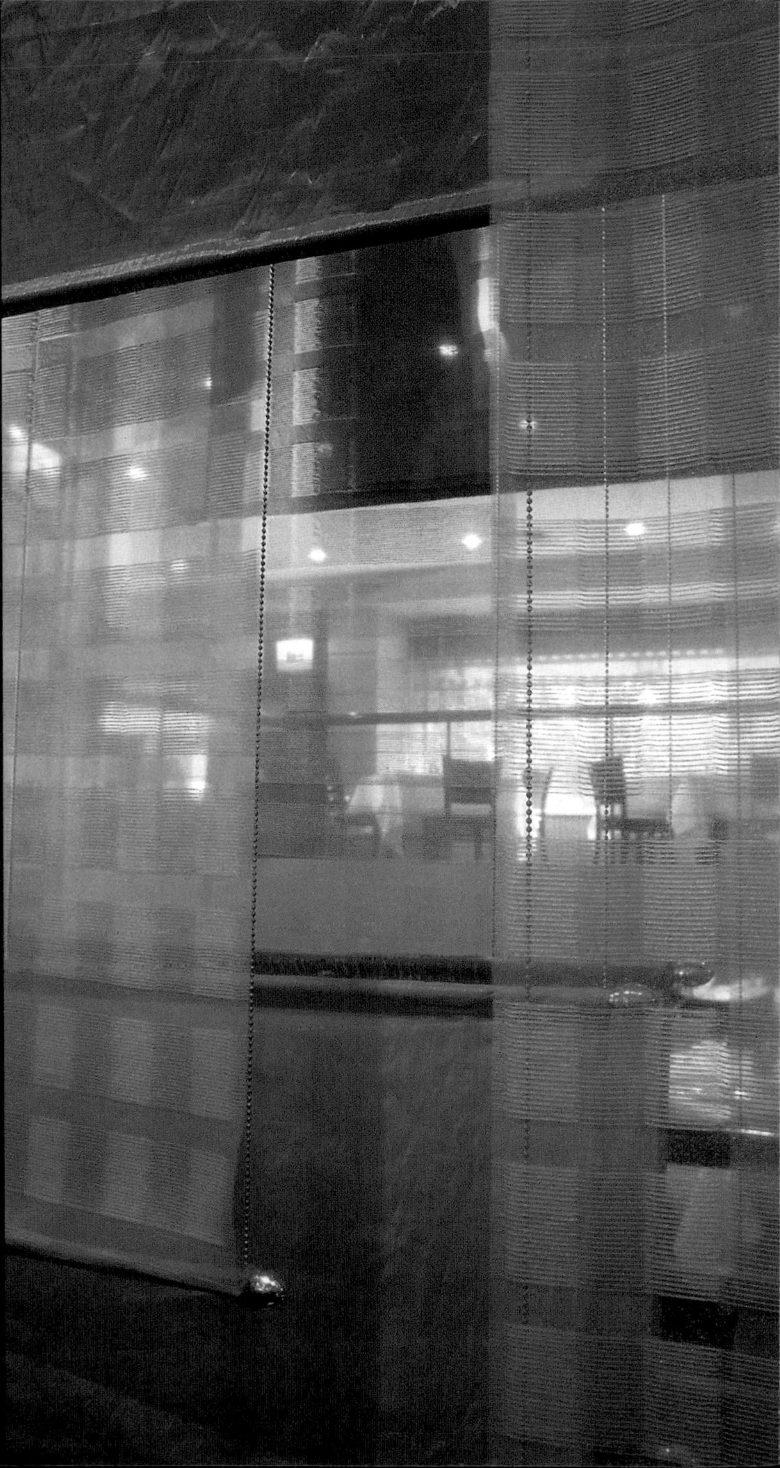

Opening Hours

Dinner can begin as early as 5.30 or 6pm, as many restaurants cater to the pre-theatre crowd (curtain 8pm), and office workers leave for the day around 6pm. Last orders for dinner are usually around 10.30 or 11pm. Most restaurants serve lunch between noon and 2.30–3pm. Opening times do vary widely, so it's always best to call first.

Prices

Eating out in New York is thought to be less expensive than in Paris or New York, but generally speaking it's not cheap. An average dinner costs about $40–50 per person including wine and tip. A prix fixe menu is usually a bargain, especially in the upscale restaurants. The prices given in this book *(see page 3)* are intended as guidelines only.

Reservations

To avoid disappointment, it's always a good idea to ring first and reserve a table, especially for weekends.

Service Charge and Tipping

The tip is not included in the bill, and is generally about 15–20% of the pre-tax total. An easy way to calculate the tip is to double the sales tax total on the bill, which in the state of New York is 8.6%. Service charges are added for large groups (8 or more).

Credit Cards

The majority of establishments take all credit cards; a few only accept American Express, others only cash, so call ahead to be certain.

Public Transportation

The New York subway is a fast and efficient way of getting around and not particularly dangerous until about 11pm at night, when the crime rate does rise somewhat. Each ride costs $2, with discounts when you buy more than 10 rides at once. Tickets come in the form of a metrocard, which can be bought from a ticket agent or vending machine at most stations, and which accept credit cards and cash.

Taxis

It's relatively easy to hail a cab on a New York street; busy avenues are generally the best place to get one quickly. The middle part of the sign on top of the cab is lit if it's available. If the entire sign is lit (meaning the "off duty" lights are on too), then it's either taken or going off shift. Cabs are most scarce during morning and afternoon rush hours (which can start as early as 4.30pm), when it's raining, or snowing. Be sure to wear your seatbelt even for a short ride – cab accidents are frequent and hospital costs can be expensive.

What to Eat Where

Good restaurants are found all over the city these days; it's the mood that changes somewhat from one area to another. Greenwich Village and SoHo have a wide selection of intimate, cozy and relaxed restaurants; the Flatiron District, Gramercy Park and Tribeca have more "event" dining with a lot of "celebrity chefs" and cutting edge spots; Midtown is more formal and bustling, and geared towards the business crowd with expense accounts, although the theater district itself offers a variety of choices; the Upper East Side is also home to some of the city's biggest named restaurants and is geared to the monied crowd; at the other end of the spectrum, the once rundown but still somewhat bohemian Lower East Side and East Village is now home to many small, adventurous and fashionable spots; the Meatpacking District has become a destination for the fashionable as well; and the Upper West Side, never known as a place to go for good dining, now boasts more than a handful of truly great restaurants.

RICE
KRISPIE
APPLE
RAISIN
MUFFIN
VESELKA
Cranberry
Muffin
VESELKA
Low-Fat
Blueberry
Muffin
COOKIE
RUGELACH

A–Z of Restaurants

African

American

Asian

Austrian

Belgian

Caribbean

Chinese

Eastern Europe

French

German

Global

Greek

Indian

Italian

Japanese

Latin American

Mediterranean

Middle Eastern

North African

Peruvian

Portuguese

Scandinavian

Seafood

Spanish

Thai

Vegetarian

A–Z of Cafes and Bars